More praise for

WAR ANIMALS...

"I can't think of another author who has done more to honor the animals of war than Robin Hutton. In *War Animals*, she brings to life the forgotten stories of countless brave military heroes—heroes with wings, hooves, and paws, whose bravery and sacrifice should never be forgotten. Hutton brings her sharp eye, careful research, and lively writing style to honor our animal friends who fought alongside their human partners. This book will delight both animal lovers and military buffs!"

—Elizabeth Letts, bestselling author of *The Eighty-Dollar Champion* and *The Perfect Horse*

"Robin Hutton has performed above and beyond the call of duty in gathering these incredible stories of service animals during wartime into one handy volume. These dogs, horses and birds (plus one amazing cat!) show over and over that bravery, dedication, and loyalty aren't just human traits. Every page brings another marvel."

—Robert Weintraub, author of *No Better Friend: One Man, One Dog, and Their Extraordinary Story of Courage and Survival in WWII*

"With a sense of humor and attention to historical detail and context, author Robin Hutton brings stories of animal warriors to the pages of *War Animals*. Readers who think they know their World War II history will discover new facts. Animal fanciers will delight in the tales of smart brave dogs and other critters pressed into military service—and maybe shed a tear or two. And we have increased respect for the handlers who worked with these talented animals on the home front, in the Pacific, and in Europe. A great read!"

—Lin Ezell, Director, National Museum of the Marine Corps

WAR ANIMALS

WAR
ANIMALS

THE UNSUNG HEROES
OF WORLD WAR II

ROBIN HUTTON

NATIONAL BESTSELLING AUTHOR OF *SGT. RECKLESS*

REGNERY
HISTORY

Regnery History™ is a trademark of Salem Communications Holding Corporation
Regnery® is a registered trademark of Salem Communications Holding Corporation

Cataloging-in-Publication data on file with the Library of Congress

ISBN 978-1-62157-658-7

Published in the United States by
Regnery History
An imprint of Regnery Publishing
A Division of Salem Media Group
300 New Jersey Ave NW
Washington, DC 20001
www.RegneryHistory.com

Manufactured in the United States of America

10 9 8 7 6 5 4 3 2 1

Books are available in quantity for promotional or premium use. For information on discounts and terms, please visit our website: www.Regnery.com.

To those who had no voice or choice—
thank you for your service, your sacrifice,
and your steadfast devotion

CONTENTS

"All of them, whatever the nature of their duty or their service, shared the heat and burden of the long days of peril and defeat, of danger and victory. All of them made their contribution to our escape from great evils. We should remember them."

—DOROTHEA ST. HILL BOURNE, Allied Forces Mascot Club

Preface

In war brief, crucial instants—defining moments—occur when someone in defiance of obvious danger steps up to do what is necessary because it's the right thing to do, regardless of personal peril. In the throes of such a moment the response is impulsive, the action without hesitation.

In that moment, a hero is born.

Only later, after the crisis has passed and there is breathing space, can we reflect on how that pivotal moment perhaps altered the course of history.

EXCLUSIVE COMPANY

To me our greatest heroes are the military men and women who have served and continue to serve in the defense of our country.

In John 15:13 the King James Bible appears to anticipate by two thousand years the spirit of the Congressional Medal of

Honor, America's highest military award: "Greater love hath no man than this, that a man lay down his life for his friends."

The Medal of Honor celebrates acts of gallantry and valor "above and beyond the call of duty" against an enemy of the United States. Created in 1862 during the Civil War, the honor has been awarded to nearly thirty-five-hundred American heroes, including some engaged in the ongoing War on Terror.

As of 2018, all but one recipient have been men. The sole exception was the pioneering Civil War physician Dr. Mary Edwards Walker. During World War II, 440 servicemen of the "Greatest Generation" earned the distinction of becoming Medal of Honor recipients.

Across the pond, the Victoria Cross is the highest honor for gallantry and extreme bravery a British or Commonwealth serviceman can receive. Dating to 1856, the Cross was introduced by Queen Victoria, initially to acknowledge valor during the Crimean War. By late 2017, the Victoria Cross had been bestowed on 1,358 Britons, including 181 veterans of World War II.

Heroes are a diverse bunch. Regardless of where they're from, they come in all shapes and sizes. Sometimes, especially in wartime, heroes can even come with feathers and wings, or fur and four legs. In 1943, amidst the horrors of the Second World War, a British veterinary association introduced a new military decoration. It honored not human defenders of the British Empire but a select, unheralded, decidedly different group of patriots: heroic animals who served the cause of Great Britain and the Allies during wartime.

THE PDSA DICKIN MEDAL

This prestigious British award is the PDSA Dickin Medal, which some call "the Victoria Cross for Animals." PDSA stands for the People's Dispensary for Sick Animals, a venerable charity serving animals in the United Kingdom. The elegant bronze Dickin medallion, inscribed "For Gallantry, We Also Serve," is the highest honor an animal can achieve for bravery in battle. While America's Congressional Medal of Honor and Britain's Victoria Cross are comparable to each another, the United States still has no equivalent to the Dickin honor.

Through 2017, the People's Dispensary for Sick Animals PDSA Dickin Medal has been presented to sixty-nine actual war heroes and one honorary one; of these, fifty-five served with Allied forces during World War II. The list of World War II honorees includes thirty-two pigeons, nineteen dogs, three horses, and one cat (yes, a cat!).

This book tells many of their stories.

DICKIN MEDALISTS STATESIDE

Although it is a British honor, the Dickin counts among its World War II-era recipients a feathered American veteran. GI Joe was a blue checked splash cock (male pigeon) who served with the United States Army Pigeon Service. Humans usually don't show pigeons much respect. But GI Joe, who received his Dickin in 1946, is an exception. He's considered the greatest war bird in American history.

Since 2002 the PDSA Dickin Medal has gone to six other American heroes—three dogs from 9/11 named Apollo, Salty, and Roselle; Lucca, a Marine Corps bomb-sniffing canine who served in Afghanistan and Iraq; Sgt. Reckless, the remarkable Korean War horse hero; and Chips, a dog who was honored posthumously in January 2018 on the seventy-fifth anniversary of his World War II heroics—and whose story you will discover later in these pages. With this honor, Chips became the seventieth Dickin Medal recipient.

This book will, however, profile more than just Dickin medalists. There were many unsung animal heroes, mostly dogs, who showed their mettle alongside American forces in World War II. Most of their stories have not been told except in obscure articles or dusty, forgotten books from the 1940s and 1950s.

Collectively, these true tales form a fascinating and until now mostly missing chapter of history. This book brings all of these uniquely accomplished heroes back from an undeserved oblivion, serving up the long overdue recognition and appreciation they richly deserve.

So sit back and enjoy reading about World War II's "Greatest Generation" of battle-tested animals.

Introduction

The People's Dispensary for Sick
Animals Dickin Medal

Veterinary charity PDSA has a proud history of honoring animals. With the blessing of the War Office, our founder, Maria Dickin CBE, instituted the PDSA Dickin Medal in 1943 with the aim of honoring the service and sacrifice of animals during WWII. In doing so, it was her hope that the status of animals would be raised in society and that everyone who came into contact with an animal—and not just a war hero animal—would see their worth and treat them with the dignity and respect they deserve.

The plight of the nation's animals had lain heavy on Maria's heart and stirred her into action some years earlier.

In 1917, while volunteering in the slums of inner city London during the Great War, Maria was struck by the terrible suffering of the animals that lived alongside the poorest in society. She saw lame horses, donkeys with overgrown and painful hooves, dogs and cats riddled with mange and dragging broken and bleeding limbs behind them. Her heart broke for these poor defenseless creatures, and their struggles kept her awake as she lay in her warm bed, with her own pet dog slumbering happily next to her.

Then she had an idea. What if there was a place where these poor people could take their sick and injured animals for free— yes, free—veterinary treatment? Maria sprang into action. She found a vet and a small basement in the poor area of Whitechapel, East London, and hung a sign that read: *Bring your sick animals. Do not let them suffer. All animals treated. All treatment free.*

As word spread, the basement was overwhelmed, with queues swelling down the street. PDSA was born, and Maria strove to supply the demand that she encountered for her very special service. And now, one hundred years on from the moment the doors opened in that tiny dark basement in London, PDSA is the UK's leading veterinary charity. We've dispensed 100 million treatments to 20 million pets. Our forty-eight Pet Hospitals across the UK treat the pets of the poorest in our society: over five thousand pets are seen across our network every day.

Maria's legacy lives on through our veterinary work but also in our Animal Awards Programme, which has earned worldwide fame thanks to the amazing acts of heroism and gallantry that the awards highlight.

We are especially pleased that Robin Hutton's book, *War Animals: The Unsung Heroes of WWII*, brings to life the stories of these unique heroes for all to appreciate and enjoy.

As the PDSA Dickin Medal states, "They Also Serve" and for their bravery and devotion to duty, we will continue to honor those animals whose service and sacrifice in the theater of war helps to protect humankind.

Jan McLoughlin
Director General, PDSA

WAR DOGS

"I want you men to remember that the dogs are the least expendable of all!"[1]

—LIEUTENANT COLONEL ALAN SHAPLEY, Commanding Officer, 2nd Marine Raider Regiment (Provisional) on the ship before storming the beach of Bougainville Island, October 30, 1943

1

Lassie Goes To War

"Dogs are becoming increasingly important and miracles are achieved."[1]

—**GENERAL EDMUND B. GREGORY,** Quartermaster General
of the U.S. Army

At the time the Japanese launched their shocking December 7, 1941, attack on Pearl Harbor, the United States had no organized war dog program. The military's limited use of canines consisted of roughly fifty sled, or "sledge," dogs working in Alaska and a few other isolated places.[2] The U.S. had made a few attempts to use canines in military situations, but for some reason the armed forces had been reluctant to bring dogs fully into the fold. But when Pearl Harbor was bombed by the Japanese and Americans leapt into the fray, they quickly brought along the dogs of war.

Surprisingly, the war dog program didn't actually originate from within the military. Instead, it was founded by a New York socialite with, well. . .dogged determination. Arlene Erlanger was a respected poodle breeder who had been raising and exhibiting dogs since childhood. She owned the famed Pillicoc Kennels in Elberon, on the New Jersey shore about fifty miles south of New York City. Erlanger was a true believer in the idea that dogs could help the Allied effort. But she needed the assistance of friends and other prominent dog fanciers to get something started.

Erlanger recognized the military's initial reluctance to use dogs and took it upon herself to kick-start a movement that deeply influenced how World War II was fought and won.

CALLING ALL DOGS!

In the wake of Pearl Harbor, Mrs. Erlanger called her good friend Roland Kilbon, a fellow dog enthusiast and, luckily for Mrs. Erlanger, also a prominent columnist with the New York *Sun*. "I must see you," she said urgently. "It's about what the war means to dogs and fanciers. I've an idea and I need your help."

Fascinated, Kilbon agreed to meet. "The dog game must play its part in this thing," Erlanger declared. "Other countries have used dogs in their armies for years and ours have not. They've got to do it. Just think what dogs can do guarding forts, munitions plants and other such places. But I don't want to propose it because somebody might think it was just something to glorify the Poodle Club or Pillicoc Kennels. Can you do it?"

Kilbon grasped the significance of her proposal, but knew they would need to tread very lightly to achieve the desired outcome. "People would think that it was a promotion idea for the New York *Sun* or Arthur Roland. It can't be the proposal of one breed, fancier or publication," he told her.[3]

Erlanger was way ahead of him. She had already enlisted the help of major figures in the then wildly popular show dog community. They included Leonard Brumby, president of the Professional Handlers' Association; Henry Stoecker, the trainer who ran Erlanger's Pillicoc Kennels and later served as an Army lieutenant; and Henry I. Caesar, a banker, sportsman, and director of the American Kennel Club. Caesar was considered "one of the most highly regarded persons in the dog game."[4]

Erlanger's idea quickly grew into a grassroots movement. Dog fanciers lent enthusiastic support, as did 402 obedience and kennel clubs around the country.

The newly—and quickly—created Dogs for Defense, Inc. (DFD) was a totally volunteer organization, with professional trainers and organizers donating their time and expertise. The American Kennel Club, the governing body of the competitive dog world, offered its blessing, largely thanks to Henry Caesar's support. "With contributions from the Professional Handlers' Assn. and the Westbury Kennel Assn.," Kilbon trumpeted in the September 1943 issue of *Popular Dogs* magazine, "the first two organizations to come to the financial aid of the program, Dogs for Defense was formally launched." Henry Caesar was named Dogs for Defense's president, Roland Kilbon handled publicity, and Arlene Erlanger served as director of finance.[5]

It was January 1942—just a month after Pearl Harbor.

Dogs for Defense recruited America's first canine army, known affectionately as the K-9 Corps. Radio announcements and newspaper articles nationwide made the extraordinary pitch for people to *donate their personal pets* to the war effort.

America answered the call, offering nearly forty thousand dogs of various breeds. Eligible war dog hopefuls flooded into Dogs for Defense centers, where the screening process was brutal. After preliminary examinations by DFD volunteers, the number of acceptable candidates was whittled down by more than half, to about nineteen thousand dogs, in the first cut. Ultimately 10,425 were accepted by the K-9 Corps and went through training for all branches of military service. The rest, deemed unsuitable for training, went home to relieved owners.

Clyde Porter presents his pal Junior to Dogs for Defense, the organization that supplied dogs to the Armed Forces. Most of the United States' nearly twenty thousand war dogs were volunteered for duty by their owners. August 19, 1942. *National Archives*

THE AMERICAN THEATRE WING GETS INTO THE ACT

While the DFD was getting organized, America's stage community was gathering at the Hudson Theater in New York City. An emergency meeting had been called by the American Theatre Wing, the organization that created and still presents Broadway's annual Tony Awards. Its members—theater and film actors, radio performers, and others—were looking for ways to help the war effort.

American Theatre Wing chairman Helen Menken was a highly respected stage actress, although today she is remembered chiefly for having been the first of Humphrey Bogart's four wives. Menken and the Wing's public relations executive met with Major General Edmund B. Gregory in Washington, D.C. As the Army's Quartermaster General, Gregory headed one of that branch's key logistical support units. Menken offered the Wing's help in any way possible, even the gift of a plane! While the general appreciated the offer, he said regulations preemptively grounded the plane idea. He didn't know of any way the Wing could help, and politely thanked Menken for "the patriotic offer of the people of the entertainment world," promising to let them know if anything came up.

Something did, and fast—in the form of a request from one of Gregory's subordinates. Lieutenant Colonel Clifford C. Smith, who ran the Quartermaster Corps' Plant Protection Branch, asked for permission to use dogs as sentries to protect Quartermaster supply depots vulnerable to sabotage. "A trained dog," the lieutenant colonel reasoned, "is better than three or even more men."[6]

The general approved Smith's request and turned to the American Theatre Wing to handle it. The Quartermaster Corps, Gregory explained to Helen Menken, didn't have the necessary funding to carry out the project. Here was one way, he told her, that the Wing could truly help. The Wing chairman loved the idea and leapt at the opportunity. Menken, who happened to be a dog lover, knew firsthand just how highly attuned to their surroundings dogs could be. As the daughter of deaf parents, she had grown up in a household where dogs played vital roles in everyday life—informing the family of visitors at the front door, or if the baby was crying.

Helen Menken took the proposal to the Wing, but it became quickly apparent that the organization had neither the facilities nor the practical knowledge to carry out the mission alone. So the Wing turned to people who did: the dog trainers and professionals working with Dogs for Defense. Menken contacted Arlene Erlanger and ultimately DFD accepted full responsibility for supplying the canine recruits, while the Wing used its radio division and speakers bureau to publicize the dog recruitment program. This was one wartime shotgun marriage that worked beautifully.

WAR DOGS HAVE THEIR DAY

It took some convincing to get the U.S. Army fully on board. But finally, on March 13, 1942, war dogs were formally recognized when Undersecretary of War Robert P. Patterson authorized the Quartermaster Corps to acquire two hundred trained sentry dogs for the Army. Colonel Smith told Henry Caesar that Dogs for Defense was now the "official procurement agency for war dogs."[7]

Besides procurement, at first DFD was also responsible for housing and training the dogs. The immediate need was to prepare the hounds for sentry and patrol duty at beaches, borders, munitions plants, airports, and other industrial facilities that might interest saboteurs. Instruction eventually expanded to include training messenger, casualty, and mine detection dogs. Most of the pups would actually remain stateside to guard the home front, but more than a thousand were deployed for duty overseas.

POOCHES IN POUGHKEEPSIE

Before fulfilling the first order for two hundred dogs for the Plant Protection Branch, Dogs for Defense secured a real-world testing ground to assess the newly-trained recruits' sentry skills.

On April 13, 1942, the first three fully trained sentry pooches went to Poughkeepsie, eighty miles north of Manhattan. There, they stood watch at the Munitions Manufacturing Company, "and are serving efficiently," the *New York Times* reported. The trio included a German shepherd, a Norwegian elkhound, and a greyhound. [8]

Brigadier General Philip S. Gage, in command at Fort Hancock, one of five key installations guarding New York Harbor, was persuaded to give the dogs a try. In early May, Arlene Erlanger delivered nine four-legged sentry trainees. The DFD was an equal opportunity war dog clearinghouse, presenting Gage with a trio of black poodles, a pair of dalmatians, an Airedale, a Doberman, a German shepherd, and an Afghan hound.

Seventeen additional dogs began standing guard at a Gulf Oil plant on Staten Island and Mitchel Field on Long Island. Mitchel was home to the Air Defense Command, which was charged with developing critical protection plans for U.S. cities, military installations, industrial zones, and other potential enemy targets. [9]

"A soldier guard and his dog keep a watchful eye over planes at the Army Air Base, Mitchel Field, N.Y. Dogs like this are procured and trained for the Army by the Quartermaster Corps." March 1943. Original photo caption. *National Archives*

HOLLYWOOD HEROES

Hollywood luminaries were quick to jump on the war dog bandwagon. Greer Garson, the 1942 Oscar winner as Best Actress for *Mrs. Miniver*, donated her poodle Cliquot. The dog had been bred at Arlene Erlanger's Pillicoc Kennels.

Arlene Erlanger (standing) talks DFD stategy with actress Greer Garson. Garson's poodle Cliquot was donated to DFD. *Sophia Smith Collection, Smith College*

Legendary silent film star Mary Pickford offered up her German shepherd Silver. Crooner and actor Rudy Vallee drafted his Doberman pinscher King. Metropolitan Opera star Ezio Pinza donated his two Dalmatians, Figaro and Boris, along with an album of his recordings. "If they get lonesome," he said with a wink, "play one of these records for them."[10]

Hollywood dog trainer Carl Spitz had pioneered the use of hand signals to direct animals from beyond camera range. He owned and trained Terry, the notorious scene-stealing Cairn terrier who played Toto in *The Wizard of Oz*. Spitz helped set up Dog for Defense's training program and personally donated many dogs. Later Spitz also trained the 1st Marine War Dog Platoon at Camp Pendleton, California, before it left for Bougainville in the Solomon Islands.

Overall, the response to the DFD's dog donation drive was dazzling. America's War Dog Program was off and running on all fours.

PETS AND PATRIOTISM

Everyday Americans making animal donations were proud of making profoundly personal sacrifices. After all, they were giving up cherished pets freely and unconditionally, receiving in turn neither compensation nor any guarantee their dogs would return safely at the end of the war. Donating their dogs was a patriotic act and a way for Americans to become personally invested in the war effort.

Each owner completed a questionnaire about his or her pet's health record, temperament, and whether the dog was gun shy or spooked by loud noises such as thunderstorms. If your dog was accepted into the program, you received a War Department certificate signed by the Quartermaster General: "Appreciation is expressed for your patriotic action in donating your dog (name) for use in connection with the Armed Forces of the United States." Owners also received a thank-you letter from the commandant of whichever war dog reception and training center received their pet.

Once a dog was trained and on assignment, strict secrecy was imposed on its whereabouts. Most communication stopped—although as we shall see, military dog handlers occasionally wrote to the owners back home with updates on how the dog was doing.

Efforts were also made to "salvage" dogs from local dog pounds. Two rescued from a Westport, Connecticut, pound won DFD approval and joined the eighteen hundred canine enlistees at the Fort Robinson War Dog Training Center in Nebraska.[11] As you might expect, some people weren't so keen to hand their four-legged family members over to the armed forces. One reluctant donor telephoned the Army to demand his dog back, explaining that since the pet's departure, his wife had "suffered a severe nervous collapse, and the attending physician declared nothing would restore her but the pet's return."[12] Was that the truth or a clever ruse to win the pup's freedom? We'll never know, but luckily for the man, his dog had not yet begun training and was sent home.

In another instance, a woman wrote in with a much more compelling (and verifiable) argument: "In answer to your recent letter, I wish to say that the Army may not have my dog. Her license number is 7220 and you can cross her off your list. The Army has my husband, two brothers-in-law, and my father-in-law, the Navy has one of my brothers and the Government has two more. I think that is enough."[13]

FURRY FASCIST FIGHTERS

At the start, in 1942, Dogs for Defense and the U.S. Army Quartermaster Corps worked with thirty-two breeds ranging

from collies and wirehaired pointing griffons to Irish setters and
Chesapeake Bays. Regardless of breed, all had to meet certain
specifications spelled out in a technical manual authored, not
coincidentally, by Arlene Erlanger herself, and published by the
War Department in 1943. The requirements for all included
Physical soundness, which meant "good bone, well-proportioned
bodies, strong backs, deep chests and strong muscular feet with
hard, well cushioned pads"; *Condition*, which meant they
"should be 'easy keepers'...must be muscular, never fat.... Eyes
should be clear and bright...coats should show the bloom of
health...Breath should be sweet... "; and *Behavior*, which
required that "Dogs should show general alertness, vigor and
energy. They should be steady, not timid or excitable. They
should show a willingness to be guided or taught, and evidence
the ability to learn and to retain what they have learned."[14]

Dogs also had to be between eighteen and twenty-eight
inches tall at the shoulder, and no more than five years old. Later,
the height standard was ratcheted up to between twenty-three
to twenty-eight inches at the shoulder, and dogs had to be
between fourteen months to three-and-a-half years old. Males
were preferred. Females were acceptable, although eventually all
females were ordered spayed; a female in heat created chaos
among the males and was difficult to handle, and so was her
litter. The manual didn't bother with polite euphemisms: "It has
been determined that the spaying of bitches is a military necessity
and to the best interests of the military service."[15]

Certain breeds were crossed off the "acceptable" list as
demand declined or when issues arose with them on the front
lines. Bird dogs were tried in New Guinea, for example, but
according to reports, "instinct led them to point (at) more para-
keets" than the enemy.[16] So they were removed from the list.

Other breeds, including the Briard, Bouvier, Rottweiler, and Wirehaired Pointing Griffon were problematic because so few of them were available in the United States.

Eventually the number of breeds was whittled down to eighteen, then finally, by 1944, to seven. While the standard poodle, for example, made the initial cut because of its "unusual ability to learn rapidly, good retention, patience, agility, versatility, courage, keen nose and hearing," poodles never served overseas, working strictly stateside assignments as sentries and guard dogs, and ultimately they didn't make the Army's final list: Alaskan Malamute, Belgian sheep dog, farm collie, Doberman pinscher, Eskimo, German shepherd, and Siberian husky.[17] Crosses of these breeds were also acceptable.[18] Ironically, just a year after Germany's surrender the German shepherd's versatility, traits, and breeding won it bragging rights as the "official dog of the US Army."[19]

KINKS IN THE SYSTEM

By June 1942, three months into the program, an Army inspection revealed that the dogs in training were making little progress. Several reasons were offered. First, overcrowding had become serious at the private kennels that were taking in such an abundance of donated dogs across the country. Second, because no training manual yet existed, standardized instruction was virtually impossible. Third, trainers with little or no military experience were unfamiliar with military conditions. Plus—and this is incredible—there was no one to instruct the eventual servicemen handlers how to work with and command the dogs. All this made for a discouraging start, but didn't change the Army's resolve to move forward.

As the program evolved, officials realized they would need far more dogs than originally believed, and in different capacities.

Big changes were coming to the war dog drive, and quickly, after early fears of sabotage soon came true.

"OPERATION PASTORIUS"

Just before midnight on June 13, 1942, the German submarine *U-202* surfaced about five hundred yards off the coast of Long Island. Under cover of fog, a quartet of Nazi saboteurs put ashore with four large boxes in a rubber boat near Amagansett, New York.[20] The Nazi agents had enough American currency and explosives to kill and terrorize for at least a year.

Four days later, four more German operatives landed in Ponte Vedra Beach, just south of Jacksonville, Florida.

The Nazis' sabotage campaign was dubbed "Operation Pastorius" after an early German settler in America. The goal: to destroy America from within. Among the intended bombing targets: the hydroelectric plants at Niagara Falls; Aluminum Company of America (Alcoa) factories in Illinois, Tennessee, and New York; the Pennsylvania Railroad station at Newark; locks on the Ohio River near Louisville, Kentucky, and Pittsburgh, Pennsylvania; and the New York City water supply. And that was just for starters.[21]

But the plotters hadn't accounted for a young unarmed Coast Guard recruit. Thanks to quick thinking by 2nd Class Seaman John C. Cullen, the terrorist plot to destroy these and other facilities, while it did create widespread panic, was discovered before it could do real harm.

Cullen was alone on his six-mile beach patrol that night when he came across the first group of agents busily burying supplies in the sand. Their leader, George John Dasch, was a German national who had left the U.S. to return to the fatherland when the war began. Dasch offered Cullen $260 to keep quiet. Cullen "took" the bribe, but once out of sight raced to the nearby Coast Guard station for help. By the time Cullen led armed Guardsmen to the site, the Germans were gone. A search of the sands quickly revealed freshly dug holes where the four wooden munitions crates were buried, along with a duffel bag of German uniforms.

Ten days later, on June 27, 1942, the then-largest manhunt in FBI history resulted in the capture of all eight would-be saboteurs. They were brought to justice in a speedy military tribunal.[22]

The incident proved what Dogs for Defense had been saying for months—that sentry dogs were needed to help protect American coastlines. The ongoing threat increased the popular desire for dog patrols along beaches and coastlines. Within a month the Coast Guard launched its new Beach Patrol.[23] Operations began in late August 1942, at the seaside park at Brigantine, New Jersey. Within a year, eighteen hundred dogs were patrolling American beaches.[24]

THE QUARTERMASTER CORPS TAKES CONTROL

A month earlier, the War Dog Program had been reorganized, with the Army Quartermaster Corps Remount Branch—responsible for purchasing and training horses and mules—taking responsibility for the handling and training of future war dogs. As part of the reorganization, on July 16, 1942, Secretary of War Harold Stimson directed the Quartermaster General to broaden the program by adding training for tactical dogs: silent scout or patrol, messenger, and mine detection dogs. Stimson's directive empowered each service branch to determine how many dogs it needed and how the animals would be deployed.[25]

In August 1942, the first War Dog Reception and Training Center was established at Front Royal, Virginia, at what had been a remount depot for horses and mules during World War

I. Front Royal would serve the nation's eastern region; by year's end, three other remount centers would open—at Fort Robinson in Nebraska, at San Carlos, California, and at Camp Rimini in Montana, a Marine post for the training of sled and pack dogs. A fifth center opened in April 1943 at Cat Island, off the coastal town of Gulfport, Mississippi. Cat Island was used for jungle training because its humidity and vegetation were similar to tropical climate and terrain. Two temporary centers were also set up in Beltsville, Maryland, and Fort Belvoir, Virginia.

The kennels at the War Dog Reception and Training Center, Front Royal, Virginia. *National Archives*

Once the centers were up and running, the U.S. Army Veterinary Corps was charged with maintaining the animals' well-being. Dogs for Defense remained the procurement agency, its volunteer force now free to focus solely on dog recruitment.

The Marine Corps set up its own training center at Camp Lejeune in North Carolina, while the Coast Guard established three training centers on the east coast, at Elkins Park, Pennsylvania, Hilton Head, South Carolina, and Curtis Bay, Maryland.

USMC War Dog Training Center, Camp LeJeune, North Carolina. *USMC Archives*

At the time of Stimson's directive, the Quartermaster Corps had no experience with training scout, messenger, and mine-detecting dogs, so it sought the experience and assistance of Great Britain's War Dog Training School. Great Britain had used messenger dogs very successfully during World War I thanks to Lieutenant Colonel Edwin Hautenville Richardson, a dog fancier and breeder who had set up and then become commandant of the British War Dog Training School in 1917. Colonel Richardson had written several books on the training of war dogs based on positive praise and reinforcement, including *British War Dogs: Their Training and Psychology*.[26] After World War I the War Dog Training School closed, but Great Britain reopened it on May 5, 1942.

On February 1, 1943, Captain John B. Garle, then-director of the British War Dog Training School, brought with him four dogs and two non-commissioned officers who were trained handlers to the training center in Beltsville, Maryland, and demonstrated the use of scout and messenger dogs. The demonstrations were so successful that the team traveled to all of the training centers across the United States teaching the trainers their techniques. The Quartermaster Corps used Colonel Richardson's books as training manuals until they were able to develop their own.

"GIVE DOGS AND DOLLARS"

As expenses mounted, fundraising efforts were launched to help pay some of the program's enormous costs—this, even though the dogs were donated and people volunteered their time—including the inspection of dogs for service and the costs of transporting approved canines to the various training centers. The Dogs for Defense slogan "Give Dogs and Dollars" began turning up "in speeches, radio talks, posters, feature stories, advertisements, cartoons, personal appeals, medals, certificates, announcements at dog shows and a V-Mail replica called K-9 mail."[27]

Corporate America stepped up with both monetary and in-kind donations. Ralston Purina Company, for example, donated all the dog food for new K-9 recruits up until they were shipped to training camps. The company also promoted Dogs for Defense donations in its advertising. A cigarette manufacturer's ads featured pictures of DFD war dogs posing with attractive women. This effectively provided Dogs for Defense with $250,000 worth of free publicity. The ads inspired hundreds of dog donations.[28]

Dog shows helped promote the "Give Dogs and Dollars" campaign. The prestigious Westminster Dog Show led the way with a $5,000 gift in 1943. Westminster scaled back on expensive trophies, using the funds on DFD recruitment instead. At some shows, dog fanciers even raffled off expensive puppies, with the proceeds going to the cause.

LEGAL PAYOFFS FOR DOGGIN' THE DRAFT

Not every canine met size, age, temperament, and other specifications for military service. And, as we have seen, many owners just weren't willing to hand over their pets to the military. DFD turned such negative situations into a positive fundraising strategy. The organization called its solution the "War Dog Fund" program.

The Fund was the creation of James M. Austin, a patent broker who, according to the *Huffington Post*, "donated some ten-thousand dollars to war charities in the name of his fox terrier, Saddler."[29] Under the professional name Ch (for Champion) Nornay Saddler, the terrier was named "by a poll of the nation's show judges as the outstanding show dog of all time."[30] Saddler laid claim to more than three hundred award cups, ribbons, and emblems, plus no fewer than fifty-nine best-in-show titles. Austin was the Fund's national chairman. Saddler was chief recruiter and good-naturedly deemed the "General of the 4-Fs"—dogs that couldn't make the cut.

For a fee, a pet would be registered with the "K-9 Home Guard" of the Army, Marine Corps, Navy, or Coast Guard.[31] A dog's honorary rank was determined by the size of the donation, which could range from just a dollar for a private or seaman designation to five dollars for a sergeant or chief petty officer. Twenty-five dollars bought colonel or captain status—and on up the donation tree to the hundred-dollar level for a general or admiral.

Owner-participants received official certificates acknowledging the pet, the amount donated, and the rank that the dollar donation represented. They also got a collar tag and a window sticker.

People lapped up the idea. President Franklin Roosevelt was an early joiner, registering his beloved handsome black Scottie terrier Fala as an Army private. While War Fund Dogs didn't ship out—or even leave home—their owners still could feel they were doing their part for the war effort.

President Roosevelt's beloved Scottish terrier Fala poses with presidential cousin Laura Delano, who shows off the pup's War Dog Fund certificate. The president was among thousands of Americans who donated to the Fund to "spare" their pets from actual war service. For one dollar, Fala was designated an honorary Army private. Fala lived until 1952. April 1943. *National Archives*

And the Fund wasn't limited to dogs. Americans signed up their cats, birds, and even turtles.[32]

Joan Crawford, the recruiting chairman for the entertainment industry, appealed to other Hollywood stars to join the effort. She also enlisted her dachshund Boopschen as a general and her cocker spaniel Honey as an admiral. The American Theatre Wing's Helen Menken in New York followed suit.[33]

The drive went international when American servicemen and commanding officers from battlefronts around the world began registering their pets. By the time Saddler finished up as the campaign figurehead fourteen months later, twenty-five thousand pet owners had donated about $75,000 to the War Dog Program.

The War Dog Fund tracked its progress on a large-scale U.S. map at its headquarters. The map was pierced with twenty-five hundred pins, each representing a city or town where a pet was registered. There were pins in every state.[34]

2

You're In the Army Now. Coast Guard Too. Don't Forget the Navy. And Hey, Marine Corps, Lookin' Good!

"They must undergo basic training, just like any other enlistee."[1]

—SATURDAY EVENING POST, September 5, 1942

Initially dog training for all branches of the military was conducted by Dogs for Defense and the Army's Quartermaster Corps. While the Coast Guard had three of its own training centers, it still acquired dogs from the DFD. The Marines accepted DFD dogs to jumpstart their program. But by late November 1942, the Marine Corps established its own recruiting and training program at Camp Lejeune, North Carolina, procuring dogs from the Doberman Pinscher Club of America.

OUT OF THE CRATE INTO THE FRYING PAN

A preliminary orientation of seven to ten days allowed the newbies in America's four-legged fighting force to adjust to their new lives. Each canine recruit arriving at a training center would be taken from his (or, yes, her) packing crate to be "inspected, weighed, groomed, even 'manicured.'"[2] After dogs were "contracted, and sworn in to 'perform active service with-out pay or allowance,'" and once they had passed a physical, they were photographed and tattooed on the left ear with a serial number for identification.[3] The pups were then promptly quarantined for three weeks. Only after that did the two-week basic training begin.

Above, new arrivals are de-crated, weighed, examined, and groomed. *National Archives*

Each four-pawed conscript was assigned a handler and underwent the basic obedience training. "The recruits were taught to perform the following fundamental commands: on leash—Heel, Sit, Down, Cover, Stay, Come, Crawl, Jump; off the leash—Drop and Jump."[4] The raw recruits learned to obey both hand signals and voice commands. They became accustomed to wearing gas masks, riding in a variety of military vehicles, and—this was vital—especially, working under the sound of gunfire.

"Stay!" *National Archives*

At the end of basic training, both dogs and handlers took final exams. Dogs passing the test then pivoted to the next phase: specialized training. During this basic training each canine enlistee had been evaluated to determine which specialized training classification best suited his talents. At that time, the dogs (except for sledge and pack dogs, who were trained separately) were divided into two groups: those destined for guard duty were sentry and attack (or "police") dogs, and those trained for tactical use were silent scout, messenger, and casualty dogs. To be selected for scout and messenger duty, a dog had to show higher levels of intelligence, willingness, energy, and sensitivity.[5] There was also a short-lived program involving about 140 mine-detection specialists, called M-dogs. When two M-dog units were deployed to North Africa with little success—handlers found that they had trouble detecting mines under combat conditions—the program was discontinued.[6]

Dogs that would be deployed overseas also needed special training to get used to the rigors they would face in war zones: smoke, the sounds of gunfire and artillery, landings, navigating jungle conditions. Yet there was no way to truly prepare them for what they would face in war.

Whether it be getting use to the sounds of fire or being lowered onto a boat, these dogs had to learn to cope with it all. *National Archives/USMC Archives/ Marine Raider Museum Archives*

The specialized training lasted from eight to thirteen weeks, depending on the specialty. Sentry dogs required just eight weeks, while scout, messenger, and casualty dogs needed more. Sometimes the dogs didn't have a clue what was being asked of them. At one training center a huge Great Dane named Duke was being taught to jump a series of hurdles. When the trainer released the Dane's chain, dutiful Duke bounded towards the first hurdle, not quite knowing what he was supposed to do. But the big dog really wanted to please his handler, so Duke "picked up the awkward wooden hurdle in his massive jaws and carried it back and laid it at his handler's feet, wagging his tail proudly."[7] Needless to say, Duke needed a few more tries to get it right, but he probably made a really good sentry dog.

SENTRY DOGS

Also known as "watch dogs," sentry dogs were taught to growl or bark if they sensed anything strange or unfamiliar nearby—from the presence of strangers to the mere scent of a fire. These pooch patrollers were required to possess "moderate to high intelligence, willingness, energy and aggressiveness. The handler must instill in the dog that '...every human, except himself, is his natural enemy.'"[8] Each sentry dog worked with a human handler, usually doing patrol duty on a short leash.

Standing guard. *National Archives/Quartermaster Museum*

ATTACK DOGS

Attack or "police," dogs also received sentry training. But unlike watch dogs they worked off leash and were trained to attack, either on command or if provoked. They were required to possess "courage, speed and strength." Every police dog had to be "heavy enough to throw a man to the ground by the impact of his body." Strong teeth and powerful jaws were also desirable attributes, since the dogs were taught to bite on command and to "cease attack instantly on command from his master or on cessation of resistance by the aggravator."[9] Each attack dog was paired with a handler, with whom he worked as a unit; sometimes an additional sentry dog and handler joined the team unit to increase security. Attack dogs worked well in darkness.

Going on the offensive. The attack dogs. *National Archives*

SILENT SCOUTS

The silent scout or patrol dog was likened to a "super sentry dog...used by reconnaissance patrols to discover whether an area is free of hostile presence."[10] There is no way to gauge how many lives these dogs saved by being able to warn their handlers of dangers as far away as five hundred yards. Marines trainer Lieutenant Clyde Henderson marveled that patrol dogs "on more than one occasion saved our patrols from falling into deadly ambushes which otherwise might not have been detected in the dense jungles."[11]

Silent scouts worked both on and off leash, depending on the hound, although they were usually on a leash for better control. These versatile dog soldiers could work effectively in either daylight or darkness, regardless of poor weather conditions and terrain obstacles. They were "silent" because they needed the maximum scope for their powerful senses to detect danger—or even just motion—either through hearing, sight, or scent. Scout dogs alerted their human handlers in different ways. Some simply tensed up. Others stopped short and crouched. Some raised their hackles. The handler might even hear a very low growl as the dog tensed. The handler had to learn to "read" his charge to know how the dog would alert to danger.

Training in the woods was essential for the silent scouts. Scout dog King leads a patrol through a jungle trail in Aitape, New Guinea. August 6, 1944. *USMC Archives/National Archives*

MESSENGER DOGS

The messenger dog was a lifeline between units—a reliable, furry conveyor of communication in dense jungles where telephone wires had been cut, or had never existed. A messenger dog was faster than a human and posed a difficult target for the enemy "because of his natural camouflage, his size, speed, and ability to take advantage of protecting cover."[12] He could find his way in daylight or darkness, through any kind of weather or terrain, and he was especially effective in the jungle.

A messenger dog's training began with exercises to desensitize the animal to the sounds of battle. According to a training technical manual, "Every known distraction must be introduced during training, such as bomb detonations, shell and gunfire,

troop and motor traffic, and the presence of moving or station-
ary troops, civilians and animals."[13]

Messenger dogs in training and in the field. *National Archives/USMC Archives*

A messenger dog could also help lay communication wire.
A coil attached to his collar unwound as he walked, enabling the
men to replace or lay wire quickly. He also sometimes worked
as a transport, moving emergency supply loads weighing up to
twenty-five pounds. If necessary, a messenger dog could deliver
two carrier pigeons in cages strapped to his back.

Every messenger required two handlers: the dog ran from
one master to the other when quietly ordered to "report." These
dogs possessed scenting abilities so powerful that they easily
located handlers who had moved from their original positions.
Nothing stopped the messenger dog from his mission. "Loyalty,
devotion, bravery, intelligence, and stamina" truly defined this
specialty dog.[14]

CASUALTY DOGS

Working with medical personnel, casualty dogs majored (so to speak) in locating the wounded. These dogged pursuits meant discovering a soldier lying unconscious on a battlefield, one buried beneath shelling debris, or even one cowering in a hiding place missed by medical patrols. These life-saving dogs worked off leash; once they found a casualty, they returned to their handler, who fastened on a leash and was led to the wounded soldier. Casualty dogs saved minutes crucial to soldiers who were suffering from shock or hemorrhaging.

Dalmatians were often trained as casualty dogs. *National Archives*

A casualty dog had to be friendly, affectionate, and trained not to bite, even when feeling threatened: an injured or delirious soldier might strike out at the dog in panic, not realizing the pup was actually there to help.

TEAMWORK

The men eventually learned how to be handlers and how to care for their dogs. Doing so made them better soldiers, sailors, and Marines as they learned about patrol and scout work, compass and map reading, military procedures, and how to conduct field maneuvers. By the end of training, a war dog and his handler melded into a single entity: a team. Together with their dogs they were assigned a post, and together they would fight to win the war.

"Cpl. Peter S. Denaga, USMC, 25, of West Islip, L.I.N.Y., shares a drink from his canteen cup with his Devil Dog mate, 'Pal' after a tough day of simulated landing maneuvers." May 1943. Original photo caption. *USMC Archives*

A breakdown of the 10,425 dogs that were finally selected for the full training and became part of the Quartermaster's K-9 Corps shows just how dramatically sentry dogs and stateside service dominated the program:

TYPE OF DOG	TRAINED FOR ARMY	TRAINED FOR COAST GUARD	TOTAL	SERVED IN US	SERVED OVERSEAS
Sentry	6,121	3,174	9,295	8,396	899
Scout	571	0	571	135	436
Sled and Pack	268	0	268	0	268
Messenger	151	0	151	0	151
Mine Detection	140	0	140	0	140
TOTAL	7,251	3,174	10,425	8,531	1,894

Fifteen war dog platoons were activated, trained, and shipped overseas for combat as part of the Quartermaster's K-9 Corps. Of these, seven platoons fought the Germans in Europe. These included QM War Dog Platoons 33rd through the 38th, plus the 42nd. The dogs in these platoons were trained as scouts and messengers, except for the 36th, which was a mine-detection unit. The other eight platoons, starting with the 25th and 26th, served in the Pacific fighting the Japanese.

SHOW-OFFS

Sometimes newly trained members of the K-9 Corps were put through their paces at dog show demonstrations to let civilian audiences know how well the training program was going. Naturally, officials hoped the doggie revues would spur more donations to "Give Dogs and Dollars." At a show in Boston, a woman in the audience recognized her own pup among the war dogs:

> Proud of her pet's performance, the woman owner could not resist telling the officer in charge. The officer, forming a sudden resolution, invited her to enter the ring. From across the arena the dog caught sight of his mistress. Ears pricked up, eyes shone with recognition, tail began thumping the ground.

"Stay," the dog's handler commanded. At the officer's urging, the woman called her dog by name. The
dog sat like a statue and never stirred, only quivering
a little. His handler, proud too now, bent his head
toward his charge and said softly, "Okay." With that
the dog darted away, racing across the ring in great
bounds. With one of those unmelodious but poignant
canine cries of joy a dog sometimes utters, he sprang
into his mistress' arms, licking at her face with loving
tongue.

Yet when his handler called him back, he instantly
obeyed. The Army could not have asked for a more
striking example of perfect discipline and training.[15]

BEACH PATROL—PAWS FOR THE CAUSE

Most of the dogs in the Quartermaster's K-9 program, as we
have seen, did sentry duty stateside. More of them were in the
Coast Guard than in any other service. The Guard's pup popula-
tion peaked at 3,649. These dogs served alongside about twenty-
four thousand Coast Guard personnel stationed at ten different
naval districts across the country.[16] All told, the Guard's war dogs
worked an area of approximately thirty-seven hundred miles.

Coast Guard war dogs on beach patrol. *National Archives/USCG Archives*

One hazard to dogs doing beach patrol duty involved sharp shards of broken seashells, which cut their paws. So the Coast Guard devised little boots for them. As you'd expect, the booties were packed in sets of four, with hundreds of sets distributed. A comparable situation developed at a camp in the West. The dogs there also needed the leather booties—because of cactus thorns.

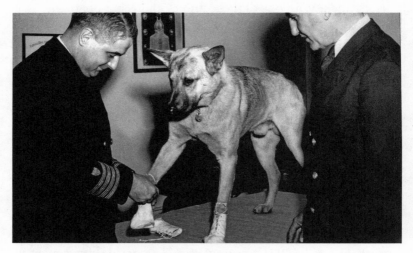

"DOG-GONE GOOD SHOES: No ration coupons are needed for the latest thing in footwear which is exhibited by Poncho, a Coast Guard dog. Captain Raymond J. Mauerman, former chief training officer of the Coast Guard Dog Patrol, examines a pair of new canvas boots which were designed to protect the war dog's feet from cuts from oyster shells while on long beach patrols." Original photo caption. *National Archives*

By the autumn of 1943, the perceived national security threat along the U.S. coastline had died down. So the dog training schools were closed and patrols were reduced by three-quarters. But the program wasn't discontinued, as many dogs were retrained for different patrols or special guard duty.[17]

NOTHIN' LIKE A GOOD FIFTY-CENT DOG

A German shepherd named Nora took a different path to Coast Guard glory. She belonged to Apprentice Seaman Evans

E. Mitchell of Chicago, who had purchased her for fifty cents from a neighbor. The sailor trained her to serve alongside him on patrol duty at the Oregon Inlet Station off North Carolina.

On a bitterly cold night in November 1943, Mitchell and Nora were on their regular tour along the isolated beach. Mitchell felt ill and fainted along the water's edge. When Nora could not rouse him, she picked up Mitchell's cap, raced to the nearest Coast Guard station some distance away, and presented it to the guardsman on duty. Chief Boatswain's Mate Thomas J. Harris studied the cap, saw Mitchell's name in it, noted the shepherd's frantic behavior, and finally put two and two together to surmise something was terribly wrong. Nora led him back to Mitchell, still unconscious and lying inside the high tide line. Nora's heroic actions likely prevented Mitchell's death from exposure or drowning.

After the apprentice seaman made a full recovery, the American Society for the Prevention of Cruelty to Animals presented the four-legged heroine with the bronze John P. Haines medal for saving Mitchell's life.

In a reenactment, a fainted Coast Guard sailor, Apprentice Seaman Evan E. Mitchell, is saved by his trusty patrol dog Nora. The dog lured a Guard watchman to the nighttime beach site where Mitchell had fainted, saving the sailor from a likely death from exposure. The German shepherd received the ASPCA's John P. Haines Medal for her heroism. *USCG Archives*

The Coast Guard conducted thousands of 'round-the-clock security patrols during the war, regardless of weather conditions or terrain. And dogs weren't their only animal assistants. Some Coast Guardsmen rode on horseback.[18]

The U.S. Coast Guard patrolled beaches and other significant homeland locations with both War Dog Program graduates and equestrian teams. *USCG Archives*

So many amazing K-9 heroes served during the war that selecting which stories to tell is difficult. Because the War Dog Program began as an experiment, the pressure was on the first wave of canines to justify the program's effectiveness, regardless of which branch they served. Mistakes were made and problems arose, but over time a lot was learned that improved dog recruitment and training.

You are about to learn the inspiring, heroic stories of just some of the first dogs in America's War Dog Program. It is because of their incredible efforts that the program still exists today.

3

Chips

America's First—and Most Highly-Decorated—
War Dog Hero

*"We went through a lot together.... He saved my life
more than once when things were tough."*

—PRIVATE JOHN P. ROWELL, Chips's first handler

COLLIE/GERMAN SHEPHERD/HUSKY MIX—QM TATTOO NO. 11A

He was the poster boy for Dogs for Defense and, outside of movie canines Lassie and Rin Tin Tin, arguably the most beloved dog in the land. A January 14, 1944, headline in the *New York Times* reflected the high esteem in which the military held Chips: "Army Dog Is First to Win DSC Award. Pleasantville Canine Hailed as a Hero with American Troops in Sicily."

Chips was America's first canine hero of World War II. He is the most highly decorated dog in U.S. military history, and one of the most respected by the troops. He received the Silver Star Medal, the Armed Forces' third-highest military combat decoration. Some news organizations even reported that Chips was originally up for the number-two medal, the Distinguished Service Cross. At one time, Chips also was recommended for a Purple Heart. But when these official honors stoked enormous controversy—including complaints that such medals were not intended for animals, only humans—they were revoked.

Still, for several months anyway, the Silver Star was rightfully his.

THE PRIDE OF PLEASANTVILLE

Chips, a collie-German shepherd-husky mix, belonged to the Edward J. Wren family in an all-American village with a name right out of Norman Rockwell: Pleasantville, New York.[1] Chips was stubbornly protective of the Wrens' daughters, eight-year-old Gail and younger sister Nancy; their little brother, John, was still a baby when Chips first joined the security detail at the Wrens' house.

The Wren children (from left) Nancy, John, and Gail proudly admire their war hero pet. *Wren Family Archives*

Before long the energetic mutt was demonstrating his athleticism by chasing the postman and biting garbage collectors.

To channel this aggressive, take-no-prisoners style, the Wrens answered Dogs for Defense's call and volunteered the unsuspecting pup for, pardon the expression, doggie duty. "When the call came for this new idea they had of bringing dogs into the service," John Wren recalled, "my parents knew that we had a very smart, very strong, very powerful dog, and that he was young and that he would be a great candidate.

"I know it was difficult for my mother and father to make this decision because they loved him dearly. . .but they felt it was a very important thing for the country for them to donate and do what they can to help the effort."[2]

PATTON'S PUPS

On May 2, 1942, two-year-old Chips arrived at the War Dog Training Center in Front Royal, Virginia, for instruction as a sentry dog. After graduation in late September 1942, he was branded with the number 11A and paired with a handler, Private John P. Rowell from Arkansas.

Two other male sentry dogs, Watch and Pal, along with one female sentry, Mena—the press dubbed her a "K-9 WAC"—were assigned to the same detachment.[3] All were trained as sentries but not scouts. This meant they provided perimeter defense at night, while in the daytime they simply followed their handlers. The dogs were based at Camp Pickett, Virginia. The Army's furry new fighters didn't know it, but by war's end their commanding officer would rank among the most legendary and controversial military figures in American history. They were attached to the 30th Infantry Regiment, Third Infantry Division of Major General George S. Patton Jr.'s Seventh Army. Eventually, Chips would be among the four-legged fighters to be sent into combat overseas.

OPERATION TORCH

Chips was barely out of training when his unit sailed from Newport News, Virginia, bound for French Morocco in October 1942. The unit was joining Operation Torch, the amphibious invasion of North Africa that would land under enemy fire near Casablanca on November 8, 1942. Torch marked the first time British and American forces collaborated on an invasion plan. General Eisenhower commanded the operation, which depended on five successful landings by the amphibious force at various locations.

General Patton commanded the Western Task Force of thirty-five thousand troops cruising in a fleet. Patton was responsible for three of the landings on French Morocco. His key goal: capture Casablanca.

Chips suffered from seasickness during his voyage. But with good care he was ready to go for the landing. At daybreak on November 8 the dogs were lowered into one of the landing crafts bound for the shoreline. But onshore forces of France's Nazi-collaborating Vichy regime surprised the invaders with heavy fire; one shell that exploded near the dogs' boat reduced poor Mena to cowering and whimpering. The violence left her sidelined for the rest of the mission, severely shell-shocked. The blasts frightened Chips, too, but only briefly. He soon settled down and went to work.

Allied aircraft flew cover overhead as the invaders hit the beach. There on the sands, the dog's handler dug two shallow foxholes, one each for Chips and himself. Chips and Private Rowell hunkered down as bombs exploded and shrapnel whirled everywhere. Soon, Rowell began to dig his hole deeper. Chips watched him for only a moment before quite suddenly his paws frantically swiped at the sand. The dog was following Rowell's lead and expanding his own hole.[4]

Once the beachhead was secured, Chips saw plenty of action—on patrols under fire and on sentry duty with Private Rowell behind enemy lines. Still spooked by the bedlam, poor Mena stayed behind, already struggling with Post Traumatic Stress Disorder.

The Nazi-surrogate Vichy resistance forces soon collapsed; Casablanca was secured two days after the landing. One report praised the performance of the dogs on the mission, noting that triumphant Allied troops had failed to identify "any soldier in an outfit guarded by K-9s stabbed in his sleep and stripped of clothes and equipment by Arab thieves—as was the fate of others."[5] The American sentry dogs had proven their worth in an early field performance.

WHEN ALLIES MEET

With hostilities over in Morocco, Chips moved on to the modest task of protecting heads of state. He assumed sentry duty at the Casablanca Conference, the critical summit between President Franklin D. Roosevelt and British Prime Minister Winston Churchill that opened on January 14, 1943. During the ten-day session the two leaders mapped out the next phase of the Allied Forces' global war strategy. The Conference was also where Roosevelt and Churchill developed the doctrine of "unconditional surrender" in dealing with the Axis powers.

Each night Chips, Watch, and Pal all patrolled the area where the leaders were meeting. Chips was able to rub shoulders with FDR and the British prime minister. French General Charles de Gaulle was also in attendance, but it's not clear if Chips made his acquaintance.

Sergeant William Haulk of Macomb, Illinois took over temporary handling of Chips shortly after Casablanca when Rowell fell ill and landed in the hospital. "We had four war dogs in our battalion," said Haulk, "and Chips was the best liked of them all. After our stay at Casablanca we moved all over North Africa and then into Tunisia. Chips missed the action in Tunisia, but after the battle for Africa was over we trained for the invasion of Sicily."[6]

WHO'S YOUR DADDY?

Around this time it was discovered that Mena was pregnant. She gave birth to nine puppies, apparently "the result of her romance aboard ship with Chips."[7] Some sources, though, claimed the father was Pal; others pointed to Watch. Regardless, Mena's adventures in motherhood ensured strict future enforcement of a rule that all female war dogs be spayed before acceptance by the K-9 Unit. Chips left Mena and her puppies behind when he sailed for Sicily. According to Sergeant Haulk, "the new father was both love sick and sea sick on the trip across the Mediterranean, but got over both amazingly quick when the firing began."[8]

Four of Mena's puppies—Marquis, Gus, Butch, and Runt— returned to the States with their mother, who never fully recovered from PTSD.[9] Drafted at birth, the four war pups went through training at Front Royal, then served their country. Marquis joined the Coast Guard in Baltimore's Curtis Bay district, Gus and Butch served with the Guard in the Pacific Theater, and Runt served with the U.S. Army. There was fierce competition within the outfit for the remaining five pups, who ultimately became mascots.

DOG'S DAY OF DESTINY

July 10, 1943: the day Chips became the first American dog hero of the war. His shining hour came during the Allied invasion of Sicily, code named Operation Husky. The historic predawn assault, a major amphibious and airborne campaign, combined air and sea landings involving a hundred fifty thousand troops, three thousand ships, four thousand aircraft—and the one dog who would ever hold America's third-highest military honor. It was one of the largest combined operations of the war, when Allied forces took the island of Sicily away from Axis control.

After Private Rowell's hospital stay, Chips had been reunited with his original handler. The duo was still attached to the Seventh Army commanded by General Patton.[10]

At around 4:20 in the morning Rowell led Chips ashore through darkness and horrible wind. They had landed at Blue Beach, just east of Licata on Sicily's southern coastline. At the break of dawn they had advanced some three hundred yards in from the water's edge when the platoon was pinned down by an Italian machine-gun team hidden in what looked like a peasant hut. Two machine guns were firing from the hut. As the platoon hit the ground, Chips bared his teeth, broke from Rowell, charged the nest, and leaped into the pillbox, seemingly oblivious to the barrage of gunfire.

Rowell and the others could only look on helplessly. They heard gunshots from inside and feared the worst.

"There was an awful lot of noise and the firing stopped. Then, I saw one Italian soldier come out the door with Chips at his throat. I called him off before he could kill the man," Rowell said.[11] Next, the handler reported, three other enemy soldiers then emerged, their hands raised in surrender. According to one of the dog's later handlers, W. H. Bryant Jr., once inside the pillbox Chips had "grabbed the machine gun by the barrel and pulled it off its mount."[12]

Chips risked his life to single-handedly eliminate the Italian hideout, thus saving the lives of many Allied soldiers. The shepherd's bravery also enabled the Allied landing party to continue advancing. By 11:30 that morning, Licata was firmly in American hands.

Chips, however, did not emerge unscathed. The courageous canine suffered a scalp wound and powder burns from the pistol shots inside the hut. He was treated, but his injuries weren't serious enough to warrant removing him from field duty. That was lucky, because later that day Chips's keen sense of smell tipped him off to the presence of ten Italian soldiers. They were quickly discovered moving silently towards the beach, apparently hoping to infiltrate the invaders' camp. Instead, all were taken into custody.[13]

"'Chips,' the dog hero of the 3d Infantry Division. Chips was wounded while invading a machine gun nest. Capua Sector, Italy, November 19, 1943. 30th Infantry, 3rd Infantry Division." November 19, 1943. Original photo caption. *National Archives*

Dogs for Defense immediately credited Chips for the capture. Overnight, press coverage made the Wrens' shepherd an international hero.

BITING THE HAND THAT COMMANDS YOU

Chips stayed with the battalion until the fighting on Sicily ended on August 17. He then joined Lieutenant General Mark W. Clark's Fifth Army, which landed in Italy a month later and participated in Operation Avalanche—the Allies' invasion of the Italian mainland. Chips saw action at the bloody Battle of Salerno on September 9 and in the Naples-Foggia and Rome-Arno campaigns, the latter of which stretched through most of 1944.

Chips's heroic reputation was already established when, after Salerno, he met the Allied commander-in-chief in the Mediterranean Theater. Like everyone, General Dwight D. Eisenhower was impressed by Chips's valor during the Sicilian landing. But Ike's face-to-face meeting with the celebrated shepherd sentry didn't quite go as planned. When the general bent over to congratulate him, Chips—trained to allow only his handler to touch him—actually nipped Eisenhower on the hand! But all was soon forgiven; after all, this was just what Chips was drilled to do.

After his heroics in Sicily, Chips meets General Dwight D. Eisenhower. *U.S. Army Signal Corps/National Archives*

"FOR GALLANTRY IN ACTION"

Once the Third Division Infantry Regiment confirmed details of Chips's valiant acts—tackling the machine gunners and helping capture the ten Italian soldiers—platoon commander Captain Edward G. Parr proposed the war dog be "cited in orders and awarded the Distinguished Service Cross for extra heroism in action."

"Chips' courageous act," Parr declared in the September 9, 1943 citation, "single-handedly eliminating a dangerous machine-gun nest and causing the surrender of its crew, reflects the highest credit on himself and the military service."[14]

Chips accepts a treat from his handler. *Quartermaster Museum Archives*

Further up the chain of command, Major General Lucian K. Truscott Jr., commander of the Third Division, liked the idea. Truscott boldly waived War Department rules barring animals from being so honored and approved not the Distinguished

Service Cross but the Silver Star for Chips. Six weeks later, General Order No. 79 from Headquarters read:

> I–AWARD OF THE SILVER STAR …a Silver Star is awarded to the following named individuals: "CHIPS," 11-A, U.S. Army Dog, Company I, Thirtieth Infantry. For gallantry in action. After landing on Blue Beach east of Licata, Sicily, at about 0420 the morning of 10 July, 1943, "CHIPS" and his handler advanced about 300 yards inland under a flurry of flares and tracer bullets. After maneuvering through machine gun fire they approached what appeared to be a native grass hut. Suddenly, a hidden enemy machine gun began firing from the hut on troops on the beach. Unhesitantly, "CHIPS" wrenched his leash from his handler's hand, dashed into the hut, teeth bared, and vigorously attacked the enemy gun crew. After a few seconds, the gun ceased firing, loud yelling could be heard and out of the hut one of the crew came running, "CHIPS" tearing at his neck. The second crewman soon followed, his hands raised high in surrender. American soldiers quickly took charge of the prisoners. "CHIPS" courageous act, single-handedly eliminating a dangerous machine gun nest and causing surrender of its crew, reflects the highest credit on himself and the military service. Entered the service from Front Royal, Virginia.[15]

The citation specifically singled out the dog's heroics on Sicily. Chips was also recommended for a Purple Heart, for burns suffered to the left side of his mouth and left eye. But when controversy about awarding military medals to a dog arose, the recommendation was revoked and he never received the Purple Heart.

Almost a month later, on November 19, Chips was formally presented his Silver Star "somewhere in Italy. . .for bravery in action against the enemy." As Chips accepted the honor, "a group of soldiers stood at attention and heavy guns pounded enemy mountain positions to the north."[16]

Chips remains the only dog in history to receive the Silver Star. "There is no question or doubt in my mind as to whether he deserves it," William H. Bryant assured the Wren family in a letter.[17]

The press was all over the story. Dogs for Defense seized on the free and inspiring publicity to step up its domestic dog donation program.[18]

But the hoopla would be short-lived. William Thomas was national commander of the Military Order of the Purple Heart. In a letter to President Roosevelt and the War Department, Thomas complained that presenting medals "to one Chips, a G.I. battle dog, decries the high and lofty purposes for which the medal was created."[19] Thomas launched a campaign to revoke the Silver Star and ensure that military honors never again be awarded to animals.

The campaign worked. On February 3, 1944, word from Army headquarters made it official: Chips's Silver Star was revoked.[20] The headline in the *New York Times* read, "Award of Soldier Medals to Dogs is Barred by Army after Protest."[21] Chips was also denied the Purple Heart. Yet on February 3, 1944, Major General J. A. Ulio, the Army's Adjutant General, wrote, that "if it is desired to recognize the outstanding services of an animal or a fowl, appropriate citation may be published in unit general orders."[22]

Medals or not, Chips proved himself a genuine hero, and his inspiring story of valor was retold in papers across America.

In a letter to the Wren family, Private Charles Zimmerman, who served with Chips in Africa, Sicily, and Italy, shared his admiration for the war hero: "Your Chips is a dog to be proud of and every member of the battalion that he is in is sure proud of him. I'm glad that we have Chips and dogs like him on our side instead of the enemy's."[23]

The *New York Times* took a playful approach, reporting that Chips "has met President Roosevelt, Prime Minister Churchill and Gen Dwight Eisenhower, and is reported to be anxious to bite Hitler."[24]

CHANGING DUTIES

By December 1943, the stress of wartime service had taken its toll on Chips. The heroic pup, by now suffering from shell fire-related combat fatigue, "retired" from frontline duty with "I" Company, 30th Infantry Regiment to Headquarters Company, 3rd Infantry Division and was reassigned to guard duty for Captain Charles G. Juneau, the executive officer of Headquarters Company.[25]

The following July, the unit left Italy to help prepare for the invasion of southern France. Captain Juneau was transferred and promoted to assistant provost marshal, or second in command of military police. But he went home to the States three months later, and Chips was assigned his last handler, W. H. Bryant Jr., a provost sergeant who supervised the prisoners-of-war enclosure.

"ONE MAN GUARD COMPANY"

In January 1945 Chips began nighttime duty guarding prisoners of war held in the Vosges Mountains near Colmar in Alsace, France. Bryant found his canine charge "a one-man guard company. The prisoners were more afraid of him than all the guns in the American Army. If one so much as moved—you can bet he knew it and wouldn't fail to let everyone know it. A few made the mistake of getting too close to him and they thought the devil had grabbed them."[26]

Bryant also maintained Chips deserved and should have been honored with the same medals awarded to his human colleagues, including the Presidential Citation with a cluster: "he earned this with 'I' Company, 30th Infantry, on Mt Rotundo in Italy and the Colmar Pocket in Alsace." Bryant also insisted that Chips deserved the highly prestigious "French Fourragere. . .the European Theater ribbon, and for all good soldiers, the Good Conduct Ribbon."[27]

Chips guards German POWs. *National Archives*

Bryant and Chips wrapped up their wartime duty in Salzburg, Austria in the summer of 1945. "Chips continued serving as a good soldier should," Bryant wrote, "which was the only way he knew."[28]

They finally headed home from Le Havre, France, on September 23, catching a ride on a Liberty ship. But the men of Chips's platoon wouldn't let him leave without first showing their appreciation. They presented him with an unofficial Theater Ribbon medal with arrowhead—for an assault landing—and eight battle stars acknowledging Chips's contributions to the fighting in French Morocco, Tunisia, Sicily, Naples-Foggia, Rome-Arno, Southern France, the Rhineland, and Central Europe.

"THE BEST FRIEND I'VE EVER HAD"

Bryant and Chips arrived in Boston on October 5. It was a bittersweet day for Bryant, who would be returning the dog he loved to the Army Remount Station at Front Royal, Virginia. There Chips would be retrained for civilian life before being discharged to the Wren family. "It was," Bryant admitted, "like giving up the best friend I've ever had."

Bryant's affection and admiration for the battle-tested dog are revealed at the end of his note to the family: "No one in the world has a better dog than you....

"We [had] quite a few nights on the same cot, bed or whatever we could get. He's the best friend I've ever had."[29]

A HERO'S WELCOME

"Mr. Chips," as it states on his discharge papers, was honorably discharged from the Aleshire Quartermaster Depot at Front Royal, Virginia on December 10, 1945, and headed home to the Wren family.

By now the four-legged veteran was quite the celebrity and, as such, was accompanied on the train ride to Pleasantville, New York, by six reporters and photographers. A boisterous crowd greeted the local hero as the 9:30 express rolled into the station. When he saw Chips, four-year-old Johnny Wren threw his arms around him.

"I remember going to the station with my father and others and having friends and all kinds of people around," John Wren said later. "But I mostly remember when I saw him in the cage and realized that was *my* dog coming home. I was quite excited, as was everybody."[30]

"Scores of adults clustered around the baggage car to greet the hero," the *New York Times* noted.[31] After a celebration and photo op at the station, the Wrens brought their conquering hero home, where he was celebrated anew by neighbors and extended family. Chips seemed oblivious to all the attention. As you might expect, the Wrens' kids were especially thrilled to have him back—young John, nine-year-old Nancy, and Gail, who was twelve.

Between the long trip and the excitement of the day's festivities, Chips was exhausted. When the public fuss played itself out, the distinguished hero of Pleasantville fell into a deep sleep. At long last he was safe at home and surrounded by loved ones.

OLD HABITS DIE HARD

Once rested, Chips settled back into his original stateside duty of guarding the Wren children. This was no honorary Fourth of July parade kind of thing. Not to Chips, anyway. Years later John Wren recalled how much he enjoyed walking Chips as a boy, showing off his very own national hero to his Pleasantville neighbors. "I had an Army uniform, of sorts," Wren said, "complete with a cap and a cowboy holster. I would walk around like a guard, up and down Orchard Street with my war dog right next to me, saluting everyone I passed. I remember it to this day. I was very proud."[32]

Then one day on guard duty, Chips had a flashback to Sicily and the war. "A kid came running out of his house towards Chips and me, firing a cap gun at us. Chips immediately sprang into action. It was like a 'growl and a rip' as Chips grabbed the gun away from him.

"He didn't charge or bite the kid, just scared him as he took the gun away. It all happened so fast. The kid ran crying into the house. My mother got all kinds of flak from the neighbors that Chips was a dangerous war dog."[33]

But even more impressive was how Chips literally saved little Johnny's life. "My mother told me the story about how we were all at Quogue Beach [on Long Island's south shore] one day," Wren recalled, "and I wandered out to the water. Suddenly the undertow took me under, and Chips was the only one who saw it happen. He ran into the water and pulled me out by my swim trunks. He was quite an animal."[34]

GOODBYE, MR. CHIPS

Sadly, Chips never had much of a chance to fully readjust to civilian life. He was home just seven months when on April 16, 1946, he succumbed to kidney failure. Contrary to published accounts, Chips was not interred in a nearby pet cemetery. In fact the beloved war hero was buried in a small, unmarked grave in woods near Pleasantville. Only the surviving Wren family members know the plot's precise location.

In September 1947, the Wrens received a letter from Private John Rowell, one which certainly must have felt bittersweet to the family. Rowell asked after Chips, unaware that his onetime comrade in arms had passed. "We went through a lot together," Rowell wrote to the family, "and he is really wonderful. He saved my life more than once when things were tough. . . .

"Mrs. Wren, I could never express in writing how I feel about him but please take good care of him."

Goodbye, Mr. Chips, and thank you. You will always be America's most highly decorated war dog hero.

4

Devil Dogs of the Marine Corps

"The dogs have proven themselves as message carriers, scouts, and vital night security.... They were remarkable and more are needed."[1]

—LIEUTENANT COLONEL ALAN SHAPLEY, Commander, 2nd Marine Raider Regiment (Provisional)

On November 26, 1942, word came from Washington that the Marines would be putting together their own war dog training facility. The authorizing directive came from no less than USMC Commandant Lieutenant General Thomas Holcomb, who ordered the unit established at Camp Lejeune, in New River, North Carolina. Brought in to run the facility was Jackson H. Boyd, a Marine captain from Southern Pines, North Carolina. A quarter-century earlier, Boyd had served as an Army artilleryman in World War I. But, significantly, he also was a dog trainer and breeder who owned seventy foxhounds.[2]

BUILDING A DOG PROGRAM FOR THE MARINES

When the order came down, Boyd and nineteen enlisted Marines were already busy training with dogs at Fort Robinson, Nebraska. The twenty-five-hundred-acre outpost tucked into the northwest corner of that state was more than eighteen hundred miles from the new K-9 training headquarters at Lejeune.

Meantime, in Maryland, four more Marine enlistees were training with canines at Fort Washington in Prince George's County.

As the new handlers completed their coursework, the commandant ordered each one from Fort Robinson to bring two dogs with him to Lejeune. Adding to these thirty-eight canines were two that Captain Boyd brought along himself. And the Marines at Fort Washington would return with two messenger dogs.[3] These forty-two draftees were joined by twenty Dobermans procured by Roslyn Terhune, a columnist and Baltimore dog fancier with the Doberman Pinscher Club of America.[4] These sixty-two dogs became the nucleus of the K-9 training unit at Lejeune.

DEVIL DOGS GET IN SHAPE

Three notable messenger dogs among those arriving from Fort Robinson were the German Shepherds Caesar (branded as 05H), Jack (09H), and Thor (12H).[5] They officially became Devil Dogs on March 3, 1942, and were the only German Shepherds in the 1st Marine War Dog Platoon to ship out to the Pacific.

Jack, Thor, and Caesar: 1st Marine War Dog Platoon's messenger team. March 17, 1944. *Marc Wortman*

Ah, the nickname. Devil Dog. It originally referred to human, not four-legged Marines. According to one popular explanation, the pet name (so to speak) dated from World War I, when the German army admired the Marines' tenacious fighting spirit so much that they began calling them "Teufel Hunden," or "Satan/devil dog."[6]

When the Marines organized their training facility, the Doberman Pinscher Club of America (DPCA) agreed to handle dog procurement. The Doberman was thought to be the breed best suited for the harsh Pacific jungle climate because of its aggressive but controlled temperament, work ethic, and short hair.[7]

The DPCA set up sixteen recruiting regions across the country that its members canvassed for recruits. Spending their own time and money, they routinely traveled up to a hundred miles from home to check out potential applicants. "Their payment for this effort," said a Marine spokesman in Washington, "is the satisfaction they get from contributing to the war effort and the promotion of their breed.

"When they examine a dog and tell us he is okay, we enroll him."[8]

Training begins for the 1st Marine War Dog Platoon. German shepherd Caesar is pictured at the back of the pack, far right. *Marine Raider Museum Archives*

RECORD BOOKS: THE PERSONAL TOUCH

The first dog to "enlist" directly in the Marine Corps was a boxer named Fritz. Naturally, he was assigned the service number 1. Like Fritz, each incoming dog underwent an indelible ink ID branding on the underside of the right earflap. (Enlistees who had originally come into the military via Dogs for Defense or the Quartermaster Corps retained their original brand numbers.)

Every dog was also issued a record book for recording stats and background information.[9] Among all branches, the Marine Corps alone maintained these biographical dog logs. According to data compiled in the *USMC Dog Service Record Books, 1942–1945*, 1,033 trained dogs served with the Marine Corps in World War II. Most were products of the Marines' own program; only 13 percent—or 132 dogs—were trained by Dogs for Defense and the Army's Quartermaster Corps.[10]

Private Dean ponders the contents of his own record book. *National Archives*

The individual dog record books provide a fascinating glimpse of military history. Each four-by-six-inch book runs forty pages and is a treasure trove of personal information on a dog. Some even include the original enrollment application, designed to be completed from the dog's perspective. Each book's records were kept current by a dog's handler and stayed with the dog wherever he or she was stationed. Many surviving record books still retain a picture taken of the canine recruit.

Honorary promotions went to dogs based on length of service. After three months, a dog became a private first class. Following that, promotions came annually: corporal at one year; sergeant after two; three years brought a platoon sergeant rank; four years, gunner sergeant; and after five years a dog rose to master gunner sergeant. Ranks achieved and the corresponding promotion dates were duly recorded in a dog's record book. It was inevitable that eventually some dogs outranked their own handlers. On paper, anyway.

The books deliver an up-close and personal portrait of each Devil Dog serving the Corps. For the reader, these modest bound paperbacks bring the dogs to life. This is especially true of each volume's "Notes on Training" section. Fritz (no. 1) is described as "a very tractable dog and excellent worker."[11] Another K-9 recruit, Sparks (no. 49), seems to have been popular: "Sparky is a good big sound dog with a happy-go-lucky personality.... He is the clown of the platoon."

Sometimes the handlers' entries are stirring to read, and it is difficult not to be touched by a dog's dedication, work, sacrifice—and by the bonds between the dog and his wartime master.

SEMPER FIDO

Since the Marines are strictly a combat organization, branch brass chose to train Corps dogs only as scouts and messengers, reasoning that "unless the dogs contributed directly to the killing of the enemy and the keeping down of casualties in outfits to which the animals were assigned," it was a waste of time and manpower to train them.[12] Some sentry training, however, was included because the dogs slept in foxholes with their handlers, remaining "on guard" throughout the night.

Butch stands guard as he lets his handler, Private First Class Rez P. Hester, catch some much-needed rest. *National Archives*

If individual Marines were dogged by doubts, the official attitude of the Corps was simple and unequivocal: "Dogs are weapons," a USMC Planning and Policies Division statement declared. "They give our men added power of observation through their acute sense of smell and hearing."[13]

The seven Marine war dog platoons trained at Camp Lejeune all ultimately served in the Pacific. Let's meet a few of the heroes who served with the 1st Marine War Dog Platoon.

THE FIRST TO WAR

Clyde A. Henderson was a chemistry instructor from Cleveland's James Ford Rhodes High School. But he wasn't recruited to lead the 1st Marine War Dog Platoon because he had mastered the periodic table. The first lieutenant (later captain) was also a Doberman fancier and trainer in civilian life. As platoon commander, Henderson would put twenty-four dogs through their paces. The 1st Marine War Dog Platoon consisted of twenty-one Doberman pinschers and three German shepherds, forty-eight handlers (two for each dog), plus six instructors and headquarters personnel. Twelve dogs were schooled as scouts, six saw service as sentries, and three mobilized as messengers. Three casualty canines also were assigned to the platoon.[14]

Henderson arrived at Lejeune in March 1943 to find a "platoon composed most[ly] of green dogs and green men," as 60 percent of the K-9 recruits arrived there just two weeks or less before being shipped out to war.[15] The chemistry teacher from Cleveland knew he had a lot of work ahead just to get everyone battle-ready. Henderson felt the pressure. "My own fears were inspired mainly by the fact that we were a rush-order outfit," he wrote the following year for a magazine, "and the success or failure of this first platoon would pretty much determine whether the Marine Corps would continue with dogs."[16]

The situation demanded a different kind of chemistry, and Henderson set about drilling everyone, dogs and men alike, into shape.

The 1st Marine War Dog Platoon left Camp Lejeune on April 30, 1943, embarking on a five-day train ride to Camp Pendleton in Southern California. As the platoon pulled out, the 2nd and 3rd War Dog Platoons back at Lejeune were starting their own war training.

At Pendleton, the dogs and men of the 1st Platoon received accelerated training from Carl Spitz, the Hollywood dog trainer who had been so instrumental in setting up the Dogs for Defense training program. A few weeks later, in June, they boarded a Liberty ship and set off into the Pacific.[17]

On the voyage, the dogs followed a strict exercise routine— a morning session, after which they were groomed, then two more exercise sessions later in the day. The men built an "outdoor head" on the sundeck where the dogs could relieve themselves. The thoughtfully designed makeshift restroom even came with sand and posts, which were stand-ins for fire hydrants or trees. The furry trainees were fed at 5:00 in the afternoon. By 7:00 p.m. they were crated for the night. To keep curious sailors and troops away, a human sentry stood a twenty-four-hour guard on the canines. Only one dog ever got seasick; the men were not so lucky.[18]

The ship landed in New Caledonia in the southwest Pacific. After a demonstration of their skills as patrol/scouts and messengers, the unit's dogs were attached to the Headquarters and Service (H&S) Company, then joined forces with the 2nd Marine Raider Regiment (Provisional). The regiment's distinguished commander, Lieutenant Colonel Alan Shapley, had survived the sinking of the USS *Arizona* at Pearl Harbor and earned a Silver Star for his gallantry. The war dog units and Shapley's regiment had a lot to learn about each other. Using dogs in combat was considered an experiment, and there were mixed feelings on the front lines.

"Many of the Marine troops doubted that dogs could be put to any practical use in combat, and grumbled that they would just get in the way," 1st Marine War Dog Platoon leader Henderson wrote. "Others were sure the dogs would go berserk under fire."[19] To ease the concerns, extra training time was lavished on the canines so that all were as prepared as possible.

On October 4, 1943, the regiment set sail for Empress Augusta Bay, Bougainville, in the Solomon Islands. It would be the first time the dogs and handlers would be under hostile fire.

BOUGAINVILLE OR BUST

Bougainville, the largest of the Solomon Islands, was temporary home to forty thousand Japanese soldiers—250 square miles of "the most miserable, impenetrable, sniper-impregnated rain forest in the world," with jungle so dense that you couldn't "see, smell or hear a man five feet away."[20] So by necessity the dogs became the eyes and ears of the Marines.

The invasion's objective was to take the port of Empress Augusta Bay, the Islands' deepest and best port, then extend the beachhead out about six square miles; the Japanese could keep the rest of the island. The Marines then planned to build and defend an airfield for American planes providing airborne security for the task forces and convoys that would invade the Philippines in October 1944. This initial landing on Bougainville was a Marine Corps operation, but once all was secure, the Army would take over.

The invasion of Bougainville began at dawn on November 1, 1943. Twelve transports carried more than 14,300 troops, including the 1st Marine War Dog Platoon.

According to the official *Journal of the 1st Marine Dog Platoon*, dogs and handlers were divided into two units. The first, with ten dogs, was part of the initial landing ("H Hour"). Two hours later, the other fourteen dogs followed in a second wave ("H Hour + 2 Hours"). The dogs were hoisted over the side of the USS *George Clymer* and lowered by rope into one of three Higgins amphibious landing crafts.

Dogs being lowered into a Higgins boat. *National Archives/USMC Archives*

The first Marines who hit the beach were met with heavier than expected enemy fire. "As we approached the shore, shells fell so close that the barge almost capsized. Shell fragments dented the ramp," Henderson recalled. "The handlers were hugging their dogs. I suspected they were trying to reassure themselves as much as the dogs.

"When our barge stalled on the sand ten yards from the shore, we leaped into the water and the dogs swam after us.

"In a few whirling seconds, all of us—dogs and men—raced across the short stretch of sand and dived into the jungle. The dogs were heaving excitedly, but ready for anything."[21]

That was the start. Although confronted with various obstacles, the landing force still managed to repel the Japanese defenders. By nightfall, all fourteen-thousand-plus troops were ashore, along with sixty-two-hundred tons of fuel, rations, and ammunition.

The Marines had landed. Now came the real work.

Canine valor helped in the operation, with three dogs really standing out: the messenger German shepherds Caesar and Jack, and a silent scout/patrol dog named Andy, a Doberman pinscher.

Jack leads the way, followed by Caesar, Thor, and their Doberman pinscher comrades on Bougainville, Solomon Islands. *USMC Archives*

CAESAR

"I would not give Caesar up for a general's commission."
—**PRIVATE FIRST CLASS RUFUS MAYO,** Caesar's handler

GERMAN SHEPHERD—QM TATOO #05H

Caesar's story really begins with the Max Glazer family of the Bronx. Or, rather, with the family's three grown sons: Max Jr., Morris, and Irving, the youngest and a student at City College of New York. The Glazer brothers wanted a dog—specifically, a German shepherd. They figured that if they pooled their money—all sixty dollars of it—each could claim a one-third interest in the new pet. Every Sunday for three months, the boys drove around Long Island looking for "the one." No dog, however, met their exacting standards—until they met nine-week-old Caesar von Steuben, who "just stood out as the best in the litter." According to one published account, he acquired the name because, even as a puppy, "he looked like a future conqueror."[22]

Caesar was beloved by the entire family. For his part, however, Caesar really took a shine to Mrs. Glazer. (Was it because she fed him? Hmmm.) Caesar proved a great watchdog, but another skill made him a neighborhood celebrity. He demonstrated the trick whenever the brothers took him along to the grocery store or bakery. After their purchases were wrapped together, they sent Caesar home with the parcel. All they had to say was, "Take it to mom," and off he went. Caesar simply would not stop until the parcel was delivered directly to Mrs. Glazer at their fourth-floor walk-up.

The German shepherd was steadfastly obedient and a quick study. Sometimes Irving took him to a park for training. When told to sit, Caesar wouldn't move again until Irving gave the word. Sometimes he stayed frozen for fifteen minutes or longer. If they were running together and Irving yelled, "Stop!," Caesar stopped on a dime.

That obedience and loyalty would serve him well in combat.

When war erupted, the draft took all three Glazer sons. With the boys away and Mr. Glazer working nights, Mrs. Glazer feared Caesar would be too much dog for her to handle alone. When Dogs for Defense began its pitch for recruits, the Glazers saw it as Caesar's opportunity to join Max, Morris, and Irving in wartime service to the country.

ALL HAIL, CAESAR

At first Caesar joined the Army, which tattooed him Dog 05H and sent him on to Fort Robinson, Nebraska, for training as a messenger dog. This training included lessons on how *not* to bark—something that would be critical when enemy soldiers were nearby. At Fort Robinson, he met two other German shepherds, Jack and Thor, who would ultimately follow him to the Marine Corps.

Thor, Caesar, and Jack with handlers. *Marine Raider Museum Archives*

On March 3, 1943, Caesar swapped service branches, transferring to the Marine Corps at Camp Lejeune and joining the 1st Marine War Dog Platoon. At Lejeune he met his new handlers, Privates First Class John Kleeman of Philadelphia and Rufus Mayo from Montgomery, Alabama. They trained together as a team until April 30, when all shipped out to Camp Pendleton. After arriving there five days later, Caesar began secondary training as a sentry and also messenger dog.

One dog handler recognized Caesar as "the smartest dog I ever knew, and the smartest in the platoon." Private Homer Finley from Longmont, Colorado, who also handled both Jack and Thor, said Caesar "was just a great dog."[23]

Caesar's own handler became so attached to him that, when writing home, Mayo had the dog send his love by pressing his paw print to the lower right-hand corner of the letter.[24]

CRY "HAVOC!" AND LET SLIP THE DOGS OF WAR

When they hit the sands at Bougainville, two dog teams went to work immediately—Caesar's as messenger, Andy's as scout/patrol. Andy worked at point, which made him most vulnerable to enemy fire. Caesar pulled up the rear, ready to deliver messages whenever needed.

They were working with M Company, a 250-man patrol moving inland to set up a roadblock on the Piva Trail before the Japanese could counter-attack.[25] Conventional communications were impossible: telephone lines had not been established in the area at the time, and walkie-talkies were useless in the dense jungle.

Thus Caesar played a critical role in the operation because he represented the only means of communication between the front line and the Marines' command center. Once the roadblock was established, Caesar was busy running important messages to the battalion command post.

"Caesar's handler, Pfc. Rufus Mayo, took Caesar into a quiet conference. . .and began talking softly about Caesar's other handler, Pfc. John Kleeman, who was back at the command post waiting," Henderson later wrote. "Insistently, Mayo kept whispering, 'Where's Johnny?' Caesar grew tense. Then with a flourish, Mayo unsnapped the leash and ordered, 'Report!'"[26]

That's all Caesar needed to hear. He raced off to find Kleeman. Rifle shots echoed ominously as Caesar disappeared into the jungle. But he made it through the enemy fire and delivered messages that afternoon and into the night.

Caesar working in the field. *National Archives*

On Day Two of the invasion telephone lines were laid, only to be cut by the Japanese. Again Caesar had to run messages and other papers between the advanced positions and headquarters. At least two runs were completed with Caesar dodging sniper fire.

At night, the brave Bronx dog stood sentry, displaying the perfect discipline and obedience he had shown the Glazer boys back home.

WOUNDED AT WAR

If Caesar performed well his first two days at Bougainville, on Day Three he truly proved his value as a sentry and showed why he had become the "darling of the raiders." Handlers had their dogs join them in foxholes. The men rested easier knowing the animals were keeping watch. "It's a harrowing thing to try and relax and sleep in a foxhole when you are wondering if a [Japanese soldier] may creep in and knife you when you [are] sleep," Clyde Henderson observed. That was no exaggeration.

At dawn, the Japanese attacked. Caesar was in a foxhole with Mayo while Kleeman remained at the command post at regimental headquarters. Caesar alone heard the attackers sneaking into camp, and his instinctive reaction was to protect his handler, Mayo, sleeping there beside him. Caesar launched out of the foxhole and raced towards the enemy intruders.

When Mayo realized what was happening, he shouted at the dog to stop and return. But as Caesar turned to obey, a Japanese soldier opened fire, sending two bullets into his body—one into Caesar's left shoulder, the other into his left hip.

In the chaos and confusion of the ensuing skirmish, Caesar went missing. "Mayo was frantic," Henderson remembered. "He was half shouting and half crying" as they searched for the dog. At last they found a trail of blood through the jungle. Caesar had raced back to Kleeman at the battalion command post, where he was discovered in the bushes, barely conscious. Kleeman didn't even know Caesar had entered the camp. Mayo rushed to gently comfort the wounded war dog.

Tending to Caesar's wounds in the field. *USMC Archives*

"Three raiders were busy improvising a special stretcher," Henderson wrote. The men chopped down two long bamboo poles, lashed two short cross poles together, then fastened a blanket to form a hammock. A dozen other Marines volunteered to carry Caesar to the regimental first-aid station.[27]

Caesar is carried in a makeshift stretcher to the regimental first aid station. *USMC Archives*

Caesar's wounds being x-rayed. November 3, 1943. *National Archives* [28]

The bullet in his hip was removed, but the other was too close to Caesar's heart. The regimental surgeon, Lieutenant Commander Steven L. Steigler, felt the bullet was too risky to remove, so he left it alone.

YOU CAN'T KEEP A GOOD DOG DOWN

But the remaining slug didn't bother Caesar, who made a full recovery and was back on active duty three weeks later. His reputation was growing, especially after he had been credited with being the first war dog to carry a message in actual combat. Lieutenant Henderson noted in his log that "Caesar made nine official runs carrying messages, overlays, and captured

[Japanese] papers. On at least two of these runs he went through sniper fire. Caesar and his handlers are real heroes."[29]

Details of Caesar's heroics were reported stateside. Among the early accounts: how he had saved his handler, Mayo, from a grenade attack. During a sneak assault Caesar reportedly tore into a Japanese soldier's arm, causing him to drop the grenade and flee before Mayo called Caesar back. An official investigation revealed that Mayo had actually called Caesar back before the war dog was able to attack the enemy soldier. The story had been embellished, apparently to give the folks back home some encouraging news. But Mayo later wrote to his parents that he "owed his life to Caesar not only on this occasion but on many others."[30]

Caesar was among four dogs wounded at Bougainville. While he survived, two of the others did not. All told, Kleeman reported that Caesar was wounded three times during his service.

The platoon left for Guadalcanal on January 12, 1944, where they joined H&S Company of the 4th Marines.

1st War Dog Platoon and the 4th Marines. *Marc Wortman*

The dogs' record books indicate that they remained there for fourteen months, until March 15, 1945, when they joined the war's largest and bloodiest amphibious assault in the Pacific

Theater: the Battle of Okinawa. The 1st Marine War Dog Platoon arrived on Okinawa on April 1, 1945.

ALL GOOD DOGS GO TO HEAVEN

Sadly, for some unknown reason many pages in Caesar's record book are missing, so details are lost. But one entry, from April 17, 1945, jumps off the page: "K.I.A."

On that day, three weeks shy of VE Day and four months short of the Allies' victory over Japan, Caesar was killed in action.

It isn't known how Caesar was killed, but presumably it was by sniper fire. What is known is that he carried that original slug, the one close to his heart, until the day he died.

Caesar is forever remembered as America's first messenger dog in combat. He sure did the Morris brothers proud.

———

JACK

"Jack is really a second Rin-Tin-Tin. Boy, is he coming swell! However I think that the officers here have too big ideas for Jack and me to carry out. We'll surely do our best, though."[31]

—PRIVATE FIRST CLASS GORDON J. WORTMAN, Jack's handler

GERMAN SHEPHERD—QM TATOO #09H

A three-year-old German shepherd, Jack came to Dogs for Defense from the Joseph Verhaeghe family of Floral Park, Long Island, a half hour drive from the Glazers in the Bronx. Verhaeghe was a painter and decorator who had immigrated to America from his native Belgium after World War I, seeking a fresh start in the New World.

But the second war with Germany brought new horrors to Verhaeghe, as many of his family members remained in Belgium. He was determined to help "rid this world of oppression once and for all."[32] Verhaeghe tried to enlist in the Seabees, but a punctured eardrum made him ineligible. Next, he tried the Merchant Marine, with the same result. Then the Belgian immigrant tried to enlist in the Canadian army, but once again it was thumbs down.

Joseph Verhaeghe, though, was a man on a mission. When he heard about the Dogs for Defense recruiting efforts, Verhaeghe hoped Jack might somehow make up for his own failure to get into the fight. But to donate the hound, Verhaeghe first needed the permission of the shepherd's actual owner: his eleven-year-old son, Bobby.

The family had rescued Jack from the local animal shelter where an Army inductee had left him. Bobby cherished the dog and Jack had quickly become a wonderful guardian for the boy.

Understand, Jack was no angel. In fact, he was something of a prankster. To neighbors, he was the notorious local ice cream thief who would snatch a cone from an innocent child and vacuum it down in a single gulp. To his credit, Jack was a gentleman thief who never bit. And Joseph Verhaeghe always kindly replaced the neighbor kids' stolen cones.

The family could never stay angry with Jack for long; he knew just how to play them. The dog's strategy was simple. Whenever Jack misbehaved, he'd stick his head under Mrs. Verhaeghe's arm. "He was as cute as the dickens and you just couldn't do anything to him," she said.[33]

So sending Jack off to war was a very difficult call, especially for his young owner. "Pop, if Jack can save lives," Bobby declared at last through tears, "I want him to go in."[34]

Thus began the saga of Jack, the War Dog.

PAWS FOR THE FIGHT

Like Caesar, Jack received his basic and preliminary messenger training from the U.S. Army, which tattooed him with the ID number 09H. During training, the Army introduced its new recruit to two other German shepherds also learning the ropes—Caesar and Thor. These three eventually made up the messenger dog unit of the 1st Marine War Dog Platoon.

Jack in training to be a messenger dog at Camp Lejeune, with Sergeant Raymond Barnowsky of Pontiac, Michigan. *National Archives*

Beyond a newly-acquired tattoo, Jack boasted at least one other characteristic that helped distinguish him from the other dogs: a somewhat abbreviated left ear. He had lost the tip in a dogfight. This especially helped differentiate him from Thor, who like Jack boasted a light-colored coat.

Jack excelled in training and transferred to Camp Lejeune and the Marines with his canine compatriots on March 3, 1943. Training continued there, this time with two new handlers, Privates First Class Gordon J. Wortman of Davis Junction, Illinois, and Paul Joseph Castracane of Cohoes in upstate New York. Wortman had prior experience training dogs, and after boot camp he had asked to serve with a war dog platoon.

The team trained together up until leaving at the end of April for Camp Pendleton in California. Once there, Jack's messenger training kicked up a notch. Per his record book, on May 5 Jack began more than four months of demanding scout/patrol instruction. Then, on September 15, the unit sailed to New Caledonia to link up with the 2nd Marine Raider Regiment (Provisional).

Wortman's letters home reflected his bonding with and respect for his foxhole partner. In one note to his parents, the Marine remarked on the "swell" job Jack was doing, and on his growing admiration for the dog: "I wish I had as much energy as Jack has," he told the folks back in Davis Junction, his rural hamlet hometown one hundred miles northwest of Chicago. Wortman's observations are peppered with forties idioms and expressions of affection for his four-legged charge. "Jack is really tops—working like a million."

In his last letter before the landing on Bougainville, dated October 21, 1943, Wortman reassured his family: "I am fine and in the best of health. Jack is also fine. I surely hope you get a chance to see him some day. . . .

"Jack is sitting here alongside me now and he said to send you his love. Don't worry about me. Jack will take care of me."[35]

Gordon Wortman and Jack. *Marc Wortman*

On November 1, 1943, Jack and his team were part of "H Hour + 2 Hours," the second wave to storm the sands on Bougainville. Jack and the entire war dog platoon were hoisted by rope over the side of the ship and lowered to the waiting Higgins boat. Despite the hostile surfside gunfire, all made it safely to shore and protection.

The first two nights, Jack worked security rounds, joining eight other dogs in general patrols for the regiment command post. On the third day—on which his canine colleague Caesar would be seriously wounded—Jack began ferrying messages between "E" Company, which was on the roadblock, and the 2nd Battalion.

JACK TO THE RESCUE

His most heroic moment came on November 7, 1943. Jack and Wortman were part of a small unit assigned to guard the roadblock at Piva Trail, deep in the jungle. Jack's other handler, Paul Castracane, remained at the battalion command post. In the early afternoon, the Japanese cut the telephone line linking the roadblock to the command center.

Having isolated the Marines, the Japanese attacked. The vicious assault brought casualties, among them Wortman, who suffered a terrible gunshot wound to the leg. Jack didn't escape unharmed, either. A machine gun slug slid, more or less, into his back. But the wound turned out to be just a deep crease; the bullet didn't actually lodge in his body. Still, Jack was bleeding heavily.

For comfort, the wounded dog leaned into Wortman, quietly whimpering. Jack's pain must have been bad, because many dogs will do anything to mask pain, to hide their weakness. Wortman, writhing in his own pain, did his best to comfort Jack.

The situation became desperate. With the telephone line cut, the Marines' only chance for survival was to get word to command that both reinforcements and stretchers were critically needed. The job was deemed too dangerous for a man.

The commanding officer made his way to Wortman. "Son, we've got to get through to headquarters," he told Jack's wounded handler. "Your dog is the only one we can send. Do you think he can make it?" Wortman looked at Jack beside him.

"I think so, sir," Wortman replied. "He's got lots of guts." With that, the officer quickly scribbled out a request for support and stretchers. Wortman stuffed it into a pouch on Jack's collar, gently stroked the dog's head and quietly said, "This is it, old boy. We're depending on you. 'Report' to Paul."[36]

The shepherd rose painfully, tentatively to his feet. Looking to his master one last time, he seemed to get a second wind and turned and bolted, headed to command. Wortman and the others held their breath as a hail of enemy bullets chased the escaping Jack. Miraculously, he made a clean getaway.

At battalion command, Paul Castracane had just stepped inside his tent to remove gear when someone yelled to him that Jack was back. The messenger dog was a sight, too—bloody, mud-caked, and utterly exhausted. "As he reached me, he dropped at my feet, blood gushing from a wound on his back," Castracane remembered.[37] He found the note in Jack's pouch and quickly ran it over to command. He then scooped up Jack in his arms and rushed off to the first-aid tent.

Thanks to Jack's heroics, reinforcements and aid were immediately dispatched to the roadblock. The reinforcements helped force an enemy retreat, during which many Japanese forces were trapped and captured. When medical help arrived, Wortman and other wounded Marines were placed on stretchers and taken to the field hospital.

Wortman's words, "Jack will take care of me," seemed almost prophetic; Jack indeed had saved the day.

In letters he sent home while he recuperated, Gordon Wortman admitted how much he missed his heroic hound. "I want you to know that Jack carried a message through after he was wounded and so. . .he is being recommended for a medal of some kind.

"He was also advanced to the rating of a sergeant. That's really going to be tough. How can I give orders to a dog when he has a higher rating than I do?"[38]

Wortman received a Purple Heart for his injury. Jack didn't go ignored. An entry on page thirty-seven of his record book reads, "Due to the wound received while in action, Jack was recommended for a medal comparable to the Purple Heart."

A newspaper story on April 24, 1944 reported that Paul Castracane had nominated Jack for the Silver Star. Sadly, Jack never received either medal—or any honors for valor.

NEW HANDLERS

While Wortman was recovering, Private Paul Castracane himself was injured. "I inherited Jack after Castacrane was wounded," recalled Homer Finley, one of Thor's original handlers. "[Jack] was so easy to train, so easy to get along with."[39]

Jack with Private Homer Finley. *USMC Archives*

Shortly thereafter, Jack found himself assigned to two new handlers, both from small town America—Privates First Class

Henry L. Denault from tiny Hudson, New Hampshire, and Francis F. Penrod of little Farmersville, Ohio. They all left Bougainville on January 12, 1944, bound for Guadalcanal. Jack transferred to the 4th Marines on February 1, and remained on Guadalcanal for more than a year, until March 15, 1945.

Wortman recovered and returned to duty February 20, 1944, only to find he would no longer be working with his brave four-legged buddy. But he was happy to see the dog thriving. That night, the private first class wrote home: "Jack is fine. He seemed glad to see me again and I was sure happy to see him. Golly, a fellow doesn't realize how much he can miss a dog!"[40]

Jack and his unit next moved on to Okinawa. His record book reports that Jack was in on the taking of Okinawa Island from April 2 to July 6, 1945. Jack managed to survive the battle that Caesar did not.

HOMEWARD BOUND

On July 31, 1945, a week before the decisive U.S. attack on Hiroshima, Jack returned to the 1st Marine War Dog Platoon. Four months later, on December 6, he came home to the War Dog Training School at Camp Lejeune. Jack was essentially "de-trained" at the base, as part of his transition back to civilian life. The debriefing provided dog handler Homer Finley, himself a short-timer at Lejeune at the same time, a chance to say goodbye to his furry fellow Marine.

"I was shown around the camp one day where the dogs were," Finley recalled in a 2017 interview, "and I saw Jack, and I said 'Oh, my God, there's Jack!' And the guy showing me around said, 'Well don't get too close because nobody else can, he's vicious.'

"And I said, 'If I know Jack, he won't bother me one little bit.' So bravely, I went to the gate and walked in, and it was just like a family reunion. He came up, put his paws on my shoulder and was licking my face.

"And these guys were dumbfounded to think I could do that with Jack and nobody else could do that. That was the highlight of my war dog experience."[41]

Accounts of Jack's heroics and those of his comrades-in-tails, appeared widely in the press. In the fall of 1945 *Courage Comics* magazine ran a five-page story about Jack under the headline "Red Badge of Courage." Jack's hometown Nassau *Daily Review Star* offered an editorial cartoon featuring the local hero seated among palm trees with a Japanese flag in his mouth, looking pretty proud of himself.

Joseph Verhaeghe sent a notarized letter requesting Jack's return to his custody on February 4, 1946. In the letter, Verhaeghe assumed full responsibility for Jack's behavior and offered to indemnify the government from responsibility for any injuries the de-mobbed war dog might inflict on account of his "vicious propensities."

February 19, 1946, was a happy day for son Bobby and all the Verhaeghes. At Camp Lejeune, North Carolina, the United States Marine Corps issued Jack an honorary discharge. Afterwards, Jack came home to Floral Park, Long Island, to live out his years as a Devil Dog war hero.

Whether he stole ice cream cones after that day has never been reported.

――――――

ANDY

"I am one mother who knows a dog named 'Andy' has saved her son and the rest of the boys in that group. He has proved his value in jungle warfare, and I am grateful to you and your dog."

—**GLADYS M. LANE,** mother of Private First Class Jack Mahoney[42]

DOBERMAN PINSCHER—MC TATOO #71

His given name had a decidedly aristocratic ring: Andreas von Wiedehurst. But everyone called him Andy. He was born July 26, 1941, and owned by Doberman breeder Theodore Andreas Wiedemann of Norristown, Pennsylvania.

Andy never competed on the dog show circuit. Maybe it was his tendency to fight—one especially brutal dust-up had left Andy's ears so mangled that they couldn't be properly repaired. On the other hand, he possessed valuable virtues, including "extremely fine conformation, bone structure and level-headedness."[43] So in his civilian days, Andy was used for stud, siring many beautiful and healthy puppies.

Andy was also a hard worker, blessed with great energy and stamina. He loved to jump and could scale an eight-foot wall.

Andy scales a wall during training. *Marine Raider Museum Archives*

Temperamentally, he was charming and affectionate. Andy's greatest asset was his desire to please his master. No matter the request, Andy always gave his best effort. If for nothing else, this eagerness to please explained why his owner figured Andy would make a great Marine and would "carry out every command to the end, even [if] it meant giving up his life to do so."[44]

A MARINE TO HIS CORE

After Andy enlisted in the Marines on April 14, 1943, his right ear received the USMC branding number 71. His formal training as a patrol/scout dog was abbreviated, as the platoon shipped out just a few days after his arrival. Andy was assigned two handlers, Privates First Class Robert E. Lansley of Syracuse, New York, and John "Jack" Mahoney of Clinton, Connecticut. Both developed strong bonds with their new Pinscher partner, proud to be working with "the best dog in the field," according to others in the platoon.

"Andy is a dog of good size and stable temperament," wrote someone—likely Lansley or Mahoney—in his dog book record. "Because of his graceful gait and bearing, he was called 'Gentleman Jim.' Although very mild and affectionate, he was one of our best attack dogs. In action, he also proved to be one of the very best point dogs."[45]

Andy with Private First Class Robert Lansley and platoon commander Lieutenant Clyde Henderson (L). Lansley, Andy, and Private First Class John Mahoney (R). January 19, 1944. *USMC Archives*

The platoon commander, Lieutenant Clyde Henderson, described Andy as "a sort of mamma's dog, very affectionate around friends. But we had trained him to be a mean hombre with strangers."[46]

Andy was among the few dogs that liked to work off leash. If he wandered too far ahead of the patrol, Lansley made a clucking sound and Andy turned to look at him. Lansley then motioned Andy back with hand signals.

Andy was also considered an easy dog to "read" when warning handlers of potential danger. He would walk along relaxed and happy but freeze if he smelled or heard anything strange. At these moments, the fur on his back bristled and he wouldn't move. Sometimes he offered a low growl while looking in the direction of the danger.

INTO THE JUNGLE

When the Marines hit the beach at Bougainville, Andy went to work leading M Company, a 250-man patrol, inland before the Japanese could counter-attack. The Japanese were using two trails—the Piva, which ran over the mountains, and Numa-Numa, which started at a different beach. The two trails diverged at a point inland, with the Piva running down to the beach where the Marines had landed. If the Marines could reach the junction with the Numa-Numa, they could set up a roadblock preventing enemy reinforcements from reaching the sands.

This was a job that Andy could help with. Working about twenty-five yards ahead of his handlers, he led the men into the interior. About four hundred yards into the jungle, Andy stopped. After a moment, Lansley assumed that Andy had probably just discovered an animal hiding in the brush. They moved on, but about 150 yards later, the dog froze again. This time, Andy's ears pricked and the fur on his back rose. He pointed slightly to the right, adding a low growl. Lansley turned to the scout leader and warned that a sniper was probably in the brush, about seventy-five yards in.

The scout leader, who never had worked with dogs, was skeptical. Still, he sent two automatic riflemen out to investigate.

"Lansley patted Andy and murmured, 'Nice boy!' But Andy was peeved," Henderson recalled. "He wanted to bark. He wanted to tear through the jungle and fly at the throat of that sniper. He had always been allowed to do that in maneuvers, because it built up aggressiveness and helped his morale. But now he had to stand by silently."[47]

Suddenly there was a rapid burst of gunfire. The Marine scouts returned to say they had sprayed a mangrove tree that looked suspicious. Sure enough an enemy soldier had tumbled out of it, dead. Just like that, Andy acquired a whole new set of admirers.

"Marine Raiders scouting out a jungle trail, in the Empress Augusta Bay region on Bougainville Island, are aided in locating Japs by a specially-trained scout dog. This picture shows the dog 'alerted,' two men have been sent ahead to see what has caused the reaction." November 3, 1943. Original photo caption. *USMC Archives*

Twice more, Andy alerted to snipers hiding on the trail, providing the men of M Company enough time to take cover, then eliminate the enemy positions or patrols. Because of Andy's sharp nose and other keen senses, M Company advanced farther than any other company and successfully established the roadblock at that critical trail junction.

"MOST EXTRAORDINARY"

Andy's actions on the fourteenth day ashore were characterized by Lieutenant Henderson as "the most extraordinary feat of the Bougainville operation."[48]

A Marine unit at the front lines encountered stiff Japanese resistance highlighted by heavy machine gun fire. No one could figure out where it was coming from, so Lansley and Mahoney volunteered to take Andy on a search for enemy strong points. "We had complete faith in Andy, and knew he would spot whatever it was out there," Lansley said.[49]

The three moved beyond the lines into heavy foliage. Andy led the way and was about twenty yards in front before he froze in place, the fur on his back again standing straight up. Clearly, something was up. "First, he turned sideways in the trail and began moving forward side-leggedly," Henderson recalled. "That was Andy's own peculiar way of saying there was a whole mess of strangers up ahead."[50]

Lansley and Mahoney continued cautiously ahead towards their fearless devil dog. "Andy stopped short, and looked to the right and left, the way he always alerted," Lansley remembered. "I crept up along a little trail behind him and saw two machine gun nests, one on each side of the trail," where Andy had pointed.[51] They were camouflaged behind some banyan tree roots. Lansley described the enemy nests as "trained in a fixed line of fire, slantwise across the trail," which would allow a deadly Japanese crossfire attack.[52]

Lansley called Andy back from harm's way. A light Marine tank moved in to attack the two nests. But rolling forward the tank hit a land mine and was blown off its tracks. Worse, when the tank commander climbed out, he was shot dead.

As Lansley described it, "I just began cutting loose with the sub-machine gun I carried, firing at one side of the trail, then the other."[53] According to Lieutenant Henderson, Lansley told Mahoney to cover him as he changed magazines and continued firing, "then raced forward and hurled grenades into dugouts he found beneath both trees."[54]

When the ensuing skirmish ended, all the Japanese snipers lay dead in their nests. Lansley and Mahoney had both suffered wounds from exploding grenades. Mahoney was evacuated to a hospital and treated for shoulder, back and hand injuries. Andy, however, escaped unharmed. "If it hadn't been for Andy," Lansley said later, "Johnnie and I'd have got it when we were testing out the line of fire. His point told us exactly where the nests were located."[55]

Andy, Lansley, and Mahoney played a crucial role in wiping out the machine-gun nests, clearing that entire sector and allowing the Marines' line to move forward that day.

A CRUEL TWIST OF FATE

Andy stayed on Bougainville with the 1st War Dog Platoon until January 12, 1944, when all were transferred to Guadalcanal for reassignment. There he and Lansley were reunited with Mahoney, who had recovered from his injuries.

Wartime can make for cruel ironies. One notorious example was the death of Major General George S. Patton. The celebrated, controversial Army general repeatedly cheated death in the war. But just seven months after VE Day he was gone, the victim of medical complications following a simple traffic accident.

Andy suffered a similar tragically ironic fate. Because combat noise had badly compromised his hearing, "Gentleman Jim" never heard the rumbling military truck moving toward him when he darted in front of it. Everything happened so fast that the driver didn't have time to react.

The last entry in Andy's record book, under Medical History, is dated March 18, 1944: "Struck by truck at 10 a.m., back broken and crushed internally, died 10:20 am." The entry ended simply: "Killed in line of duty."[56]

Even the toughest Marines serving with him wept openly at the loss of Gentleman Jim.

CORPORALS ALL

In a lengthy report to Washington, Lieutenant Colonel Alan Shapley, commander of the 2nd Marine Raider Regiment (Provisional), cited the heroics of six war dogs—Caesar, Jack, and Andy, plus Otto, Rex, and another dog also named Jack—all Doberman Pinschers like Andy. On December 20, 1943, each received a personal Letter of Commendation for outstanding performance and service from no less than Marine Corps Commandant Thomas Holcomb. Notices of the honors were mailed to their owners back home.

All six dogs were also promoted to corporal.

WINS AND LOSSES

Officially, the dogs and their handlers were credited with leading 350 patrols and taking out more than 300 enemy soldiers.

The miracle of Bougainville was that of the twenty-four dogs involved in that ten-week campaign ending January 12, 1944, only two, both Dobermans, were killed there—Rolo (no. 16) and Kuno (no. 131). Rolo was, in fact, the first Marine Corps war dog to die in action. Kuno suffered severe head and stomach wounds from a Japanese grenade and was put down. The platoon buried him with honors.

Two handlers also became casualties—Privates First Class Russell T. Friedrich of Andover, Connecticut, who was Rolo's partner, and William N. Hendrickson of Keyport, New Jersey, who teamed with yet another Doberman, Rex (no. 26).

Rolo was regarded as a great scout dog, second only to Andy. Rolo also preferred to work off leash. Only three days before his death, Rolo had acquired a new second handler, Private First Class James M. White of New York City, who had enjoyed an affectionate rapport with his previous dog, Judy (no. 42), also a Doberman. But like many of the female dogs, Judy suffered from shell shock and was removed from the fighting, at which point White was teamed with Rolo.

Four days before Christmas 1943, Rolo and his two handlers were assigned to a new Army unit temporarily attached to the Marines. The unit's mission was to discover and identify various Japanese positions along the Torokina River. The Army personnel were unaccustomed to working with war dogs.

Rolo, White, and Friedrich went to work. About three thousand yards into the jungle, Rolo gave a strong alert that enemy soldiers were hiding up ahead and to the left. This surprised the Army lieutenant in command because Japanese soldiers had not been reported in the area. So he ignored Rolo's alert and ordered his men to push farther into the jungle. Moments later the Americans literally walked into a deadly ambush of gunfire coming from the spot Rolo had indicated.

Rolo was killed, and moments later Friedrich was shot. White suffered a head wound when a bullet pierced his helmet and grazed his scalp. The unit retreated, but when the men regrouped, Friedrich was discovered to be missing in action. The Marines could only presume he had been taken prisoner by the Japanese.

Private First Class Friedrich was never heard from again.

On the night of the seventh day of the operation, Rex (no. 26) successfully alerted his handler, Private First Class William N. Hendrickson, that Japanese soldiers were lurking nearby. "As a result of Rex's warning," his citation reads, "the Marines were prepared for the attack and were successful in repelling it."[57] But Hendrickson was killed during the attack.

Lieutenant Colonel Shapley's report had nothing but high praise for the four-legged heroes: "The War Dog Platoon has proven itself to be an unqualified success, and the use of dogs in combat was on trial.

"The dogs have proven themselves as message carriers, scouts, and vital night security; and were constantly employed during the operation of extending the beachhead. They were remarkable and more are needed."[58]

Shapley's findings were endorsed by Major General Roy S. Geiger, who led the U.S. ground forces on Bougainville, and Marine Division Commander Major General Allen H. Turnage.

The dogs of Bougainville more than proved the strategic value of canines serving in war.

Left to right: Jack (Dobie), Jack (German shepherd), Otto, and Caesar with their handlers on Bougainville. *USMC Archives*

5

More than Mascots

"There wasn't a military camp or installation in this country or abroad, that didn't have its quota of pet dogs during the war.... Their contribution to victory was one of morale. They didn't fight like their comrades in the K-9 Corps, but there is no denying that to the men, far from their families and sometimes facing death daily, that a devoted four footed pal was a link with home and the peaceful life."[1]

—**TOM NEWTON**, K-9 History

Not every four-legged fighter serving with American armed forces in World War II came to serve in the war through established channels such as Dogs For Defense. Some of America's canine heroes just kind of fell into the fight. And many of these pups, too, inspired their human comrades with displays of remarkable valor.

Here are two amazing stories.

SINBAD THE SAILOR
USCG K9C CHIEF DOG (PETTY OFFICER)

"Perhaps that's why Coast Guardsmen love Sinbad— he's as bad as the worst and as good as the best of us."[2]

—**EDDIE LLOYD**, editor, *Coast Guard Magazine*

MUTT: "WITH A BIT OF BULLDOG, DOBERMAN PINSCHER AND WHAT-NOT. MOSTLY WHAT-NOT"[3]

Coast Guard cutter WPG-32, christened the USCGC *George W. Campbell*, was named for a now-obscure early American

statesman with the patriotic name George Washington Campbell.[4] An incident on a cold night in 1937 would dramatically
change life aboard the 377-foot cutter. The *Campbell*, then just
a year old, was preparing to set out from New York Harbor on
a patrol run of the eastern seaboard and Ensign A. A. "Blackie"
Rother, the ship's chief boatswain's mate (or master seaman), was
returning from shore leave.

Moving quickly and quietly, gingerly toting his liberty bag,
Rother boarded the ship. Inside his bag was precious contraband:
a stocky black-and-tan mixed breed pup (translation: mutt) with
expressive white eyebrows. Rother had purchased the dog to keep
his girlfriend company while he was at sea, but her apartment
manager turned out to have a "no pets" policy. So the sailor stuffed
him into his duffel bag and spirited him aboard the *Campbell*.[5]

Hey, Rother figured, the ship needed a mascot, right?

As events played out, the ship got an adorable mascot—and
much more. The men of the *Campbell* really took to the newcomer, who proved himself a dedicated fellow crewmember
worthy of their affection—and of the international attention he
soon would receive.

They got Sinbad the Sailor.

The afternoon after Rother had smuggled the puppy aboard,
the *Campbell*'s captain was addressing the crew during the daily
"muster."[6] He found himself distracted by a little black dog who
was sashaying across the quarterdeck, looking for the sailors he
had made friends with overnight. The crew gasped. Rother
stepped forward to explain the situation and plead his case for a
mascot. But Sinbad was his own best advocate. From the captain's stern tone, the little dog sensed that he'd done something
wrong. So he took matters into his own paws, ambled over to the
captain, looked him straight in the eye. . .and barked, wagging
his tail as hard as he could.

The men of the *Campbell* had their mascot.

Sinbad the Sailor. *USCG Archives*

Sinbad was described as "rough, tough and rowdy. . .a liberty-rum-chow-hound, with a bit of Bulldog, Doberman Pinscher, and what-not. Mostly what-not."[7] He became a full-fledged member of the crew, with his own service number, medical history, uniform, special collars, and his own seabag—his name stenciled on the side so no other dogs could steal it. The cruising canine even had his own bunk and battle station assignment.

The very intelligent mixed breed quickly learned the ship's routine. Sinbad had a personality all his own, and he seemed to make friends with everyone. He seemed happiest in a group, as though he was "one of the gang."

Everyone was Sinbad's master; he took orders from any crewman and knew he had to follow them to the letter. If he did something to anger a crewmember, Sinbad always tried to make things right; he couldn't stand having anyone onboard mad at him. He especially loved being around the enlisted men because they played and talked with him. He didn't always seem comfortable around officers, but he was always respectful.

A hound of humble tastes, Sinbad's favorite toy was a simple round metal washer, with which he used to play "roll-and-catch." Sinbad would place the washer in front of a member of the crew and sit down and wait until a crewman picked it up and rolled it away. The dog's job was to chase and capture the gasket before it whirled to a stop. Sinbad never tired of the chase. Afterward, he hid the washer, always careful to remember exactly where he had stashed it.

Somebody taught the dog another trick with the washer. Sinbad would set it down, then sit on his haunches very straight, as if begging a magician's assistant to help him with the trick. A crewman would take the bait and place the washer on the tip of Sinbad's nose. The dog then proceeded to flip the flat, coin-sized metal ring into the air and catch it in his mouth. This was a huge hit with everyone.

A sensitive guy, Sinbad intuitively recognized when someone felt sad, worried, or in distress. At those moments the pup would race to retrieve the washer and set it down at the man's feet to cheer him up with his tricks.

The furry stowaway was a fabulously successful morale booster to the men of the USS *Campbell*.

A LOVE OF LIBERTY

Sinbad helped lighten the strain of wartime on the seas, and as for most sailors, going on liberty became his favorite pastime. He loved going ashore with the crew. He would wait eagerly for his collar to be put on because that was his "liberty card," and he was always the first one off the ship. At every port where the *Campbell* docked, Sinbad won admirers. Well, almost every port.

In the spring of 1940, as the chaos of the war in Europe was building, Sinbad caused an international incident. It happened in Greenland and almost cost the mascot of the USCGC *Campbell* his life, much to the chagrin of the *Campbell*'s new captain, James Greenspun.

Greenland was a Danish territory, so when Denmark fell into Nazi hands, an alarmed U.S. worked to prevent the same thing from happening to Greenland, because of the latter's strategic advantages. The *Campbell* was dispatched to cruise the waters offshore and to help secure diplomatic ties with Greenland. The crew was on strict orders to be on their best behavior.

After a week, the men were permitted ashore on liberty. But they found little to do in the local village, which was quite deserted. Sinbad wandered off on his own, making his way up hills where sheep grazed in pastures. He had never seen sheep before, and they stirred his curiosity.

At first the sheep seemed friendly, but they scattered at the sight of a strange dog racing towards them. Sinbad mistook their fear for playfulness and chased the sheep until he grew tired, then headed back to town and returned to the ship.

This went on for a week. Sinbad couldn't wait to reach land to go play with his new friends each day. He made a game of it and had a grand old time. Local shepherds discovered what he was doing and tried to chase him away. But Sinbad even made a game of that. It wasn't a game for the sheep, though. Some of them suddenly died from exhaustion, and others were too nervous to graze properly.

So the shepherds followed Sinbad back to the pier, discovered he was from the *Campbell*, and appealed to the port's Danish overseer for help.

Relations with the Greenlanders were growing strained because of this "wild animal." Government officials sent a formal letter of demands to Captain Greenspun. Not only did they want Sinbad's actions to stop; they demanded he be "disposed of."

The captain was predictably upset. He wasn't about to sacrifice Sinbad, though he did acknowledge the spirited dog ought to be punished. To prevent further attacks, to dissuade Greenlanders from from taking matters into their own hands, and to prevent the "riot and possible diplomatic repercussions" that "might result" from Sinbad's truancy, a "Captain's Mast" was held to try the dog and determine his punishment for his crimes. Sinbad was deprived of liberty privileges while the ship remained in Greenland's territorial waters.[8]

The pup seemed saddened by his disgrace. But the men of the *Campbell* had a good laugh over it, teasing the dismayed dog.

The *Campbell* remained in and around Greenland for months, but Sinbad never again went ashore. Eventually, the Greenlanders forgave the dog—after they had spent time with him aboard ship. But Sinbad never forgave them for getting his liberty revoked.

WAR COMES TO THE *CAMPBELL*

Even before the U.S. entered World War II, ominous clouds were gathering. Several American ships were attacked or sunk in 1941, even before Pearl Harbor. On November 1, 1941—five weeks before the Japanese attack—jurisdiction of the Coast Guard was transferred to the Navy. New faces and duties came with the changes. A new ship's commander for the *Campbell*, Captain James Hirshfield, was one of those faces.

The cutter ship had been converted to convoy escort duty, complete with big guns to defend itself and the merchant ships it

was escorting. Sinbad's battle station was below deck and theo-
retically out of harm's way. But most of the time he stood watch
on deck. Sinbad projected the sense that, as a good sailor and
mascot, his place was with the men. Nevertheless, he was
required to wear his life jacket, and when the alarm sounded for
"Battle Stations! All Hands," Sinbad knew enough to get out of
the way until hearing the all-clear.

Sinbad keeps his eye on the convoy from the bow of the ship. *National Archives*

February 22, 1943, marked the two-hundred-and-eleventh
birthday of George W. Campbell's namesake, President George
Washington. It was on that national holiday that Sinbad truly
earned the respect and admiration of crewmates—after the
Campbell was seriously damaged in an attack by the Nazi submarine *U-606.*

The ship was escorting a convoy from Northern Ireland to
Newfoundland when it found itself stalked by a "wolf pack" of
German U-boats.[9] One of the convoy's ships, the Norwegian
freighter *Nielsen Alonso*, was struck by torpedoes and began

sinking at the stern. The *Campbell* followed orders to circle back and rescue fifty stranded crew members, all of whom were grateful to make it safely aboard.

But the operation played right into a Nazi ambush. The *Campbell* was fired upon. Luckily, the torpedo missed, setting off a chase after the U-boat that lasted all day.

The rescued seamen were examined by the ship's doctor, and then were given food, coffee—and some morale boosting. Sinbad, good mascot that he was, "always seemed at his best when things were going worst."[10] The four-legged emcee became a one-dog USO show, befriending and entertaining the visitors, helping relieve what surely must have been incredible stress. But the dog show was short-lived. Several enemy U-boats were spotted, and *Campbell* crewmates raced back to their battle stations.

Campbell personnel sighted a German periscope. They raced to the German U-boat's location and released a string of depth charges. But the stubborn sub's deathblow was to be old school: the *Campbell* simply, and violently, rammed the U-boat. When the German crew bailed out through the submarine's conning tower and into the water, Sinbad was still on deck, "barking defiantly at the sub and its Nazi crew, his teeth bared, his tail stiff and his eyes ablaze with anger."

His ship. His fight. The *Campbell*'s mascot was ferociously defending the ship from an enemy that had attacked them.

While the ramming destroyed the submarine, the cost was incredibly high for the *Campbell*. She now had a gaping hole in her hull and began to take on water. The engine room flooded, the power went out, and the cutter was essentially a "dead duck on a sea full of U-boats."

Captain Hirshfield had been injured by flying splinters. Sinbad, in an uncharacteristic move, visited the captain's cabin to check on him. According to author George Foley, "The skipper was hurt and the sensitive dog cocked his head from side to side, as if to find out how badly....

"When he saw the captain smile at this unusual visit by the mascot, he sensed all was well and scampered from the cabin to rejoin the crew on the deck."[11]

All but essential personnel were ordered off the ship and onto the nearby Polish destroyer *Burza*, which had returned to protect the helpless *Campbell*. A handful stayed on board to patch up the hull, ensuring the ship stayed afloat while she was towed to safety. Asked about Sinbad, the captain didn't miss a beat. "Sinbad will stay aboard. Nothing will happen to the *Campbell* as long as Sinbad is standing by her."[12] The pup had more than earned his place on the ship. He was, as author Michael Walling declared, "as important to the ship as its engines and guns."[13]

Battle stations! *USCG Archives*

A LIVING LEGEND

Sinbad's reputation steadily grew. At hundreds of ports on two continents, people knew him by name. He was a favorite in Londonderry, Ireland, and the feeling was mutual. When the *Belfast Telegraph* ran a story about him, "from then on the town was his." It was reported that "Sinbad not only gets the keys of the city, he gets the whole lock, stock and barrel."[14] Whenever he went ashore, Sinbad made the local society columns. When he was guest of honor at a dinner for the crew at historic Guildhall, the papers ran with that story too.

But Sinbad was no saint. For one thing, he loved to drink— and evidently could really put it away. A July 19, 1943, headline in *Life* magazine revealed his tippling ways: "An Old Sea Dog Has Favorite Bars and Plenty of Girls in Every Port." The magazine described how Sinbad liked to jump onto a barstool, bark, be served a shot of whisky with a short beer chaser, lap them up, then stagger on to the next haunt with his crew. The men willingly paid his tab.

Serve 'em up! Sinbad waiting outside Kubel's, and at the bar. *USCG Archives*

As can happen in the case of any hard-drinking sailor, there were a few times that Sinbad did not make it back in time and missed the ship.

Once in Iceland the *Campbell* was scheduled to leave, but Sinbad was nowhere to be found. Unbeknownst to the crew, he had been detained by a policeman who mistook him for a stray dog. The crew begged Captain Hirshfield to wait, but he had his orders to ship out.

What happened next was like a scene straight out of a Lassie movie. Sinbad managed to break away from the police officer, but by the time he reached the dock, his ship had sailed. The men of the *Campbell* spotted Sinbad on the pier and informed the skipper, but he wouldn't turn back—until Sinbad took matters into his own paws. The beloved mutt jumped into the ice-cold waters and swam frantically after the cutter. The captain was finally convinced to go back for him: "If that dog wants to be aboard that much, swing about and pick him up."[15]

The *Campbell* did just that.[16]

But it was when he missed the boat in Sicily that Sinbad really caused a stir.

Notice of his absence had been posted with the Shore Patrol and the Army when the *Campbell* sailed. Sinbad had been missing for almost a week when Shore Patrol spotted and secured him. An American destroyer happened to be leaving for the United States, so Sinbad hitched a ride home to the East Coast. As the destroyer pulled into port, Sinbad noticed the *Campbell* in the next berth and began barking furiously. The skipper of the destroyer alerted the Coast Guard that Sinbad was aboard.

As he returned to his ship, Sinbad thought he had been for-given, but he was wrong. He was logged in as AWOL and had to face another Captain's Mast. Sinbad was busted and "restricted to the ship while in port and 'under no conditions was he to be permitted liberty in any foreign port in the future.'"[17]

This would have been fine for any other mascot, but then "it isn't every ship's mascot which has a girlfriend in almost every port."[18]

A WELL-DESERVED PROMOTION. . . FOR LESS THAN A DAY

While Sinbad served honorably, he nevertheless was busted in rank a few times for minor infractions.

Not long after the submarine incident, Sinbad was up for promotion from "Dog, First Class" to "Chief Dog." The official letter read, "Subject dog is in all respects deemed qualified for advancement to the Chief Petty Officer grade."[19]

The proposed promotion was approved by the District Coast Guard Officer, who decided, "The subject dog is deemed more than qualified for advancement to the rate suggested."[20]

The formal advancement ceremony was set for the *Campbell*'s arrival at its home port. But the simple gathering that was planned quickly became a much bigger to-do. News photographers and well-wishers vied ferociously for shots of the suddenly famous four-legged figure.

Flanked by his officers, Captain Hirshfield recited the citation, Sinbad at attention on his hind legs, his forepaws dangling and his head facing forward attentively. When he finished, Hirshfield leaned over and re-clasped Sinbad's neck collar with Sinbad's new chief's insignia.

The captain earnestly addressed his ship's heroic hound. "I am very happy to make this announcement to you. The promotion is well-deserved. My congratulations."[21]

Sinbad raised his right paw, and the captain shook it as flashbulbs exploded.

Sinbad's classic pose. *USCG Archives*

Hundreds of pictures later, Sinbad grew tired of posing. So he picked his moment—and bolted down the gangplank. Unfortunately, the new Chief Dog had forgotten he was under orders to stay for pictures. Now he was AWOL. Sinbad returned about six hours later to find a very angry captain determined to punish him for disobedience.

At yet another "Captain's Mast," Sinbad hung his head while the charges against him were read. Ultimately, Hirshfield ordered Sinbad "reduced to the next inferior grade in his rate, effective immediately." In short, Sinbad was busted from Chief Petty Officer, his rank for only a few hours, back to where he started: Dog, First Class. Oddly, he actually seemed happy about it. Sinbad was content to be just one of the gang again.

TIME MOVES ON

Sinbad remained aboard the *Campbell* for the duration of the war—and beyond. Except for a second mishap in Casablanca, life was pretty uneventful.

After the war, in 1946, Sinbad's biography was published. *Sinbad of the Coast Guard* was written by Chief Specialist George F. Foley Jr., of the Coast Guard Reserve. For years it remained the only published life story of a Coast Guardsman. The book fortified Sinbad's international celebrity. The heroic hound helped sales by joining the author's promotional book tour. In 1947, Universal Pictures made a short war-years documentary on Sinbad titled *Sinbad: Dog of the Seven Seas.*

On his book tour, Sinbad talks strategy with author Chief Specialist George F. Foley Jr. *USCG Archives*

On September 28, 1948, after eleven years of faithful service on the *Campbell*, Sinbad retired from duty, honored with an aboard-ship ceremony.

On the left, Sinbad's retirement ceremony aboard ship. At right, his final walk down the gang plank. *USCG Archives*

Sinbad moved to the Coast Guard Light Station at Barnegat, New Jersey. There he lived out the dog days of retirement until his passing on December 30, 1951.

Sinbad was buried with full military honors at the base of the Barnegat station flagpole. A bronze marker identifies the war hero's final resting place.

Sinbad, the salty sailor. *National Archives*

Eddie Lloyd, editor of the old *Coast Guard Magazine*, summarized Sinbad's story with refreshing honesty: "Sinbad was a salty sailor but he's not a *good* sailor. He'll never rate gold hashmarks nor good conduct medals. He's been on report several times, and he's raised hell in a number of ports. On a few occasions, he has embarrassed the United States government by creating disturbances in foreign zones. Perhaps that's why Coast Guardsmen love Sinbad—he's as bad as the worst and as good as the best of us."[22]

Sinbad the Sailor—his legend still lives on.

SMOKY
THE FIRST THERAPY DOG

*"...without the presence of this 'angel from a foxhole,'
I wouldn't have bothered to take cover."*[23]

—CORPORAL WILLIAM A. WYNNE of the 26th Photo Reconnaissance Squadron

YORKSHIRE TERRIER

"What kind of beast is this?" wondered Cleveland native Corporal William A. Wynne. He was referring to the little bitty critter trying to hop onto him in the dark tent of the 5212th Photographic Wing motor pool in Nadzab, New Guinea. Looking closer he saw a tiny, gray-blue female dog with a golden head and black button nose. "Her head was the size of a baseball, her ears resembled miniature windmill blades, and her weight was almost nothing at all," Wynne recalled. "She was no taller than my GI shoes and not much longer."[24]

It was March 1944. Wynne soon learned that the tiny stranger was a four-pound, seven-inch tall Yorkshire terrier. How she happened to join Wynne, the 5th Air Force, and the Photographic Wing motor pool was a remarkable story.

Ed Downey, Wynne's bunkmate from Norristown, Pennsylvania, was driving on a small primitive road through the New Guinea jungle when his jeep suddenly quit. As Downey peeked under the hood, he heard whimpering coming from the side of the road. He followed the sound.

That was when the GI saw "a furry blonde head bobbing up and then disappearing."[25] Inching closer, he found a little dog desperately trying to climb out of a foxhole. She appeared to be in bad shape, and there was no telling how long she'd been stuck down there. Downey picked up the pint-sized pup, put her in the jeep, and turned back to the errant engine.

When it finally kicked over, Downey and dog returned to the motor pool. He offered the mini-mutt to a friend, Sergeant Dare, who promptly chopped off her long hair because of the heat and gave her food and water. Dare also dared to give her a name: "Smokums."

That's how Wynne met her.

Bill Wynne had been wanting a dog, and he offered to buy this one. Dare first asked for three Australian pounds ($9.66 USD) but settled for two ($6.44 USD) because he needed the money to get back into a poker game.

At that pivotal moment, "Smokums" became "Smoky." The abbreviated name seemed more appropriate, given her unique smoky coloring. The wartime shaggy dog adoption changed both her life and Wynne's.

"Smoky became a tremendous morale booster. . .She gave me an escape from the loneliness of the New Guinea jungle," Wynne would write later.[26]

Corporal Wynne was an aerial photographer and photo lab technician with the 26th Photo Reconnaissance Squadron, later known as "Spies in the Skies."[27] Smoky followed him everywhere, and they soon were inseparable. For almost two years

Smoky traveled in a heavy canvas musette bag. In the beginning Wynne kept her hidden, but after a while she became part of the crew. Being together, Wynne reasoned, was better than being apart. He and Smoky were a team.[28]

Smoky survived the adverse conditions of extreme heat and humidity. She slept in Wynne's tent on a green felt card table cover and shared Wynne's C-rations of "Spam, heavily salted ham and bacon, dehydrated eggs and potatoes."[29] The corporal also gave her his military-issue vitamin pills.

Curiously, Smoky never became ill—a lucky break because, unlike the officially sanctioned and formally trained war dogs of the war years, pick-up warriors like Smoky had access to neither veterinary medicine nor healthier food. At one point she and Wynne were stationed on Biak Island, just northwest of New Guinea, where she walked on coral for four months. Fortunately, she didn't develop pad problems like those suffered by Coast Guard dogs who patrolled the eastern shoreline. Through it all, Smoky remained, as they said in the forties, "in the pink."

SMOKY THE CIRCUS ACT

Wynne, who knew a fair amount about dog training, put Smoky through his own obedience course. This included teaching her many tricks for entertaining the troops. "She would respond either to my voice or hand signals," Wynne remembered. "She had a great eagerness to please."[30]

Smoky mastered so many tricks that the men could have felt they'd run away to join the circus. Wynne taught her to spell her name using large cut-block letters. Soon she was walking a tight-rope while blindfolded—after climbing up and down the ladder to the platform.

There was the fine art of barrel rolling—she jumped on and off a wooden keg without a leash. Wynne taught her to ride the custom scooter he built for her.

Smoky standing on a drum. © *Smoky War Dog, LLC*

She did the "grapevine," passing through and around Wynne's legs while he walked. Wynne even taught his dog to sing.

But Smoky's own favorite pastime was a game called "Dead Dog": when Wynne pointed at her and shouted, "Bang!" Smoky fell onto her side and froze. Indefinitely. Wynne could poke Smoky, pick her up by the hind legs, roll her between his hands, even walk away—but the dog remained eerily motionless. But once he gave the command "Okay," Smoky sprang to life and rushed to him. Good dog!

Once during barrel training, Smoky stopped obeying commands, something that was very out of character for her. Wynne took her to his tent where, without warning, a small, furry black ball popped out from his pet. A puppy! Wynne was astounded.

"Unfortunately the arrival of the puppy cost Smoky a Good Conduct Medal. A year of good behavior passed before she had earned it back," Wynne quipped. [31]

Frank Petrilak, another soldier in the unit, adopted the pup and named him Topper.[32]

PRIDE OF THE SOUTHWEST PACIFIC AREA

Around this time, *Yank Down Under*, a specialty magazine published by the U.S. Army, ran a contest looking for the best mascot in the Pacific region. Wynne entered Smoky to compete for Best Mascot of a Unit and attached a couple of photos to the entry. One was a simple portrait of Smoky nestling in Wynne's helmet. But it was probably the other shot that really caught the judges' attention. In it Smoky is parachuting to earth, wearing the custom chute and harness that Wynne had fashioned for her. A friend had climbed a tree and released Smoky, who floated thirty feet to the ground as the camera clicked away. Wynne and another G.I. held a blanket to ensure her safe landing.

Smoky in a helmet and floating down in a parachute. © *Smoky War Dog, LLC*

Smoky won first prize and was named "Champion Mascot of the Southwest Pacific Area in 1944."

Yet Smoky was much more than a prize-winning mascot. She is actually the first therapy dog on record.[33]

HEALING HEARTS AND SAVING SOULS

Shortly after entering the magazine contest in July 1944, Wynne wound up in the 233rd Station Hospital in Nadzab, New Guinea. He was suffering from a mosquito-borne viral disease called dengue fever. The hospital was also treating battlefield casualties from the Biak Island invasion under way from May 27 to August 17. After Wynne's third day in the hospital, Smoky was allowed to visit him. She was such a huge hit with everyone that nurses began taking her on rounds to visit other wounded and sick soldiers.

Major Charles W. Mayo, a medical doctor whose father founded Minnesota's acclaimed Mayo Clinic, was stationed at the hospital. He gave Smoky permission to stay with Wynne, sleeping on his bed at night. Smoky joined with medical teams to tour the facility on twelve-hour rounds. Nurses came by for her at 7:00 in the morning, returning her by 7:00 at night after she had been fed. "The nurses said the guys loved her because she was one of them," Wynne wrote later.[34]

Wynne, granted two weeks of recuperative leave in Australia, took Smoky along, and together they visited hospitals in Brisbane. "Besides in New Guinea, she served in three other hospitals overseas, doing twelve wards a day—two in Australia, both Army and Navy/Marines '44 and at Manila '45."[35] Smoky performed her many tricks, putting on quite a show for patients.

Thus began Smoky's twelve-year career of therapy service.

Smoky the therapy dog. *American Red Cross Photo*

ANGEL FROM A FOXHOLE

Wynne also credits Smoky with saving his life in January 1945, while they were sailing as part of an invasion convoy bound for Luzon, the Philippines' largest island. She alerted Wynne to an incoming enemy shell that took out eight other men.

"She guided me miraculously to duck incoming shells on an LST—for without the presence of this 'angel from a foxhole,' I wouldn't have bothered to take cover," Bill Wynne wrote later. "On deck, booming and vibrating from the anti-aircraft gunnery, and lying beside a jeep, we fearfully watched kamikazes being shot down while diving on our ship. That move saved us because eight men who had been standing next to us were hit."[36]

It was after the Luzon landing, however, that Smoky truly earned her stripes.

LANDING STRIP HEROICS

At Luzon's Lingayen Gulf, a new communications cable was needed at a landing strip. Normally the job would have required three days to dig up the strip, lay the cable, and then repair the runway. This meant that forty aircraft would have to be moved to another field, thus exposing those planes and the personnel moving them to a Japanese air attack.

But communications Sergeant Bob Gapp approached Wynne with an idea. He proposed tying a string to Smoky's collar, then cajoling her to walk through an eight-inch pipe under the landing strip for just over sixty feet. If successful, this would allow the communications team to easily thread the lines through the pipe. Ah, but there was a slight catch. Some spots in the pipe had only four inches of clearance because of sand that had seeped in through pipe joints.

It would be a tight squeeze, even for little seven-inch Smoky. Wynne only agreed if, should the dog get stuck, Gapp would immediately begin digging from the top down. "Absolutely!" the sergeant replied. So Smoky "volunteered" for the mission.

Smoky strings communication wire. © *Smoky War Dog, LLC*

Wynne affixed kite string to Smoky's collar and directed his dog to stand still. Then he ran to the other side, got into position, and commanded, "Come, Smoky, come!" She hesitated at first and started to turn back. But when he called again, she seemed to get the idea. The delicate little Yorkie entered the pipe and crept slowly in the direction of her master's voice. At first Wynne could make out Smoky's silhouette. But as she moved deeper into the pipe, dust began to cloud his view. As he frantically called to her, Gapp assured Wynne that the line was still moving through. At one point, she actually did become stuck. But Gapp tugged on the string, dislodging Smoky and allowed her to continue moving toward the expected light at the end of the tunnel.

Finally, with about twenty feet left, Wynne saw "two amber eyes" and heard a faint whimpering sound. At fifteen feet she "broke into a run and flew into my outstretched arms. Gapp was laughing as he hurried over, pulled a few more feet of line through, and cut Smoky loose. The Yorkie was as pleased as we were."[37]

Thanks to Smoky's selflessness, three thick cables were threaded through the pipe, making possible teletype and phone communications to combat squadrons. Smoky's role in the operation was thought to have saved 250 men (and the forty planes) from likely enemy attacks.

For her valor, Smoky was awarded a nice, juicy steak dinner, although, truth be told, the beef was only the size of a miniburger. No matter—she was a mascot no more. Now, Smoky was a bona fide (or bona Fido) war dog.

SEA TREK: THE VOYAGE HOME

In her eighteen months in combat, Smoky was credited with twelve combat missions and awarded eight honorary battle stars. Along the way, she survived a typhoon on Okinawa and 150 air raids in New Guinea. But at last, the war ended and it was time to go home. Not back to New Guinea, but to Wynne's home in a place called Ohio.

Small dog, big problem.

Army regulations were depressingly explicit: "No dogs or mascots will go back to the U.S. on a War Department ship."[38] For weeks, Wynne plotted to sneak Smoky on board the ship with him. Naturally, he was terrified they'd be caught and she'd be taken from him forever. On November 1, 1945, Wynne got the call: they were shipping out the next morning.

To Bill Wynne's great relief, he made it safely on board with Smoky and without detection. But later the good luck ran out and Wynne was summoned to the ship's office. Wynne expected the worst—that his beloved dog would be confiscated. His fears were groundless. All Wynne had to do was sign a release clearing the ship of any responsibility for "one dog." Oh, he also might be forced to pay a bond, once they arrived stateside.

It was smooth sailing the rest of the way.

Wynne's discharge from the Army Air Forces came through a few weeks later, on November 27. Ironically, when the duo arrived home in Cleveland ten days later, it wasn't Bill Wynne who received the hero's homecoming. The headline on the Home section of that day's Cleveland *Press* read: "Tiny Dog Home from the War." Four pictures of Smoky accompanied the coverage. Her inspiring story had pushed aside coverage of General Yamashita, the Imperial Japanese Army general, who had just been sentenced to death for war crimes during the occupation of the Philippines in 1944.

Smoky's story exploded stateside, and she received requests for print and radio interviews from across the country. Wynne and Smoky were also in big demand for appearances and performances in local hospitals. Smoky didn't disappoint, always reaching into her bag of tricks and putting on a great show, to the delight of children and adults alike.

Less than a year after his discharge, Bill Wynne married his high school sweetheart, Margaret (Margie) Roberts. Their honeymoon was a road trip to Los Angeles along legendary Route 66. Smoky came along for the ride.

SMOKIN' HOT STAR

Smoky became a national, then a global sensation. Wynne took her to Hollywood and later around the world. Audiences loved seeing the tricks Wynne had taught her during the war, especially the blindfolded tightrope walk.

Indeed, Smoky provided her partner with a high-profile career he might not have otherwise enjoyed. In Cleveland the pair, billed as "Mr. Pokie and his dog, Smoky," became regulars on a live local children's show, *Castles in the Air.* The furry four-pound decorated heroine performed a live trick weekly for forty-two weeks—and never repeated one. Later, the duo hosted their own television show, *How to Train your Dog, with Bill Wynne and Smoky.*

In 1946, Sinbad the Sailor was on tour promoting his book. During a stop in Cleveland, he met Smoky and Wynne. The photo op produced some truly charming images of two "more than mascots" war heroes.

Smoky with Sinbad. 1946. © *Smoky War Dog, LLC*

Smoky retired from the limelight in 1954 and died peacefully in her sleep three years later, at age fourteen. The Wynne family buried her in a shoebox near the tree in Cleveland Metropark on which Bill and wife Margie had carved their initials when they were teenagers.

Smoky: truly an angel from a foxhole.

6

Great Britain's
War Dogs

*"I would like to pay tribute to another army which has taken
part in the struggle.... I speak of our gallant and faithful dogs,
who guarded our airfields at home and abroad, carried Red Cross
supplies, detected mines and detected casualties buried under the
debris of our bombed cities. They too laid down their lives for their
country. Let us never forget them."*[1]

—CORPORAL A. MCLELLAN, RAF

The British had no existing war dog program on September 3, 1939, the day Great Britain declared war on Germany. But unlike the U.S., which wouldn't enter the war for another twenty-seven months, the Brits already knew a lot about using canines in combat, something they had already done during the Great War.

Those World War I dogs, as we have seen, were trained by Lieutenant Colonel Edwin Hautenville Richardson, a dog fancier and breeder. Richardson's *British War Dogs, Their Training and Psychology* was among several of his published manuals used by the Army's Quartermaster Corps in the American K-9 program before the U.S. training tract *War Dogs Training Manual TM 10-396* was written and disseminated.

Richardson started with just two Airedale terriers, Wolf and Prince, whom he trained as messengers. The two performed so well on the front lines in France that in 1917, Britain's War Office asked Richardson to establish the War Dog School using animals donated by the public. Under Richardson's supervision, thousands of trained dogs successfully served in World War I as messengers and sentries. The training school was disbanded at the war's end, although Richardson continued to personally train dogs.

Twenty-odd years later, at the outbreak of World War II, the British military at first thought that because of technical advances in warfare, dogs wouldn't be as effective anymore.

Then food rationing early in the war inspired a panic among British pet owners, who had good reason to fear that they would be unable to feed and care for their pets. A horrible situation turned tragic. In London alone, thousands of pets were destroyed because of public concern and panic over bombings and food rationing. Thankfully, that would change.

But it would take time. At first, the Brits couldn't loan their dogs to the war effort as they had in the Great War; the British war dogs program no longer existed. There are conflicting reports about the role of Lieutenant Colonel Richardson, so instrumental in the Great War's dog program, in its revival. Two accounts do indicate that Richardson privately trained a few canines as sentries, along with Lieutenant Colonel James Y. Baldwin, an Alsatian dog advocate and breeder. ("Alsatian" was the name for German shepherds in the United Kingdom because of anti-German feeling after World War I—and during World War II). Then the two lieutenant-colonels convinced officials that sentry dogs remained much more effective than human guards in protecting vital military installations from saboteurs.

But the paws of British dog warfare moved slowly. Not until March 1942, more than two years after Hitler invaded Poland and Britain declared war on Germany, did the British military finally go to the dogs. The specific War Office orders came from Brigadier Murray, CBE, who headed the Army's Veterinary and Remount Services.[2] Murray demanded the immediate training of twenty-five-hundred dogs, particularly guard dogs to guard over factories and military installations. Finally, on May 5, 1942, the Greyhound Racing Kennels at Northaw near Potters Bar, an existing facility north of London, became the new home of the British Army's revived War Dog Training School. This school was eventually headed by Captain John B. Garle, who in 1943 would take a team of two handlers and four dogs to the United States to help train American war dogs.

A second canine school, the Ministry of Aircraft Production (MAP) Guard Dog School, soon opened in Gloucestershire. This school's existence was a product of both connections and genuine need. It came about after Lieutenant Colonel Baldwin's close friend, Captain Moore Brabazon, was named Minister of Aircraft Production. In this position, Brabazon oversaw airfields and storage depots around the country—not to mention thousands of expensive aircraft.

Baldwin convinced Brabazon that dogs represented the most effective and economical strategic tool to protect those critical war assets. So Brabazon cleared the way for the MAP Guard Dog School. Baldwin helped establish the school and became its Dog Advisor and Chief Training Officer. The facility focused on instructing dogs and handlers in anti-sabotage and patrol work. The Royal Air Force (RAF) handled daily administration of the school.[3]

Later in the war, the Brits set up additional war dog training facilities in Burma and Egypt.

PET OWNERS STEP UP

Once the schools were operational, the public was once again asked to lend precious pets to the cause. Groups spearheading dog procurement included the Royal Society for the

Prevention of Cruelty to Animals, the National Canine Defense League, and the Animal Protection Society of Scotland and Northern Ireland. These organizations administered preliminary health exams and registered the canines before sending them off to the various training schools. Of nearly ten thousand dogs originally offered and inspected, only about three thousand made the cut.[4]

The Brits' preferred breeds included Alsatians, Airedales (they had been used heavily in World War I), boxers, Kerry Blue terriers, farm collies (as messenger dogs only), bull terriers, labradors, and curly coated retrievers. Many cross-breeds, however, also were deemed suitable.

Around this time, the Special Air Service began using trained "para-pups" who parachuted into danger zones to work usually as scout dogs with soldiers behind enemy lines. Mine detection dogs were also being trained as para-pups.

Members of the Auxiliary Territorial Services, the women's branch of the British Army, worked at the War Dog Training School as kennel maids, caring for and exercising the dogs.

As we have already seen, the American war dogs program got its start with assistance from the Brits. The U.S. Army Quartermaster Corps used American dog teams trained by Britain's Ministry of Aircraft Production Guard Dog School. The first eight teams, each composed of a handler and a dog, underwent five weeks of sentry instruction at their school at Cheltenham. The dogs were on loan from British civilians; all of the men were volunteers. By the end of 1943, twenty-two trained sentry teams were guarding storage facilities and other installations from theft. The program proved so effective that an American guard dog school was organized, also at Cheltenham, under the Depot Branch of the Quartermaster Corps.

By D-Day, June 6, 1944, fifty-six American dog teams were trained and working with QM technical services and combat units.[5]

A month earlier—two years after Captain John B. Garle opened his British dog-training academy and about a year after he helped jump-start the American K-9 Corps—Garle's War Dog Training School graduated nearly seven thousand dogs. Many more were trained in the Middle East, then attached to the Royal Air Force for sentry duty at camouflaged airfields and other secret military installations.

BRITAIN'S BRAVEST—THE DICKIN MEDALISTS

Most of the dogs honored with the PDSA Dickin Medal were attached to various military and civil units. But a handful of free agent pups—none a part of any organization—charmed their way into battle, where they did amazing things. What follow are a few stories of heroic hounds who earned the "Victoria Cross for Animals": the prestigious PDSA Dickin Medal.

SHEILA

COLLIE
DATE OF DICKIN MEDAL: JULY 2, 1945 (D.M. 24)

"For assisting in the rescue of four American airmen lost on the Cheviots in a blizzard after an air crash in December, 1944."[6]

Sheep dog Sheila, a beautiful black and white border collie, belonged quite appropriately to a shepherd, John Dagg of Dunsdale, Kirknewton, England.[7] Sheila is the only "civilian" animal recipient of the Dickin Medal; she served with neither the Armed Forces nor any civil defense unit. She didn't heed "the call" to join Britain's K-9 Corps.

Sheila already enjoyed a perfectly respectable "reserved occupation" as a sheep dog in the Cheviot Hills of Northumberland, on the border separating England and Scotland. This would prove a very lucky break for the airmen of the U.S. Army Air Force B-17G Flying Fortress no. 44-6504.

Sheila with John Dagg. *PDSA Archives*

Nine days before Christmas 1944, John Dagg was at home with his family in College Valley at the foot of the Cheviot, the highest peak among the scenic border hills. The Daggs heard what proved to be a plane in distress, followed by the violent sound of a horrible crash. Dagg had already assisted in one plane crash rescue on the Cheviot, the year before, and he and Sheila rushed up the mountain to help.

The American plane was attached to the 303rd Bomb Group—also known as Hell's Angels—of the 360th Bomb Squad, U.S. Eighth Air Force. Flying only its third mission, the plane was among a squad of forty aircraft operating out of the Royal Air Force (RAF) Molesworth base in Cambridgeshire. Besides its nine-man crew, this particular Boeing Flying Fortress was also carrying some dangerous cargo: six 500-pound bombs.

The squad's destination was the railway marshaling yards at Ulm, Germany. But poor weather had forced the Army Air Force to abort the mission. The planes were ordered to return to various bases across Britain to reduce the risk of mid-air collisions. They broke formation and headed back.

Second Lieutenant George A. Kyle, the pilot of Flying Fortress no. 44-6504, did a 180-degree turn and headed back towards England. But during its descent the plane somehow became separated from the pack. Kyle requested headings and got them. The information, however, was not from command but from bogus German transmissions. Twice he found himself heading towards France—and too far north to reach any airbase suitable for a safe landing in England.

Worse, Kyle was still carrying those bombs. Most of the other planes had managed to jettison their bombs into the North Sea as a precaution. But Kyle couldn't do that—visibility was so bad he wasn't sure if he was over land or sea, and he couldn't risk dropping them on an English village. So he descended below the clouds, to three thousand feet, hoping to get a visual on his location and to set up for a forced landing, if necessary.

Instantly, the snow-covered Cheviot peak loomed in front of him.

At 2,634 feet, the Cheviot is among Britain's tallest mountains. The plane slammed into the West Hill beneath the summit and skidded across the shoulder of the hill and past the peat bog before slogging to a halt at Brayden Crag. By some miracle, the aircraft stayed intact and the bombs did not explode on impact. Still, a fire broke out from the ruptured fuel and hydraulic lines.

Sergeants Howard F. Delaney, George P. Smith, William R. Kauffman, and Joel A. Berly Jr., were back in the fuselage. Berly struggled to put out flames in the bomb bay, but became trapped when his foot busted through the plywood floorboards and got stuck in peat. Kauffman had been knocked unconscious but regained his wits just in time to pull Berly free. He also helped Smith escape the burning plane.

Once outside, they found Delaney, suffering from a severe head wound and wandering around in deep snow. All four took shelter in a ravine a hundred yards away from the plane, not knowing if their five other crewmates had survived.[8]

"I was eleven at the time and heard the crash," Dagg's son, also named John, recalled years later. "Then my father and Sheila set off up the mountainside."[9] Young John and his mother stayed behind and contacted authorities.

Reaching the mostly inaccessible Braydon Crag was notoriously difficult, but that's just where Dagg and Sheila headed. On the way they ran into Frank Moscrop, another local shepherd who had also heard the crash. Weather conditions were worsening, and daylight was fading fast. At the top of the hill, Sheila became excited and, sensing something up ahead, ventured out alone. With the plane still burning and a blinding snowstorm minimizing visibility, Dagg and Moscrop navigated their way by following the trail of smoke and smell.

Several hours into the makeshift rescue, Sheila finally found the four airmen who had taken shelter in the ravine. Never trained in rescue protocol, Sheila ran straight to Sergeant George Smith and began licking his face. The dazed Smith realized what was happening and started shouting. Sheila responded by barking loudly. Hearing the commotion, Dagg and Moscrop followed her yelps straight to the lost airmen. Addled, barefoot, and freezing, the four men nonetheless had survived the crash with only minor injuries.

Dagg wrapped the men's feet in parachute silk. He and Moscrop decided to move them down the hill rather than risk leaving the men alone while seeking help. They had a compelling reason: the Army air corpsmen remained dangerously close to the still-burning plane. After a quick but fruitless search for other survivors, they ventured down the hill in a blizzard so brutal that visibility was "practically nil."

It was a painfully slow and treacherous climb down, and the snowstorm was only getting worse. Trusting in Sheila's sense of direction, the team followed her lead down the hill. The *London Gazette* reported that it was only through "dogged perseverance, patience and tenacity of purpose that the rescuers were able to get the four men to safety."[10] Just as they reached Dagg's cottage, the plane exploded, shattering some of the windows in the home.

It's safe to say the decision to bring the injured down the mountain was a good one.

Dagg's daughter Margaret ran two miles in the storm to telephone for the help that ultimately transported the airmen to the RAF hospital in Berwick. There they learned the fate of their crewmates.

The pilot, Second Lieutenant George Kyle, who had suffered a broken jaw in the crash, had been pulled from the cockpit by his co-pilot, Flight Officer James H. Hardy. The third cockpit crewmember, Sergeant Ernest G. Schieferstein, had also escaped. Together, Hardy and Schieferstein had helped their pilot down the hill. Trudging through the storm, the trio eventually found shelter in a shepherd's farmhouse in nearby Mounthooly. They had assumed they were the only ones to get out of the plane alive, and found out otherwise only when they were transported to the same RAF hospital as the other four.

The bittersweet reunion revealed the sad truth: the flight's two other airmen, in the nose of the plane, had perished in the crash. Sergeant Frank Roderick Turner Jr., who as togglier would have released the bombs on the cue from the lead plane, and Flight Officer Fred Holcombe, the aircraft's navigator, were both killed on impact.

HEROES ALL AROUND

In June 1945, John Dagg and Frank Moscrop were recognized for their heroic rescue by King George VI of England, who presented each with the prestigious British Empire Medal for Meritorious Service (BEM).[11]

A month later there were more honors for the two men, this time from Allied air forces. But this time, Sheila was really the star of the ceremony. On a lovely hillside in Southern Knowe, the four-legged civilian received her Dickin Medal.[12]

The unique ceremony was led by Sir James Ross, representing Britain's Air Ministry and the Royal Air Force, and U.S. Army Air Force Colonel Eugene A. Romig of the 303rd Bomber Group. Besides saluting shepherds Dagg, Moscrop, and Sheila the sheep dog, they also thanked the other shepherds and "women folk" of the Cheviot district for their many wartime rescue efforts.

Framed memorial scrolls were presented to the Southern Knowe School by the RAF (the Air Ministry Commendation) and the U.S. Army Air Force (the Eighth Air Force Commendation) for permanent display "to commemorate the rescue of airmen in distress by the shepherds and their wives and daughters during the war."[13]

Commendations were also bestowed on Dagg and Moscrop. "Your gallantry, skill and kindness in searching for our men, conducting them to shelter and caring for their needs, will ever be remembered," recited Colonel Romig directly from the Eighth Air Force scroll. "You showed towards them in the fullest measure the friendship and helpfulness which have marked our partnership with the people of Britain. Your deed has drawn closer the bond between us and enriched our common heritage for which we have fought."[14]

Sir James Ross formally presented the Air Ministry Commendation to the two shepherds and the village.

Sir James's wife, Lady Ross, presented Sheila with the Dickin Medal. But Sheila turned surprisingly shy in the spotlight. As Lady Ross struggled to attach the medal to her collar, the squirming sheepdog "even lay on her back and waved her legs in the air during the ceremony."[15] "The star of the day was Sheila," reported one newspaper. "She neither wanted her medal nor her photograph, and much hilarity was caused when her part of the ceremony took place. She was as temperamental as an operatic star."[16]

Sheila was also named an Honorary Member of the Allied Forces Mascot Club.

SHEILA'S LEGACY

After the death of her son, Sergeant Frank Roderick Turner, Sallie Turner wrote to John Dagg to thank him for the rescue of her son's crewmates. She also expressed a desire to buy one of Sheila's puppies, should she ever have a litter. Dagg was happy to agree, and Mrs. Turner's wish was fulfilled in the form of a little white female pup, Tibbie.[17]

Mrs. Turner's senator, Olin D. Johnston of South Carolina, helped arrange the delivery of Tibbie to her new home in Charleston via Trans-World Airlines.[18] The news media trumpeted the feel-good canine interest story. One typical headline: "Cheviot Collie to Be Flown to America: Hill Shepherd Gives 'V.C's' Puppy to Airman's Mother: Crash Sequel."[19] Papers on both sides of the pond covered the story. Dagg's son, John Jr., tearfully dropped his beloved puppy off at the Kirknewton rail station. She shipped out in a special carton onto which the young John Dagg had scrawled, "Be kind to Tibbie."[20]

One newspaper summed up the dog's role in the postwar lives of Sallie Turner and her husband: "Now Tibby, an excited tail-wagging bundle of white, is on her way, more than willing to try her best to fill two empty hearts."[21]

She did just that—and much more. Tibbie lived to eleven, to the end of her happy life the town pet of Columbia, South Carolina.

BING

ALSATIAN—WAR DOG 2720/6871
DATE OF DICKIN MEDAL: MARCH 29, 1947 (D.M. 48)

"This patrol dog was attached to a Parachute Battalion of the 13th Battalion Airborne Division. He landed in Normandy with them and, having done the requisite number of jumps, became a fully-qualified Paratrooper."

Betty Fetch was heartbroken when her family loaned their beloved Brian to the British Army. The Alsatian-collie mix was the runt of his litter. Yet at age two his appetite was off the charts and the Fetches feared Brian might eat them out of house and home. Wartime food rations were understandably tight, especially the meat allotment. So the family from Loughborough, Leicestershire, reluctantly sent Brian to war because they simply couldn't afford to feed him.

DARING YOUNG PARADOG

In January 1944, Brian arrived at the War Dog Training School in Hertfordshire, where for reasons unrecorded he acquired a new name—"Bing"—and was given identification number 2720/6871. Lance Corporal Ken Bailey had gone to the school in search of dogs for the 13th (Lancashire) Parachute Battalion, 6th Airborne Division. "I received instructions from the CO to investigate the possibility of parachuting war dogs into action together with the parachute troops," Bailey would later write. The canines were to be part of a scout and sniper unit, and they were required to already have patrol training. "The commandant and chief instructor gave me a free hand to select those I thought most suitable, and after a fortnight's testing, four dogs were selected as possible and journeyed back to Larkhill with me."[22]

Three made the final cut: Bing and fellow Alsatians Monty and Ranee. Ranee ultimately became the only female parachute dog of the war. Lance Corporal Bailey started out as her handler, although he also worked with Bing.

"Training began from the moment of kennelling," Bailey recalled. "Two months later, all the theoretical work was ready for practical testing."[23] In addition to their patrol dog training, the animals were also trained to sniff out landmines. But first they had to get used to the noise and movement of battle. So they sat for hours in a transport aircraft, taxiing with propellers whirling and engines at full throttle. Once they were accustomed to the din and sense of movement, the dogs' training really took off: They learned how to jump from planes in canine parachute maneuvers. Each hound had its own harness and a static line parachute, which opened automatically once a pup was plummeting.

To make jumps easier, parapups weren't allowed to eat or drink anything before a leap. But they knew the trainer had meat in his pocket, a treat each would receive upon landing. So parapups were trained to jump immediately after their handlers did. No problem, because they really wanted the treat! According to one account, the routine was simple: "Jump, land, eat: with each training jump, the dogs started enjoying their job more."[24]

Bing made his first jump April 3, 1944. And soon he made six more successful jumps, happily wagging a triumphant tail after each.

THE INVASION OF NORMANDY

June 6, 1944. D-Day—universally acknowledged as a pivotal point in the war. All the training in the world could not fully prepare either dogs or soldiers for the magnitude of Operation Overlord, the code name for the D-Day landing at Normandy, the kick-off of the Allied invasion of German-occupied Western Europe.

Bing and the 13th Parachute Battalion were part of Operation Tonga, the airborne operation to back up the storming of five French beaches.

The 13th Battalion comprised three planes, each carrying twenty men and a dog. All seemed to go as planned. The planes took off for France at 11:30 on the night of June 5, reaching the Normandy coast eighty minutes later. The battle was on.

Bing's plane was quickly riddled with enemy fire. The Alsatian mix and his handler were the last two to jump. And Bing appeared to be having second thoughts. "The dog had followed all the others to the door," recalled the pilot, Flight Lieutenant P. M. Bristow, "and as it came to its turn to follow its handler, backed away from the door and retired to the front of the fuselage. Doug [Strake, the jump master] had had to unplug himself from the intercom, catch the dog and literally throw it out."[25]

This wasn't the worst of Bing's problems. In training he had been a champ. But this time, in his first real combat jump, Bing's parachute became snagged in tree branches, leaving him to dangle helplessly for more than two hours. When his handler finally found him, he had to wait to retrieve Bing because of the shelling.[26] When he finally rescued the dog, Bing had two deep cuts to the face, most likely from German mortar fire.

Once on the ground, though, Bing proved himself more than deserving of the respect and admiration of his human colleagues. "Despite wounds to his neck and eyes," recalled Private David Robinson of the Anti-Tank Platoon, "he took his place in the line with his handler."[27]

One account underscores Bing's remarkable spirit: "Anywhere there was trouble, even after [Bing] was wounded by mortar fire, he was there to sniff it out. And when something didn't seem quite right, he would freeze and point towards the danger with his nose. During rest breaks, he kept watch over sleeping British troops; on the move, he pioneered the advance through potential danger zones. His fearless excursions through perilous terrain and behind enemy lines were credited with saving hundreds of servicemen from ambush."[28]

The unit advanced as far as the Seine before being withdrawn to England.

Sadly, Monty and Ranee did not fare so well. Monty was seriously wounded in the landing—but survived to fight another day. Ranee, on the other hand, became separated from Bailey and was never heard from again.

After Ranee's disappearance, Bailey began working with Bing. Over the next few months, they were an effective combat team. Even after Bing suffered head and eye injuries, he still continued providing patrol and mine sniffing duties.

TIME MARCHES ON—AND SO DOES BING

Three months after Operation Tonga, the unit went to Belgium to help counter German advance in the Ardennes. Today, historians call the fight the Battle of the Bulge.

Bing and his Scout Platoon near Wismar. 1945. *Airborne Assault Museum. Duxford, England*

Bing was sent back to England to rest but returned to his unit in March 1945 with a new handler, Corporal Aaron "Jack" Walton of the Scout Platoon, in time for Operation Varsity on

March 24. The valiant parapup was part of the tumultuous airborne assault crossing of the River Rhine into Germany. Sixteen thousand paratroopers in several thousand aircraft participated in Varsity, which was not only the war's last airborne operation but also the largest airborne operation in history conducted at one location on a single day. Ultimately, Bing marched alongside his men a full 350 miles to the Baltic Sea.

During that march, on a very hot April 6, the men—parched and eager to drink and refill their canteens—stopped in a village for just ten minutes. But when they started to pull out, Bing was missing. "After a frantic search," recalled Lieutenant Peter Downward of the Scout Platoon, "we found a barn door with a clearance from the ground of about 12 inches, and there was Bing, who had found a large basin of clear liquid and obviously had slaked his thirst in it.

"It was a drip tray under a huge wine butt and I suddenly realized that we had an intoxicated war dog on our hands. He was bundled into the back of a Jeep together with his handler, and we set forth."[29]

HOMEWARD BOUND

After the war, Bing remained on active duty in Germany for a year, mostly guarding airfields and ammunition dumps. The Army reached out to Betty Fetch to ask if Bing could remain in Germany with his men a bit longer. But Miss Fetch declined the request, and three weeks later, Bing was reunited with the Fetches. According to one account, after his return home, "...for three or four weeks Bing acted very strange and [Betty Fetch] was thinking of returning him to the Army. Then one morning he had completely changed; he was back to knowing her."[30]

On April 26, 1947, Bing received his PDSA Dickin Medal for gallantry, presented by Air Chief Marshal Sir Frederick Bowhill.

Betty Fetch looks on proudly as Bing receives his Dickin Medal. April 26, 1947. *PDSA Archives*

Bing lived out his days quietly, dying of natural causes at age thirteen on October 26, 1955. He is buried at the PDSA Ilford Animal Cemetery outside London. His Dickin Medal and a model of him are on display today in the Imperial War Museum, Duxford.

RIFLEMAN KHAN
ALSATIAN—WAR DOG 147. 6TH BATTALION CAMERONIANS
(SCOTTISH RIFLES)
DATE OF DICKIN MEDAL: MARCH 27, 1945 (D.M. 19)

"For rescuing Lance Cpl. Muldoon from drowning under heavy shell fire at the assault of Walcheren, November 1944, while serving with the 6th Cameronians (SR)."

Khan, a handsome blonde Alsatian, had belonged to the Harold Railton family of Tolworth in Surrey since he was a puppy. The Railtons' twin daughters June and Joy loved the "mischievous bundle of fur." But it was their brother, eight-year-old Barry Railton, who had the most intense bond with the dog.

Barry Railton and his beloved Khan. *PDSA Archives*

From an early age Khan loved to play games, which showcased his keen intelligence and eagerness to learn. "You've never seen such a loving little chap as he was," Mrs. Railton remarked. "If he did any wrong, he would go straight under the table and peep out."

When the appeal came from the War Office in 1942, the family faced a tough decision. "We realized that Khan would be in his element," Mrs. Railton said later, "but we did not want to part with him." But the Railtons were presented with the same dilemma as the Fetches. "Food, however, was getting [to be] a problem, and finally we put down his name."

At the War Dogs Training School, Khan officially became War Dog no. 147. "I think there were tears in all our eyes as Khan went off to war," Mrs. Railton said. "Barry, who claimed him as his own dog, was only consoled by the fact that his pet was going to do his bit to win this war."[31]

Khan was considered a star pupil and excelled in patrol training. He specialized in finding explosives. After his six-week course, the Alsatian was attached to the 6th Cameronians, a battalion of the Scottish Rifles based at Lanarkshire in Scotland's central lowlands. There he teamed with Lance Corporal James Muldoon, whose bond with Khan rivaled that of Barry Railton. Handler and dog were inseparable from the start.

James Muldoon and Khan. *PDSA Archives*

Khan and Muldoon were soon seeing action in Normandy and elsewhere in Western Europe. While the dog repeatedly proved himself, the true test of his mettle came November 2, 1944, at the battle of Walcheren Causeway in Belgium, part of Operation Infatuate. It was there that he earned the nickname Rifleman Khan.[32]

OPERATION INFATUATE

Two months earlier the Allies had captured Antwerp, Belgium, but they couldn't use the port because the German occupation of Walcheren Island and South Beveland, in Dutch territory, blocked it. Operations Vitality and Infatuate were phases three and four, respectively, of the Battle of the Scheldt, aimed at capturing South Beveland and Walcheren Island to open the mouth of the Scheldt Estuary—enabling the Allies to use the port of Antwerp as a supply route for troops in northwest Europe. Both Walcheren Island and the causeway connecting it to the mainland were guarded by the German 15th Division.

At the time of Operation Infatuate, the 6th Cameronians were attached to the 2nd Canadian Infantry Division. The operation was launched at 3:30 in the morning of November 2, under the cover of darkness, Khan and Muldoon in the thick of it. The attack on the island took place across a narrow sea causeway made perilous by German snipers.

Muldoon and Khan were aboard a landing craft making its way across to the muddy bank. But before it could reach shore, the snipers began spraying heavy artillery fire. An enemy shell hit the craft, cutting it nearly in half and sending the troops, equipment, and Khan flying into the cold, black waters of the Sloe Channel.

"I was rather badly wounded and was unconscious when the assault craft in which I was lying, and which was under heavy fire, was capsized," Muldoon recalled. "Thrown into the sea, I regained consciousness and saw that I was seventy yards from the shore."[33]

The men, sitting ducks, were even easier targets because of their heavy backpacks. And if the snipers didn't get them, the Germans had also laid hundreds of mines along the banks of the canal.

Khan, however, was not burdened by a backpack or other additional weight. He fiercely dogpaddled to the bank, only to become stuck in the muddy ooze. He managed to free himself quickly, then began a desperate search for his master on the shore.

James Muldoon was not a swimmer. He struggled to stay afloat and to keep his gun dry. And soon he was losing the battle to keep his head above water. Muldoon was hopelessly trapped in the mud and about to sink from the weight of his pack.

He cried out to Khan for help.

The war dog, running on the bank, instantly stopped, his ears pricked forward in a display of intense focus. Through all the sound and fury of the intense battle—mortar shells pounded overhead, gunfire whizzed by, men barked orders or screamed for help—one sound pierced through the chaos: his master's cries. Khan pinpointed Muldoon's location in the darkness and water.

The dog didn't hesitate. Khan took off like a bullet, returning to the treacherous, black, unnerving waters. He made a beeline for Muldoon, fighting through the tide of soldiers wading the opposite way, trying to reach land.

"My shouts for help brought Khan out to me," Muldoon recalled.[34]

Khan grabbed his handler's tunic at the collar and pulled, but Muldoon didn't budge. A second try. Still nothing—Muldoon was really stuck. But after repeated attempts, Muldoon somehow managed to relax. He shook himself free from the mud's clutches, and

Khan dragged the exhausted soldier through the muck to safety. Once they hit the bank, Muldoon coughed up the muddy water he had swallowed and Khan shook himself, spraying water all around. Khan grabbed Muldoon's tunic one more time and pulled him to firmer ground as the battle continued to rage all around them.

Many lives were lost that day, including that of the company commander, Colonel Sixsmith. But thanks to Rifleman Khan, Muldoon survived to tell their story.

HONORED FOR HEROICS

When Muldoon was sent to an army field hospital to recuperate, Khan refused to leave his master's side. Four months later, on March 27, 1945, while still in service with the Scottish Rifles, Khan was awarded his PDSA Dickin Medal.

Khan proudly wears his Dickin Medal. *Muldoon Family*

The Railton family knew nothing of Khan's heroics or his status as a decorated war hero. They had waited for news about him, but details didn't arrive until a year after the battle in which their dog had demonstrated such heroism. In November 1945 they received a letter from Army Veterinary Services saying that it had "received a request from Rifleman Muldoon to be allowed to keep the dog who had saved his life."[35] How, the Army agency asked, did the Railtons feel about that?

What? Suddenly the family wanted to know exactly what Khan had done. Barry pushed his mom to ask for details.

A note about Barry: while Khan was away, the boy had contracted polio, "but he never forgot his dog and longed for the day when he could come back again."[36] After much deliberation, the family's answer to the Army was a firm no—the Railtons wanted their pet back.

Barry and the Railtons subsequently received details of Khan's heroism from the commanding officer of the 6th Battalion Cameronians, who also let them know about the award he had won: "For this gallant, loyal and faithful action, Khan was awarded the Dickin Medal, which was presented to him at a full battalion parade by the commanding officer. I would like to express to you on behalf of the battalion our grateful thanks for the loan of Khan, who stood firmly by us through all our battles."[37]

The Railtons' understandably proud son couldn't wait to have his four-legged friend home again: "I am longing for the day when he can take me out. . .I am sure he will look after me well after what he has done in the war."[38]

On May 9, 1946, Khan and Muldoon went their separate ways. How painful that must have been for both. Especially because after being "demobbed" Khan was obliged to spend six months in quarantine before he could be reunited with the

Railtons. During his confinement, Khan received the highest honor bestowed by the Royal Society for the Prevention of Cruelty to Animals: a collar with the inscription "For Valor."

REUNITED (AND IT FEELS SO GOOD!)

More than a year passed before Muldoon and Khan met up again. The reunion came July 16, 1947, at the newspaper-sponsored National "Star" Third Dog Tournament at Wembley Stadium. Fifteen other Dickin Medal recipients had been invited to the event; ten of them would participate.[39] Muldoon unexpectedly received a letter from Barry Railton asking if he would like to lead Khan in the event's Parade of War Dogs. Muldoon jumped at the chance.

When Khan saw his beloved handler on the big day, it was as if their year apart had never happened. The moment moved everyone who witnessed it: "At the first glimpse of Muldoon, Khan dashed toward him and, standing up, put his great paws on the man's shoulders, licking his face and giving little joyous whines, while his tail wagged with unbelievable speed and violence. After a few seconds he seemed to remember his owners; leaving Muldoon he ran to Mr. and Mrs. Railton and their young son Barry. He thrust his nose into each in turn, wagged his tail as if in thanks and farewell, then turned back to Muldoon saying unmistakably, 'I belong to you and I'm coming with you.' Khan had made his choice and in the most courteous way imaginable."[40]

Barry's father was deeply moved by Khan's loyalty to his wartime handler. After a brief family meeting, Harold Railton ambled over to Muldoon, shook his hand, and said simply, "The dog is yours."[41]

Khan died in 1955. The four-legged hero of the Scottish Rifles is thought to be buried in the animal cemetery at Edinburgh Castle in Scotland.

ROB
THE "SKY-DOG"
COLLIE—WAR DOG NO. 471/332—SPECIAL AIR SERVICE (SAS)
DATE OF DICKIN MEDAL: JANUARY 22, 1945 (D.M. 11)

"Took part in landings during North African Campaign with an Infantry unit and later served with a Special Air Unit in Italy as patrol and guard on small detachments lying-up in enemy territory. His presence with these parties saved many of them from discovery and subsequent capture or destruction. Rob made over 20 parachute descents."

Rob may be the only Dickin Medal recipient whose heroism stirred challenge and controversy many decades after his service to country.

A beautiful cattle collie, Rob belonged to Edward Bayne, a farmer in Ellesmere, Shropshire, and his family. Bayne had paid five shillings (about twenty U.S. dollars today) for the six-week-old puppy, born in July 1939. Bayne's wife described Rob as "mostly black with a white face with black spots, white waistcoat and 'stockings,' and a long black bushy tail with a white tip."[42]

Mrs. Bayne spoiled the newest member of the family. She tolerated Rob's love of the good life; the dog preferred to sleep on comfy chairs in the house rather than in the farm's musty old barn. A canine of taste, Rob also favored eating off the family's best china. But Edward Bayne put Rob to work herding cattle, bringing the cows in for milking, rounding up pigs, and keeping the chickens out of the garden. For fun, Rob loved riding the tractor with his master.

To hear Mrs. Bayne tell it, Rob "was so gentle that even the chicks knew him and were not afraid of him. He used to help settle them in their houses at night, picking them up in his mouth when they had strayed away—he had a wonderful mouth—and tucking them in under their mothers."[43] Toddler Basil Bayne learned to walk by clutching Rob's coat and, well, toddling along beside him.

Because he was a beloved pet, parting with Rob was wrenching for the Baynes when the war dog trainers came calling. But food (especially dog biscuit) was getting scarce, and with other members of the family already serving their country, the Baynes felt Rob should do his part.

WHAT'S IN A NUMBER?

So off Rob went to training at the War Dog Training School at Northaw, Middlesex, where he became War Dog 471/332. He excelled in the program, which prepared him for patrol and sentry duties, plus messenger work. After graduation, Rob was placed with an infantry regiment in North Africa. Later, he then joined the elite 2nd Special Air Service (SAS), participating in frequently dangerous landings in North Africa and Italy.

It's unclear exactly when and how Rob began parachuting assignments, but he evidently loved them. Rob jumped without hesitation, and once on the ground lay still until his handler arrived to remove the doggie chute. Overall, Rob was credited with an impressive twenty parachute descents.

Just exactly what duties Rob performed on the missions isn't publicly known; the secretive SAS wanted it that way. It is known that the courageous collie once jumped behind enemy lines with SAS personnel and remained there for several months.

Rob never failed to fulfill his guard duties, and his diligence saved an untold number of team members from discovery or capture. Although no details are available, evidently one of Rob's jumps into Italy was part of a mission to rescue Allied airmen and servicemen.

In several mostly vague letters, the War Office reassured the Baynes that Rob was "fit and well and doing a splendid job of work."[44] The dog's valor was borne out in a January 1945 "Very Secret" War Office note to the family:

> I am directed to inform you that it is proposed to award the 'Dickin' medal for Gallantry to War Dog No. 471/322, "Rob," which you were good enough to loan for War Service on the 19th May, 1942.
>
> Since the dog has been with the Armed Forces he has given invaluable service, and it is hoped that you will agree to this presentation to commemorate his conspicuous devotion to duty.
>
> Subject to your approval, it is hoped that the medal will be awarded on the 8th February, 1945, and I should be grateful if you would kindly confirm that you are agreeable to this presentation. A pre-paid envelope is attached for your convenience in replaying.
>
> May I take this opportunity of again expressing our appreciation of your patriotic gesture in loaning 'Rob' for service.

The letter was signed by Lieutenant Colonel J. C. Bennison on behalf of Brigadier General George Kelly, director of the War Office's Army Veterinary and Remount Services.[45]

Later, the War Office allowed Rob's Dickin award to be made public. Rob was a special recipient in that he was the only animal recommended by the War Office for a Dickin Medal. The citation submitted to the PDSA read: "Took part in landings in the North African Campaign with an Infantry Unit.

"From September 1943 he served with a Special Air Unit in Italy. Most of these operations were of an unpleasant nature.

"He was used as a patrol dog and guard on small parties which were lying up in enemy territory. There is no doubt that his presence with these parties saved many of them from being discovered, and thereby from being captured or killed."

The Baynes weren't alone in their excitement; the news media ate it up, and the publicity buoyed the spirits of the military units Rob had worked with. On February 6, 1945, one of them sent the SAS Regiment a simple message: "Brigade sends heartiest congratulations to Rob on award of the first V.C. to S.A.S. troops."[46]

Rob, getting ready for his close-up. *PDSA Archives*

Just two days later, while "on a special 24-hours leave," and joined by men from his unit, Rob was presented with his Dickin Medal. He received the honor from Major the Honourable William Philip Sidney VC (by then also known as Lord de Lisle and Dudley), himself a Victoria Cross recipient for heroism at Anzio in the Italian campaign. The ceremony was held at the Prisoner of War Funds Exhibition at the Rover Showroom in Piccadilly.

Members of Rob's SAS regiment honor him (left). The Honourable William Philip Sidney VC congratulates Rob on his award (right). February 8, 1945. *PDSA Archives*

Soon after, Rob received the "Red Collar and Medallion for Valor" from the Royal Society for the Prevention of Cruelty to Animals and so is regarded as a "Double V.C."

When the Special Air Service disbanded in October 1945, Rob was finally cleared to go home. On November 27, the Baynes welcomed their freshly "demobbed" war hero at a rail station reunion. The conquering hero arrived with a soldier escort. That day Rob met the newest member of the family, daughter Heather.

Rob and his family: Basil (left), baby Heather, and Edna Baynes. *PDSA Archives*

He quickly fell right back into familiar farm duties and old habits, "as if he had been away three hours instead of over three years."[47] Except that thanks to his wartime responsibilities, Rob was now useless as a cattle dog. "No longer would he remain behind them; he had to lead the cattle, or encircle them—up on the right, down on the left—as he had done on patrol."[48] By the time he arrived home, his Dickin Medal somehow had gone missing, but the War Office stepped in and arranged for a replacement.

Like many Dickin medalists, Rob participated in numerous postwar fundraisers and functions. He was a wonderful draw. Rob was joined at many appearances by Judy, Irma, Rifleman Khan, Thorn, Jet, Peter, and others.

Rob died January 18, 1952, at age twelve. As with all Dickin medalists, the PDSA offered a resting place for Rob at their Ilford Animal Cemetery. But the Baynes declined, preferring to bury the beloved pet on their farm. That way, he'd always be close to the family.

Rob's headstone reads:

> *To the Dear Memory of Rob, War Dog No. 471/322. Twice VC. Britain's First Parachute Dog who served three-and-a-half years in North Africa and Italy with the 2nd Special Air Service Regiment. Died 18 January 1952 aged twelve-and-one-half years. Erected by Basil and Heather Bayne in Memory of a Faithful Friend and Playmate 1939–1952.*

HERO OR HOAX?

But Rob's story wasn't over. When a display called "The Animals' War" opened at London's Imperial War Museum in 2006, questions over his service record arose. The exhibit prompted news reports that Rob's deeds were either exaggerated or wholly fictional. The questions were resurrected from an obscure 1998 autobiography, *Who Cares Who Wins*, written by a decorated wartime SAS lieutenant, Jimmy Quentin Hughes. In the book, which had gone virtually unnoticed when published eight years earlier, Hughes contended Rob did not in fact make parachute jumps. Instead, Hughes claimed, Rob had merely served as a companion for the battalion quartermaster, Captain Thomas Burt.

Hughes insisted that Rob's accomplishments had been exaggerated because the Bayne family had requested their dog be returned, Captain Burt had grown attached to Rob, and he didn't want to let the dog go.[49] So, Hughes wrote, both he and Burt "contrived to keep him by telling the family he was indispensable, and exaggerating his exploits."[50]

Hughes died in 2004, two years before the Imperial War Museum exhibit opened. But his friend Mickey King told newspapers that he remembered how Hughes laughed about the alleged hoax. "Quentin said that nobody survived twenty parachute drops, let alone a dog," King maintained. "You were lucky to survive three."[51] The media picked up the story; a headline in the July 21, 2006, edition of the *Daily Telegraph* was typical: "SAS reports of canine heroics 'just a shaggy dog story.'"[52]

Where is the truth in all this? It's impossible to say, since all who served with Rob are gone. There is no definitive way to confirm or debunk the details of the Dickin honoree's war record. This leaves Hughes's claims forever just so much hearsay.

And it is important to note that it was the War Office that nominated Rob for the Dickin. It seems highly unlikely that the War Office didn't perform the routine yet serious due diligence necessary to confirm the truth of Rob's exploits. And the War Office wouldn't have needed to look far for proof, since it was responsible for compiling and maintaining SAS service records.

Moreover, it remains difficult to believe someone of Captain Burt's high character and reputation—he received the prestigious Member of the British Empire (MBE) medal at the same ceremony at which Rob received his Dickin Medal—would lie to superiors and the War Office just to keep the dog around. It just doesn't make sense.

And in the bigger scheme of things does it really matter if Rob actually made all twenty jumps? The unalterable fact remains that he served the 2nd SAS effectively, heroically, and with distinction, along the way winning the deep respect and appreciation of everyone in his unit. It's not inconceivable that the officers and men might exaggerate the number of his jumps to keep him with them. But if that were the case, why wouldn't Rob fully deserve his Dickin Medal anyway?

I guess we'll never know. But Rob gets my vote.

———

RICKY
WELSH COLLIE/OLD ENGLISH SHEEPDOG
DATE OF DICKIN MEDAL: MARCH 29, 1947 (D.M. 47)

"This dog was engaged in cleaning the verges of the canal bank at Nederweert, Holland. He found all the mines but during the operation one of them exploded. Ricky was wounded in the head but remained calm and kept at work. Had he become excited he would have been a danger to the rest of the section working nearby."

Ricky earned his Dickin Medal with his nose. He took on one of the riskiest jobs asked of a war dog: bomb sniffer.

A beautiful short-legged Welsh collie-sheepdog mix, Ricky belonged to the Litchfield family of Bromley in Kent. Mr. Litchfield, serving on Home Guard duty in Hastings at the time, had purchased the four-month-old pup from a destitute family.[53] He paid seven shillings and sixpence. Later the Litchfields moved to Kent, where they eventually faced food shortages of their own and loaned Ricky to the war effort in 1944.

Ricky underwent training at the War Dogs Training School as an "M"—mine detection—dog, sometimes affectionately called a "sniffer." Upon graduation he was assigned to the 279th Field Company, Royal Engineers of the 15th (Scottish) Infantry Division. His handler was Maurice Yielding, who in peacetime made his living as a circus artist.[54]

Ricky also proved himself quite an artist—in mine detection. At first bomb-sniffing dogs were trained to sniff out mines made of metal. But late in the war, in 1944, the Germans developed non-metallic mines. At that point Ricky and other M-dogs were trained to search for soil that had been recently disturbed. When Ricky located a mine, he'd lie down about five feet away, face the danger spot, and refuse to move until his handler neutralized the mine.

Many dogs weren't cut out for this job. It required a canine who was highly intelligent, sure-footed, nimble and—most important—disciplined and quiet. In the heat of the moment the dog had to remain still and calm. A dog without the right temperament and skillset might bolt, unwittingly setting off another landmine buried nearby.

After D-Day, Ricky and Yielding worked their way across France and Belgium and into Holland. The Germans were retreating and as they went placing mines and other incendiary devices intended for advancing Allied forces. Because the Netherlands was the last line of defense before the Allies entered Germany, the Third Reich plastered that country with bombing devices. Roads, riverbanks, and canals were all loaded with non-metallic mines.

PERILS OF WAR

Ricky was very good at his job, even locating mines buried deep under gravel or thick mud. But he could not control the actions of everyone in his unit. On December 3, 1944, Ricky and Yielding were working along the canal banks in Nederweert, in southeastern Holland. Ricky had already located several clusters of mines, all of which were successfully removed.

Ricky and Yielding working the minefields. *Cape Kingdom Neutraceuticals*

But as Ricky stood by, the section commander, who was probing for mines nearby, took a tragically wrong step. The resulting blast killed him and blew Ricky off the riverbank and into the mud.

"We were actually within three feet of the mine and in the middle of a minefield," Yielding wrote to the Litchfields. "I am confident [Ricky] was as steady as the Rock of Gibraltar and I think it was his coolness that brought us out of a sticky patch safely."[55]

Ricky was struck in the head by a piece of shrapnel. He bled profusely—the wound so close to his eyes there was fear he might lose his sight. But the dog was so "chill" that he lay there motionless until help finally arrived. Had he panicked and possibly set off other mines, the additional loss of life might have been huge.

But as soon as cool hand Ricky was bandaged up, the four-legged mine sweeper went right back to sniffing the area. The M-dog successfully cleared all the remaining mines hidden in the vicinity.

Ricky so impressed the War Office that on the day of his scheduled release the military offered the Litchfield family twenty-five pounds—the maximum amount they were legally allowed to offer—if they could keep Ricky in the service. But Mr. Litchfield said no. The family missed their beloved Ricky.

On April 26, 1947, Ricky was awarded his Dickin Medal in a double presentation ceremony alongside Bing. Ricky received the honor from Air Chief Marshal Sir Frederick Bowhill.

Sir Frederick Bowhill pets Bing as Ricky relaxes, awaiting their ceremony. April 26, 1947. *PDSA Archives*

Also bestowed on the collie-sheepdog mix that day: the Royal Society for the Prevention of Cruelty to Animals' "For Valor" medal and collar, for his heroism.

Over the years Ricky did fundraising for the PDSA, and attended dog shows promoting the war dogs of Britain. On December 17, 1947, Ricky helped "bless" the first motorized PDSA caravan dispensary at Westminster, alongside Olga, a Dickin Medal war horse (story appears later).

Ricky lived peacefully with the Litchfields until July 20, 1953, and they buried him at Ilford Animal Cemetery. But the family continues to keep Ricky's memory alive. Their family business, a line of natural dog products, is named after him.

You can't miss the packaging, which features Ricky's beautifully tousled furry face.

Ricky wears his medal proudly. What a face! *PDSA Archives*

ANTIS

ALSATIAN

DATE OF DICKIN MEDAL: JANUARY 28, 1949 (D.M. 52)

"Owned by a Czech airman, this dog served with him in the French Air Force and RAF from 1940 to 1945, both in N. Africa and England. Returning to Czechoslovakia after the war, he substantially helped his master's escape across the frontier when after the death of Jan Masaryk, he had to fly from the Communists."

"Get your hands up!" Czech air gunner Václav Robert Bozděch shouted in halting French. "Show yourself now!" Bozděch kept a tight grip on his pistol while inching his way toward the sound of muffled snoring escaping the kitchen of a bombed-out and apparently abandoned farmhouse.

It was a very cold morning in January 1940. Bozděch's plane had just been shot down while on a reconnaissance mission in the no-man's land between German and French lines. Bozděch and his French pilot, Pierre Duval, were desperately looking for a place they could be safe from capture by the enemy, and snatch a little rest. Plus, the Czech airman needed to treat the wounds Duval suffered in the crash.

Bozděch entered the wrecked structure and crept towards the sound, which now seemed to emanate from the room's only notable contents: a pile of rubble including a stove and an overturned chair. "Wake up!" he snarled. "Show yourself!"[56]

No answer. Except for what sounded, curiously, like—a yawn? What insolence! Bozděch's adrenaline surged as he stole forward, then peeked ever so slowly behind the chair. There, staring down the barrel of his pistol, was a little gray and brown ball of fur sporting huge ears. Bozděch had discovered a four-week-old German shepherd puppy. The little pup, curled up beside the chair, "stumbled to its feet unsteadily and was peering up at him anxiously, growling out a throaty little challenge."[57]

Whew! Feeling a bit foolish, the Czech aviator put away his gun, picked up the puppy by the scruff of his neck, clutched him to his chest, and petted him reassuringly. The little guy's initial resistance melted a little more with every stroke. So did the airman's heart.

"He unzipped his leather flying jacket and slipped the puppy inside. 'You're coming with me, boy,' he said. 'We're in this together.'"[58]

Thus began a great, true story of mutual love and devotion between a man and a dog. The lifelong friendship would be filled with valorous, death-defying adventures in the skies over war-torn Europe.

CZECH MATE

Airman Robert Bozděch had fled to France in 1939 when the Germans invaded his native Czechoslovakia. There he joined the French Air Force, served as a turret gunner, and was shot down in the 1940 incident that was the beginning of his relationship with the German shepherd puppy.

Following their crash, Bozděch and Duval were rescued by French soldiers, and back at their French airbase the Czech presented his furry new friend to his squadron mates. The others loved the dog so much that they declared him their mascot. They named him "Ant"—which sounded more like "aunt"—a reference to the Russian ANT Pe-2 dive-bomber they had enjoyed flying back home with the Czech Air Force. Eventually, the name somehow evolved into Antis.

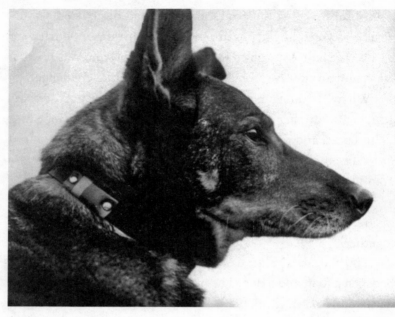

Antis. *PDSA Archives*

When the Germans invaded France, Bozděch and the squadron made their way to England. They brought Antis along, smuggling him in a kit bag to evade strict quarantine laws. Antis served with Bozděch in both the French and Royal air forces from 1940 to 1945, seeing action over North Africa and England.

WHO NEEDS TRAINING?

Antis helped save countless lives.

The dog had an extraordinary gift: he could sense enemy warplanes long before they were detected by the human eye and ear. One night when Antis and Bozděch were stationed with the Czech-manned No. 312 Squadron at RAF Speke in Liverpool, Bozděch was walking back to base from the town with Antis and another Czech airman named Stetka. The dog suddenly began to whine, and Bozděch knew the look in his eyes meant danger was near and closing fast. The whining intensified and the anxious Antis shook his head and stared up at the stars. Air raid sirens began wailing, but before the men could find a shelter, German bombs began falling from the sky.

Robert Bozděch grabbed his little friend and hit the ground, shielding the dog beneath him until the explosions stopped and the planes vanished. The trio rose to find the three houses right in front of them leveled. Screams of the injured and those pinned in the carnage punctuated the darkness. The airmen and the dog raced toward the nearest-sounding cries.

A man was pulled from the rubble, alive but shaken. Seeing this, Antis began pawing at the ground. A Civil Defence worker, who quite reasonably mistook Antis for a search-and-rescue dog, directed the two Czech airmen to follow him into the site. Bozděch, with his limited English, couldn't articulate that Antis wasn't trained for this kind of work. And the Alsatian himself didn't know that he wasn't qualified for the job. He simply ran to a spot and began digging and barking. Rescuers hurried over and pitched in. Soon, an injured woman was safely lifted out and carried to an ambulance. A few minutes later, Antis did it again, this time discovering a man.

Unless you knew otherwise, you'd swear Antis had worked in search-and-rescue all his life.

Bozděch wrote about how well Antis teamed with the rescuers. Typically, the Alsatian stopped and barked at a particular spot until rescuers "started to work without question—and so four people were rescued from certain death beneath the debris."[59]

The Czech and the canine were heading for another spot when they were separated by a collapsing wall. The panicked

Bozděch frantically dug for Antis, fearing his friend was buried deep in debris. His biggest fears: Antis either was crushed and in pain, or had suffocated beneath the dust and rubble. But then he heard Antis's bark, which steadily grew louder. Rescuers scaled the mound of mess to find the dog on the other side, unhurt, standing in what appeared to be the remains of a bedroom.

Robert Bozděch sobbed with relief before the reality of war reasserted itself: Antis discovered a mother, a baby in her arms, both partially buried in the rubble. Neither had survived.

By the time they reached base late that night, Antis's paws were bleeding from all the digging. Robert carried him most of the way home, tending first to the dog's wounds before addressing his own. When Bozděch's head finally hit the pillow, the brave dog was already out cold. "The hero of the evening slept," Robert Bozděch wrote, "and for once, his snores went unrebuked."[60]

BARKING FOR BOZDĚCH

After several months of inaction at the RAF base, Bozděch and two grounded compatriots grew increasingly eager to return to the air—and the fight. Their chance came with a transfer to the No. 311 Czechoslovak Squadron of Bomber Command, stationed at RAF Honington in Suffolk, England, and utilizing East Wretham Airfield.

When Bozděch had been flying for the French, Antis was allowed along on missions, during which he lay quietly at his friend's feet. Antis loved to fly—or maybe he just loved being with Bozděch. They performed low-altitude reconnaissance with the ground attack unit, flying at heights that didn't require an oxygen mask. This made it easy for Antis to tag along.

But when Bozděch began flying with the Royal Air Force, the rules were different. British regulations forbade animals on aircraft. So on every one of Bozděch's missions, Antis watched

Robert's plane take off until it was just a speck in the distance. He then took up his place in the dispersal area—the spot near a runway usually used for parking aircraft. There he waited, refusing to move until his master returned. During those nervous hours while Bozděch was away, "not a morsel of food would pass his lips."[61]

Antis knew the exact sound of Bozděch's 1598-C Wellington bomber. The "C" was for the plane's nickname, Cecilia. He could distinguish its pitch from that of any other, virtually identical Wellington bomber. When he heard Cecilia on approach, even before she became visible, the war dog couldn't contain his excitement: "Suddenly, Antis was on his feet and he barked loudly, beginning the wild war dance for joy. . .tearing around and around the group of waiting men as if he'd gone half mad."

Robert Bozděch had taught his adopted pal to be mindful around aircraft, neither to cross a runway nor to approach a plane when its propellers were spinning. So only when the engines were cut did Antis run to greet his friend, "waiting at the bottom of the ladder as Robert climbed down."[62]

PSYCHIC PUP?

On June 12, 1941, Cecilia and seven other bombers left on a mission two hundred miles away, over Hamm in northwestern Germany. Antis waited patiently, falling asleep at his post until, at 1:00 in the morning, something jolted him awake. Standing stiffly, the furry aviator trembled, then pointed his nose toward where the returning planes should have been approaching. Then the inconsolable Antis howled, mournfully, in a "hollow, full of loss, spine-chilling" fashion.

"Cecilia's in trouble!" screamed an airman to his comrades. "Antis can sense it! God knows how, but he can."[63]

Sure enough, at that moment Bozděch's returning plane had been hit by enemy fire. A piece of metal pierced and shattered the gun turret before crashing into Robert's forehead. Blood gushing downward into his eyes momentarily blinded him. But while he lost a good deal of blood, Bozděch remained conscious.

Five of the mission's eight bombers approached the airfield. But they mattered little to Antis, who sat motionless, gazing at the horizon, waiting for Cecilia. "Every now and again he raised one of his paws, seemingly to point toward the stretch of sky where the Cecilia should appear, then lowered it, whimpering softly," author Damien Lewis wrote.[64]

Miraculously, Cecilia sputtered along over the North Sea before making a successful emergency landing at RAF Coltishall, hours away from East Wretham. Robert was rushed to a hospital, where he remained several days for treatment.

During that time Antis refused to leave his post, no matter how much the men cajoled or tempted him with food. He even refused his favorite, roast liver. When nighttime rain wouldn't budge him, squadron mates covered him with a blanket. Antis bared his teeth if anyone tried to move him, something very much out of character for him.

The poor dog's anguish touched the whole squad, since he was considered one of them. There was no way to convey to Antis that his beloved friend was alive and would soon return. The airmen feared the dog would die from lack of food, water, and sleep before Robert could get back.

In desperation, the chaplain urged that Robert be released from the hospital in Norwich and returned to base. Squadron Leader (soon to be Wing Commander) Josef Ocelka was so worried for Antis that he quickly made the arrangements.

When Bozděch arrived, he was overcome at the sight of his devoted friend, and sank to the ground beside him. Through tears, he tried to reassure Antis he really was back for good. But the loyal dog, disoriented from worry and the lack of food and water, didn't recognize Robert at first. Between the bandages on his head and face and the smells of iodine, disinfectants and other hospital scents, he just wasn't sure. Finally, it was Robert's familiar voice that got through to his friend. Antis weakly licked his master's face.

Antis tried to climb into Robert's arms, but he was too weak. So with all the strength he could summon, Robert lifted his best friend and carried him to the car. They spent the next few days together in the base hospital, recovering.

SEPARATION ANXIETY

Nearly two weeks passed before Cecilia was again airworthy. The target of the June 25, 1941, mission was the city of Bremen, a key industrial and port complex on the River Weser in northwest Germany. The huge mission employed 1,000 Allied aircraft, including almost 470 Wellingtons and all twenty bombers from East Wretham.

Unbeknownst to any of the men in those bombers, they also were deploying a secret weapon that day: one determined dog.

Robert and Antis were going through their usual pre-flight ritual. But when Bozděch went to suit up, he couldn't find the Alsatian air dog anywhere. Robert had little choice but to focus on the mission.

Antis, suffering acutely from separation anxiety, refused to be left behind this time. Just how he managed to sneak aboard Cecilia remains unclear, but the furry stowaway boarded the bomber undetected. He hid in the plane's belly beneath a canvas sling meant for an injured airman.

Fifteen thousand feet up and somewhere over the Dutch coast, Antis revealed himself. Bozděch felt a touch on his elbow. He assumed it was the flight navigator, until he saw that the route planner was deep into his charts. "Puzzled, [Bozděch] stared into the darkness around him. In the dim glow of the orange light above his panel, he saw the vague shape of the dog motionless on the floor behind him.

"It was impossible. It couldn't be. . .and yet it was. Antis lay with heaving sides, struggling to breathe."[65]

The altitude was suffocating the airborne Alsatian. Acting quickly, Robert unstrapped his own oxygen mask and placed it over Antis's muzzle. Soon the canine's breathing stabilized and, incredibly, he stood and offered his paw to shake—a peace offering and mea culpa for having stowed away. But Robert refused the gesture. Instead, he pointed to the floor, then moved Antis between his legs so they could share the oxygen mask. They would soon be over Germany, and Bozděch needed the use of both hands.

It turned out that luck was on their side that perilous night. Ice was forming on Cecilia's wings as all the Allied aircraft flew into an electrical storm. Lightning struck Cecilia, which caused an instrument failure and forced the 1598-C Wellington to turn around. She dropped her bombs into the sea and headed home.[66]

Safe again on the ground, Antis bounded from the plane and "went through an extra-ebullient and noisy war dance for joy, completing several wild circuits around the aircraft."[67] This became his ritual. The flight crew considered Antis a lucky charm, a special talisman that brought the plane good luck. So while animals were barred from RAF aircraft, Antis was declared an exception and made part of the combat team. Newspapers later dubbed him the "Dog of War."

From then on, Antis sat at Airman Bozděch feet in the gun turret, breathing through an oxygen mask fitted especially for him. The crew "got an added sense of peace from having their dog flying into the heart of death with them. It was almost as if they were more worried for Antis' welfare than their own, and that took much of their anxiety away."[68]

For his part, Antis was one happy hound.

One happy man and his dog. *PDSA Archives*

July 1941 was a busy month. Cecilia went on bombing missions every other night, targeting Essen, Münster, Cologne, Bremen, Hanover, Hamburg, Mannheim, and Brest. At month's end, Bozděch was awarded a bar for his Czechoslovak War Cross.[69]

By the time he finished his tour of duty at East Wretham, Bozděch had completed thirty-two sorties, with Antis at his feet on most of the runs.

A COOL CAT

One amazing thing about Antis was that he didn't panic in battle, not even when injured. He was wounded twice. The first time, a shell fragment pierced his oxygen mask, cutting Antis's nose, left ear, and paw. Bozděch didn't notice until after they landed and Antis performed his earthbound jig of joy. The wounds were dressed and not at all disabling, although as Antis aged, his big left ear had a noticeable permanent droop.

But the second wound, suffered in a bombing run over Mannheim, was serious. After dropping her payload of explosives, Cecilia was heading home when she came under heavy attack and was badly damaged.

When the plane was finally out of harm's way, Robert reached down to pet Antis, as he had several times that day. But this time he received no thank-you lick on the hand in return. The turret gunner looked down to see his friend unconscious, lying in a pool of blood. A shell fragment apparently had caught him in the chest hours earlier, causing a deep wound.

"He didn't whine, he didn't panic, he just lay at my feet," Robert said later.[70] Not once had Antis "tried to hinder or distract [Bozděch] from his duty. Silently he had lain there, staring mutely at his master and bearing his pain with a fortitude not often found even amongst the bravest of men."[71]

Upon landing, Robert rushed Antis to sickbay, where the brave Alsatian eventually made a full recovery. But Antis's flying days were over—at least in wartime.

On August 15, 1945, with World War II finally over, twelve converted and updated Liberator bombers of the No. 311 Czechoslovak Squadron flew in formation to Prague, flanked by fifteen new Spitfires the British government had given Czechoslovakia for that nation's new air force.[72] Robert was aboard one of the Liberators, with Antis once again resting at his feet, joining other surviving Czech airmen on the journey home.

While they received a hero's welcome, their plans for a new life in Czechoslovakia were shot down less than three years later. The communists seized power on February 25, 1948, forcing the former turret gunner and his four-legged best friend to flee the country on foot. Antis helped guide Bozděch and others through woods and trails, even alerting them of approaching communist patrols. On one occasion, he actually chased off communist troops.[73] "He saved my life during the war," Robert later told a reporter, "and saved it again helping me escape from Prague."[74]

They settled in Great Britain, where Bozděch rejoined the RAF.

THE FIRST-EVER FOREIGNER

On March 14, 1949, Antis received a PDSA Dickin Medal acknowledging the audacious Alsatian's wartime exploits. The high-profile, well attended ceremony was held during the annual Ideal Homes Exhibition in Olympia, London. Making the formal presentation was Field Marshal Lord Earl Wavell, who addressed the honoree directly: "Dog Antis. . .You have been in action a great many times, and have been wounded, and you have inspired others by your courage and steadfastness on many occasions...."

"You are the first foreign dog to receive this award, which you have worthily earned by the steadfastness, endurance and intelligence for which your race is well known. You have been your master's guardian and saviour. I am sure everyone will join with me in congratulating you on your award, and we wish you many years in which to wear it."[75]

Young Diana Astley, Lord Wavell's granddaughter, congratulates the hero. March 14, 1949. *PDSA Archives*

NEVER CAN SAY GOODBYE

Alas, Antis had but four years to enjoy wearing the medal. In early 1953, his health began to fade. Bozděch consulted a veterinarian, who gently recommended that Robert end his friend's suffering. Bozděch sought the advice of friends at the PDSA. The organization's return telegram read simply, "Advise putting old friend out of misery. Grave reserved."[76]

On August 10, 1953, Bozděch took Antis for one last walk before they boarded a night train to London. For Robert, the two-hour ride became a journey of reflection. Their destination: the animal sanatorium at Ilford.

Robert Bozděch, who published several books after the war, later wrote poignantly of his last moments together with Antis:[77]

"Gently placing his friend on the operating table, he laid his own head against that of his much loved pet and, with tears streaming down his face, murmured his last words of encouragement to the dog.

"To the end Antis had his dignity. As if knowing that his story was written, he lay quietly with his tired head in his master's hands. Almost instantly, as the surgeon did his work, a drowsy feeling crept over Antis. All seemed over, then at the last moment, using his last remaining strength Antis slightly raised his head and gazed into the grief stricken face of his master. For a second [Bozděch] caught a startled look in the dimming eyes, then sighing gently, Antis was asleep."[78]

At age fourteen, Antis took his final flight, this time solo, on August 11, 1953. Antis was buried at Ilford Animal Cemetery. His headstone includes a brief, moving poem by author John Gibson Lockhart, taken from an 1842 letter he wrote to a fellow Scot and literary giant, Thomas Carlyle:

There is an old belief
That on some solemn shore,
Beyond the sphere of grief,
Dear friends shall meet once more.

Etched beneath the Lockhart lines is the phrase "VERNY AZ DO SMRTI," Czech for LOYAL UNTO DEATH.

Robert Bozděch never owned another dog. He wouldn't even allow his children to have one.

7

Home Front Heroes

The "Digging Dogs"

*"We want the work of these dogs to be made public because
it will give confidence to the civilian to know that if he is so
unfortunate as to be buried alive by wreckage we now have the
means of swiftly locating and rescuing him."*

—LIEUTENANT COLONEL W. W. DOVE, MAP Rescue Party Dog Team

T ea time in London, September 7, 1940. A year and four days
had passed since Great Britain declared war on Hitler's Germany. Around 4:00 that afternoon, an estimated 350 German
bombers reached the British capital, having flown across the
English Channel after takeoff from airfields in German-occupied
France. The enemy planes' furious bombing assault on London
lasted until 6:00 that evening. After a two-hour respite, Hitler's
bombers returned for a second raid, this one stretching until 4:30
the next morning. When it finally ended, about 330 tons of
deadly explosives had rained down on the vulnerable city.

The two attacks marked the beginning of the notorious
Blitz—in German, *Blitzkrieg*, or "lightning war." The intense
aerial bombardments targeted London and other English cities
and continued until May 11, 1941, when Hitler called off the
raids to focus on Germany's invasion of Russia.[1]

In the Blitz's first month, the German Luftwaffe dumped a
devastating 5,300 tons of high explosives over twenty-four days

and nights. The aerial assaults didn't let up for fifty-seven consecutive days. At first the attacks were conducted quite brazenly in the daytime. But in late October 1940, the Luftwaffe switched to nights to evade counter-attacks from the Royal Air Force.

"Digging Dog" Rip surveys the devastation following a V-1 attack in Latham Street, Poplar. The bomb crater is full of water. 1941. *Imperial War Museum*

"For Londoners there are no such things as good nights," wrote Mollie Panter-Downes, a Britain-based columnist for the *New Yorker* magazine, "there are only bad nights, worse nights and better nights [as] the *Blitzkrieg* continues to be directed against such military objectives as the tired shop girl, the red-eyed clerk, and the thousands of dazed and weary families."[2]

Four days into the Blitz, in a radio address titled "Every Man to His Post," Prime Minister Winston Churchill told countrymen, "[Hitler] hopes by killing large numbers of civilians and women and children that he will terrorize and cow the people of this mighty imperial city and make them a burden and anxiety to the government....

"Little does he know the spirit of the British nation."[3]

Thirty-two-thousand civilian lives were lost to the Blitz. Another eighty-seven-thousand were injured, while fully one million other people were left homeless in the devastation.

The PDSA adapted to wartime by converting its ambulances and caravan dispensaries to animal rescue squads and placing them throughout the country, but especially in London. The group adopted a wartime slogan: "The PDSA Goes Where the Bombs Fall." Each of its rescue teams included at least one dog.

Rescue teams searched burned-out buildings and pored through rubble, frantically looking for human and animal survivors. Too often the rescue searches morphed sadly into recovery operations. Rescue squads provided aid and treatment for more than a quarter-million pets and other wounded animals, starting with seven thousand in the first week alone. The PDSA also provided longer-term care for those animals who were displaced when their homes were destroyed. Reunions between owners and homeless pets became dramatic morale boosters. In this way alone, the PDSA's contribution to the war effort was immeasurable.

What follows are seven stories of brave, four-legged Home-front Heroes, those search-and-rescue canines dubbed "The Digging Dogs." Their actions were considered so heroic that all were honored with the PDSA Dickin Medal.

TIPPERARY BEAUTY
THE ORIGINAL SEARCH-AND-RESCUE PIONEER
IRISH WIRE-HAIRED TERRIER
DATE OF DICKIN MEDAL: JANUARY 12, 1945 (D.M. 8)

"For being the pioneer dog in locating buried air raid victims while serving with a PDSA Rescue Squad."

Beauty, as friends called her, was born January 4, 1939. The PDSA didn't have to look far to find the Irish wire-haired terrier. She belonged to the association's own superintendent, Bill Barnet, who was working that year in Tipperary, Ireland, when he chose Beauty from a litter of four. The pups and their mother had been brought to the PDSA Caravan Dispensary for Barnet to inspect. Barnet named her "Beauty," so the story goes, because his wife's first reaction was, "Oh, what a beauty!"[4]

In London, Barnet led a Blitz-era rescue squad for animals. Beauty began accompanying him on these missions. She wasn't trained in search-and-rescue. It didn't exist back then. Beauty simply began saving animals trapped in the rubble on her own initiative.

Beauty with Bill Barnet. *PDSA Archives*

It started on a 1940 mission, when Beauty wandered away from Barnet and began digging on her own, "pausing every few minutes to cock her head on one side and listen."[5] Her digging grew desperate. With paws flapping furiously, Beauty burrowed deeper into the dirt until finally turning to catch Barnet's attention. Intrigued by his dog's frantic determination, Barnet directed the squad to continue what she had started. With a bit of work, they finally found the source of Beauty's passionate heroics: an injured cat pinned beneath a collapsed table.

Beauty at work. *PDSA Archives*

The feline was the first of sixty-three animals, including a goldfish, that Beauty found and rescued during the war. Rarely was her intuition wrong.

Beauty and Mr. Barnet look after two wounded dogs they rescued. April 1, 1941. *PDSA Archives*

Indeed, Beauty was so good at rescue work that when her paws were raw and bleeding from digging in rubble, she was given two sets of protective leather booties.

Beauty was considered such a leader in search-and-rescue that in May 1941, the PDSA awarded her its Pioneer Medal, something only humans usually received. More honors awaited. In 1944, the deputy mayor of Hendon in suburban London presented her a silver mounted collar bearing a huge medal: "For Services Rendered."

Another award included a special honor that read simply "Freedom of Holland Park." This unusual designation granted Beauty a unique privilege: total, unrestricted park access to "all of the trees therein." She was the only canine on Earth permitted the run of that public park.

DICKIN DAY

Beauty's greatest honor was bestowed January 12, 1945. The PDSA Dickin Medal was presented by another English hero, Antarctic explorer and Admiral of the Fleet Sir Edward Evans KCB DSO SGM, 1st Baron Mountevans, who was serving as London Regional Commissioner for Civil Defence.[6]

Admiral Sir Edward Evans presenting Beauty with her medal (L). January 12, 1945. Beauty shows off her Dickin Medal to the Mayor and Mayoress of Stalybridge, Councillor and Mrs Kenworthy (R). January 29, 1948. *PDSA Archives*

Two other heroic search-and-rescue dogs, Jet and Crumstone Irma, were similarly honored that day. (Their stories follow shortly.)

Beauty participated in numerous War Savings parades and PDSA fundraisers, alongside fellow Dickin medalists Judy, Rifleman Khan, Rob, Peter, Rex, Irma, and Jet. After the war, she enjoyed a satisfying five-year retirement, dying peacefully on October 17, 1950, shortly before her twelfth birthday. Beauty is buried at Ilford Animal Cemetery in Essex, northeast of London.

RIP

MONGREL
DATE OF DICKIN MEDAL: JULY 1945 (D.M. 27)

"For locating many air raid victims during the Blitz of 1940."

Rip was a scruffy little London mongrel who turned up homeless and hungry after a Blitz raid in September 1940. Rather than wait for a human to take him in, Rip simply claimed an ARP (Air Raid Precautions) warden on Southill Street in Poplar, London, as his master. "I thought that after a feed, he would have gone away," Mr. E. King remarked later. "But he attached himself to me."[7]

Rip in the rubble. Who can resist that face? *Imperial War Museum*

At first Rip was a mere mascot for the ARP unit. But not for long. "As my post (B132) was in the dock area," King explained, "we had many bad incidents, and Rip soon proved his worth."[8]

Like Beauty, Rip was involved in search-and-rescue work. But significantly, he was the war's first canine to assist in saving *human* lives. "He was very valuable in helping us to locate persons trapped in the debris," King said. "During the alerts, heavy gunfire, and incendiary raids, Rip was always out on duty. Never in the way, but always eager to do his bit."[9] Keeping in mind his own hardscrabble fight for survival, Rip seemed to project a sense that it was his duty to rescue others.

Rip accompanied King everywhere, including on the warden's nightly visits to street shelters. He had a wonderful spirit and personality, and always seemed to be smiling.

No wonder Rip made friends wherever he went.

Rip, in a reenactment, shows us how it's done. *Imperial War Museum*

The war mutt became a local hero, thanks to an uncanny ability to locate survivors trapped in rubble, despite the deafening chaos of Blitz blasts. Rip so impressed War Office officials that they quickly established a training center at the MAP Guard Dog School to teach dogs how to sniff out victims.[10] Yet, according to King, "Rip's training was gained the hard way. When I came across Rip sniffing around on the job, I always knew that there was someone trapped in the ruins."[11]

In *Animals in War*, author Jilly Cooper put a literary spin on Rip's heroics by referencing a character in the Beatrix Potter story *The Tale of Mr. Tod*: "How welcome to the victims must have been the first sounds of those scrabbling paws and shrill terrier yaps, and the first sight of the grinning Tommy Brock face with its merry friendly eyes."[12]

In his five years of active service, Rip assisted in more than a hundred rescues. He received the Dickin Medal in July 1945, and wore it on his collar every day.

Rip shows off his medal. July 1945. *PDSA Archives*

REST IN PEACE

How old was Rip when he joined the rescue operations? No one knew, although he clearly was an older dog. Unlike Beauty, however, Rip never had the chance to savor a long retirement. A year after the war, Rip was diagnosed with dropsy (or edema), an abnormal build-up of fluid under the skin. He died in the autumn of 1946 and was the first Dickin Medalist laid to rest at Ilford Pet Cemetery.

JET OF IADA

ALSATIAN

DATE OF DICKIN MEDAL: JANUARY 12, 1945 (D.M. 9)

"For being responsible for the rescue of persons trapped under blitzed buildings while serving with the Civil Defences of London."

The Ministry of Aircraft Production didn't add a search-and-rescue training program until later in the war. For its initial trial, MAP selected fourteen dogs. Incredibly, five of them went on to win the Dickin Medal. Jet was among those five.

As the name suggested, Jet was beautiful and dark as night—a pure Black Alsatian. Born July 21, 1942, he descended from great stock and was raised by a well-known breeder, Hilda Babcock Cleaver of Liverpool, who lent five of her dogs to the program.

Jet and Mrs. Babcock Cleaver. January 12, 1945. *PDSA Archives*

Jet was a mere nine months old when he began anti-sabotage training, becoming the first dog "officially" attached to the Civil Defence Services for search-and-rescue operations after completing the course.

By the time he began sniffing duties, Jet was already a veteran of anti-sabotage work. First he had been stationed in Northern Ireland, working at various airfields for eighteen months. While there Jet also worked with the U.S. Army Air Force and was described as "the favorite of the American troops."[13] It's not clear, though, exactly what duties he performed for the Americans.

The Black Alsatian then returned to school for additional training.

Jet arrived in London with his handler, RAF Corporal C. Wardle, in September 1944, following a V-1 "doodlebug" (or "buzzbomb") attack. Jet was not a good traveler; he was car sick for much of the hundred-mile ride on a truck transport. But duty called, and within two hours after his arrival Jet was digging through rubble. He quickly located an injured missing person, who was treated for his injuries.

Jet saw a lot of action after that.

The Black Alsatian used two methods to identify casualties: if a survivor was involved, Jet would become agitated and whine trying to reach the (presumably wounded) person. But if he discovered a place where a corpse was buried beneath debris, Jet sat calmly at the spot and patiently waited for excavators to retrieve the remains.

A HERO IS BORN

Perhaps his most impressive rescue came in October 1944. Jet and his handler were called to the shell of a bombed-out hotel. Crews had already spent eleven long hours pulling survivors and bodies from the site. With the work seemingly finished, the rescuers were preparing to leave. But Jet would not stand down. The agitated Alsatian seemed to indicate that whoever scent he detected was above ground—and still very much alive.

It was a head scratcher. When rescue workers, trusting the adamant Alsatian's instincts, pressed on, it was to no avail. Only when they raised and scaled a longer ladder did they find a woman in her mid-sixties, trapped on a top floor ledge of the ruined hotel. She was exhausted, covered in dust and debris... and very much alive.

Eventually, she made a full recovery, thanks to Jet.

Jet at work. November 14, 1944. *PDSA Archives*

Of course, not all rescue efforts had happy endings. But even the recovery of human remains provided a valuable service, not just for health and public safety reasons, but because they provided emotional relief to victims' surviving families. Of the 125 people Jet located from September 1944 to war's end, more than fifty were pulled out alive. According to author Jilly Cooper, Jet once found twenty-five people trapped together in the rubble.[14]

Never once did Jet give a wrong indication of a body, alive or dead, to Corporal Wardle.

On January 12, 1945, Jet, joined by Beauty and Crumstone Irma, whom we shall meet shortly, went to a bomb site in Hendon to receive his Dickin Medal, presented by Admiral Sir Edward Evans KCB DSO SGM, 1st Baron Mountevans. "I have seen these dogs in action around London, and I know how well they work," the admiral said. "We have very great faith in their powers of rescue and I know they will continue to be successful during these latest spite methods of Hitler's."[15] The medal presentation was the prelude to a public demonstration of the dogs locating a "casualty" buried in the Hendon ruins.

VICTORY PARADE

VE Day—marking the Allies' victory in Europe and Germany's unconditional surrender—was celebrated May 8, 1945. Overall, World War II formally ended September 2—V-J Day—when Japan finally threw in the towel. Over the following months, liberated Allied prisoners of war came home and the world began to heal from the war's chaos, ravages, and grief.

By mid-1946, Britain was at last ready to celebrate with a huge Victory Parade on Saturday, June 8. Jet and Crumstone Irma had the honor of leading the Civil Defence Services section in which they proudly served. "The crowd remembered and cheered," as Jet strode proudly in the parade attended by the royal family, former Prime Minister Winston Churchill, and his successor, Clement Attlee.[16]

Afterward, it was time for Jet to go home. He returned to the waiting arms of Mrs. Cleaver and lived out a retirement that included appearing at fundraisers for the PDSA and other charities.

On October 18, 1949, Jet, just seven years old, passed away prematurely from heart and kidney failure. The fearless Black

Alsatian was buried in the rose garden at Calderstones Park, Liverpool, where he and Mrs. Cleaver enjoyed a daily walk.

A beautiful memorial, paid for by the city, remains there in his honor.

CRUMSTONE IRMA

ALSATIAN
DATE OF DICKIN MEDAL: JANUARY 12, 1945 (D.M. 10)

"For being responsible for the rescue of persons trapped under blitzed buildings while serving with the Civil Defences of London."

Irma belonged to Mrs. Margaret Griffin, a well-known breeder and trainer. The beautiful Alsatian descended from the Crumstone line, believed by breeders to produce dogs with exceptional intelligence and strong devotion to duty. Mrs. Griffin had brought Irma's grandmother, Echo, to England from New Zealand. When the war began, Echo was at the relatively advanced age of nine. Still she served a year as a patrol dog. When she retired at ten, Irma took over her grandmother's work.

The high-achieving family also included a thespian. Storm—Irma's father and Echo's son—portrayed Black Wull in the 1938 British film *Owd Bob*.[17] During the war, Storm worked as an emergency messenger, and Irma did too before entering search-and-rescue work. When telephone lines went down, Storm and Irma carried messages from the Leatherhead Air Raid Precautions Post to the Surrey Report Centre for Civil Defence Services. The dog delivery program had skeptics, but Storm proved his value when he raced three and a half miles in under fourteen minutes to deliver a message.

Irma's owner stepped up when the call arose for war dogs. Mrs. Griffin became chief trainer at the MAP program. "As soon as the dog training school was started in January 1942, I shut up my house and lived in a hut and caravan to do this work of training war dogs," she told an interviewer. Mrs. Griffin claimed to be the first woman handler of Civil Defence search-and-rescue dogs.[18] She personally handled Irma and Irma's half-sister, Crumstone Psyche, when they began search-and-rescue duties in October 1944. For her role in bringing dogs to the war, Mrs. Griffin would be awarded the British Empire Medal (BEM).

The respected breeder kept a diary of her work, sending detailed reports to the Allied Forces Mascot Club. The entries present a rare and intriguing peek at a slice of British history that might otherwise have been lost to the winds of war.

What follows are a few of the remarkable moments she recorded about Irma:

October 10, 1944

At 12:15 am, the dogs answered a call in Ilford, where a series of homes had been hit. Irma searched the first house and made an indication. Searchers found the body of a woman below the spot. In the next house, Irma indicated a particular location where, as it turned out, a woman was trapped. She was successfully freed. Next, Irma found the bodies of three other women, all buried about fourteen feet under debris. But Irma found nothing in the next home, even though the woman who lived there was reported missing. The next morning, however, her body was discovered in a garden, fifty yards from the blast site.

Twelve hours later, a V-2 rocket hit in Leytonstone. Irma and Psyche discovered three bodies at the scene.[19]

March 1945

"I was called out in the morning following an incident as persons were still missing," Mrs. Griffin wrote. "Irma and Psyche *together* suddenly ran to a point in the debris. Beneath this rubble we found a collapsed floor. A woman was trapped there between two floors. She had been there over nine hours and was still conscious. We got her out and, after examination, the doctor said she had a good chance of recovery. This was a wonderful find, as the position of the floors was quite hidden by a mound of rubble and the woman's presence was quite unexpected."

Sadly, the woman's baby did not survive.

Around the same spot, the dogs indicated another survivor was near. So the rescuers resumed digging, and found a small collie, quite alive, "who was little the worse for his experiences."[20]

In a letter dated March 19, 1945, Mrs. Griffin described another search-and-rescue success: "At a later incident Irma gave the position of victims under a collapsed house and although there was some doubt in the minds of the men who were working on the ruins, excavations were made. As a result they discovered two girls, both alive."[21] This rescue was especially impressive because Irma refused to give up on the location, and kept returning to it, even after two days. Only because of her tenacity did the two girls survive.

Irma working alongside Jet. *PDSA Archives*

THE RAVEN RESCUE

At 2:30 on the morning of February 6, 1945, a V-2 rocket struck in the northeast London district of Chingford. Some of the homes were destroyed, others badly damaged. A ruptured gas line compromised air quality, making a bad situation worse. Casualties were mounting when Mrs. Griffin and her girls were brought in.

Irma quickly made an indication towards a thirty-foot dividing wall left standing, ever so precariously, between two houses. She and Psyche quickly scaled a twenty-foot mound of rubble, whereupon Irma indicated a suspect spot. Rescue workers began digging. They stopped about twenty minutes later, after hearing a crying baby, followed by faint sounds they believed could be the child's mother. Digging furiously once more, rescuers were fifteen feet down when they banged into the top of a Morrison shelter, a heavy steel box that was designed to serve as an indoor air-raid shelter but also doubled as a table. Inside, they surmised, was a woman, her baby and a second young boy.

It took another two hours of careful digging before rescuers finally pulled the Raven family from their prison of debris. The two boys were safe, but by then the mother had died of asphyxiation.

At the time, her husband, the boys' father Edward Raven, was at his job. "I was called from work and told that the house was down. When I arrived they were just getting the boys out." Mrs. Raven was among four fatalities in the attack; forty-five others were injured.

This Raven family story has an uplifting ending. On February 10, 1950, the baby, Keith Raven (by then, seven) and nine-year-brother John reunited with Irma and Psyche for the first time since the tragedy. The pre-arranged meet-up came when their father brought them to the annual Crufts Dog Show at the historic Olympia exhibition center in West Kensington, London. Irma was wearing her beautiful Dickin Medal for the occasion, and the "two boys and two Alsatians played and romped in the gallery of the arena—united after five years."[22]

CANINE ESP?

The most important quality in a search-and-rescue dog is a good nose. If a canine can smell a victim eight to ten feet away, the dog is considered to possess a good range. But Irma could do much better than that. She once found a victim under twenty feet of rubble. On numerous occasions, her detective's nose was accurate from ten to fifteen feet down.

Incredibly, Irma even had the ability to discern whether a victim was alive or dead. If she sensed life, Irma let out a special bark, then began to dig. But Irma had a distinctly different bark when she believed a fatality was involved. In those instances, she stood stoically and respectfully over the area and waited for rescuers to reach the grim find.

If they recovered a body, Irma felt compelled to lick the victim's face or hands, as if hoping a last-ditch effort might wake the person. When this didn't work, she'd gaze at her handler as if pleading for help.

Once Irma's bark indicated that she had found a live body. But when the man was pulled from the debris, he was lifeless. Rescuers were crushed; they had reached him too late. Irma refused to accept that conclusion. Instead of licking his face and hands as she usually did with dead bodies, she resumed barking—and the man stirred.

He was alive after all! Irma's remarkable instincts had once again proved correct.

Irma licking the hand of a casualty on a stretcher. *PDSA Archives*

As effective as Irma was on patrol duty and message running, she saved her best for search-and-rescue. In all, Irma and sister Psyche located 233 victims of German air raids, twenty-one of whom were found alive. Sadly, more often than not, search-and-rescue turned into search-and-recovery. "I hope soon the bells of peace will be ringing out," Mrs. Griffin noted in her diary, "and there will not be any more of these tragic scenes for us to witness and our dogs to work upon."[23]

HOUND HEROICS HONORED

Irma received her Dickin Medal on January 12, 1945, sharing the spotlight that day with fellow Dickin honorees Beauty and Jet. But Irma wasn't done yet. Irma continued search-and-rescue work in the five months that followed—until VE Day on May 8.

A month later, on June 10, Irma proudly wore her Dickin medallion when she joined Peter, a Scotch collie and another celebrated MAP war dog, in the Civil Defence Services' Stand-Down Parade in Hyde Park. Irma's growing celebrity translated into her formal presentation to the King, Queen, and their daughter, Princess Elizabeth. Mrs. Griffin led Irma and Peter in the parade march.

That November, Irma rejoined Peter for his own moment in the Dickin spotlight. Peter's medal presentation was held at the United Charities Fair at the Grosvenor Hotel. Eight months later, at London's huge Victory Parade, Irma again led the Civil Defence Services' section of the parade, accompanied by Jet. Irma is among a dozen Dickin medalists buried at Ilford Pet Cemetery.

THORN

ALSATIAN
DATE OF DICKIN MEDAL: MARCH 2, 1945 (D.M. 12)

"For locating air-raid casualties in spite of thick smoke in a burning building."

Thorn, a great-grandson of Echo (Crumstone Irma's grand-mother), was handled by his owner, Malcolm Russell. Thorn was courageous, particularly when burning buildings were involved. Although he didn't make as many finds as some other dogs, Thorn's accomplishments remain inspiring.

Thorn seemed to simply shrug off any fear of smoke and fire, sometimes performing duties at great risk both to himself and Russell. He willingly went "where others quite literally failed to tread."[24]

Blessed with an uncanny sense of smell, Thorn could detect the presence of bombing victims right through the powerful, distracting scents of smoke and burning rubble. Russell's account of one incident was part of the Dickin Medal citation presented by Sir Edward Warner, DSO, Senior Regional

Officer for London Civil Defence: "We were working at houses which were on fire. One dog would not go into the smoke. Thorn went in slowly, step by step into the thickest smoke. He repeatedly flinched, but [when] encouraged on, he reached a spot approximately over the seat of the fire. There, he gave positive indication of having found someone, and casualties were later recovered from this spot. In my opinion the work of Thorn on this occasion was the best I have yet seen from any rescue dog. I personally found it impossible to see in the smoke and had to be helped down to where the air was clearer."[25]

Russell's own actions that day earned him the British Empire Medal (BEM) for bravery.

Thorn was named a Dickin medalist on March 2, 1945. The award presentation was held seven weeks later at the Civil Defence Football Cup Final at Wembley Stadium. Thorn accepted the honor from Sir Harold Scott, KCB, KBE, Metropolitan Police Commissioner and Permanent Secretary of the MAP.[26]

Thorn and Rex display their medals. *PDSA Archives*

A STAR IS BORN

After the war, Thorn wasn't content to return to obscurity. In his next career move, Thorn followed the lead of American war hero Audie Murphy:

He became a movie star.

There was logic to this, since he was related to Irma's father, Storm, who had already carved out his own career on the big screen.[27]

Wisely choosing to start small, Thorn appeared in a short educational film demonstrating techniques he had learned at the ARP school of mine detection and mountain rescue.[28]

Irma's multi-talented relative went on to appear in *Daughter of Darkness* with Anne Crawford and Maxwell Reed, based on the stage play *They Walk Alone*. He and Ms. Crawford spend their time on screen tracking down a murderess.

The press had a grand old time with the story, reporting that Thorn earned at least seventy-five pounds a week for the role and was insured for a thousand pounds during production. One newspaper account claimed Thorn was "coddled as much as any human star," and had been "given a stuffed stand-in to save him from strong studio lights, and this traveled on location with him. Unfortunately he became furiously jealous of it, and [barked] a long time to get over his suspicions of his 'double.'" One reviewer wrote, "His bow will be more of a bow-wow, for Thorn is an Alsatian dog whose performance, I am told, will probably make him the British Lassie."[29]

YOU CAN'T KEEP A GOOD DOG DOWN

No dedicated thespian wants to miss his first movie premiere. But in Thorn's case, a gunshot wound nearly kept him away—a sadly ironic twist of fate for a dog who had survived such a tumultuous war.

In mid-January 1948, almost two weeks before his big screen debut, Thorn was mistakenly shot near the village of Hever, Kent, by a farmer who had just had lost four sheep to a different, rampaging dog. When he saw Thorn—who was on a rabbit hunt at the time—near his sheep, the farmer mistook the Dickin honoree for the culprit and fired at him.

The bullet crashed into Thorn's shoulder. At first he wasn't expected to survive surgery to remove it. His owner remained loyally at Thorn's side. "For five days it was touch and go," Russell told a reporter.[30] But within a week, his recovery improved, and, incredibly, by January 21, Thorn was ready for his close-up.

After all that excitement, Thorn lived out his retirement in relative peace with Malcolm Russell.[31]

———

REX

ALSATIAN
DATE OF DICKIN MEDAL: APRIL 25, 1945 (D.M. 20)

"For outstanding good work in the location of casualties in burning buildings. Undaunted by smoldering debris, thick smoke, intense heat and jets of water from fire hoses, this dog displayed uncanny intelligence and outstanding determination in his efforts to follow up any scent which led him to a trapped casualty."

The talented fire rescue dog Rex was surprisingly young when he was paired with an experienced handler, Dorothy Homan, for war service. As a six-week-old puppy, Rex had been purchased for thirty shillings by Captain J. Wright of Northumberland Gardens, Jesmond, Newcastle-upon-Tyne. Wright had had his own distinguished military career. A twenty-two-year veteran of the 8th King's Royal Irish Hussars, he had served in the Middle East and India. [32]

Even before Rex was fully trained, he demonstrated impressive physical prowess and natural ability. One memorable demonstration occurred in January 1945. Rex was brought to a bomb site in Lambeth, in London's South Bank district. While being led over the grisly scene, he stopped and began to scratch the ground. The more Rex dug, the more blood rescue workers saw mixed with the loose dirt.

Digging a little deeper, Rex discovered blood-stained bricks, which rescuers assumed belonged to casualties that had previously been removed from the area. But Rex saw things differently, and when he wouldn't back down, the men held him back and resumed digging.

That was when they uncovered the corner of a bed.

Rex could be held back no longer. With a typical display of his natural physicality, the Alsatian warrior leaped back into action. He urgently dug at the earth for some time until he uncovered bedding—which he dragged from the debris literally by his teeth. At last the surprised crew could appreciate Rex's dogged insistence that day; he had correctly located bodies they hadn't expected to find at that spot. "There can be no question that he fully understands what is expected of him," an official report noted, "and he shows determination in exploration which has so often produced results." [33]

Two months later, a factory in Heston was hit by a German V-2 guided ballistic missile. The building was still ablaze when Rex and Homan arrived. They entered a weakened part of the structure, but were forced to withdraw when the burning roof began to collapse.

"[Rex] was unwilling to leave and had to be dragged away," Homan wrote, adding that the dog likely had "caught some scent which would then have given us an indication—an indication he did, in fact, give later in the day."

Hours later, Rex was allowed to reenter the factory building. By then the fire was largely under control, although some parts of the structure remained hot and the target of firehose sprays. "Despite the heat, Rex made his way across the debris in many places and gave indications of five casualties within the first four minutes," Homan wrote. "The bodies were recovered within fifteen minutes of the dog's indication."

Rex returned to the scene on two successive days. On the second day, he was coming from another site where he had inhaled a large amount of gas. By the time he reached the factory, Rex was quite ill, vomiting several times. Yet the dedicated rescue dog struggled valiantly to fulfill his mission. When Homan finally led Rex away from the site—for a rest—it was "much against the dog's will."[34]

Rex's uncanny sense of smell again made the difference at one of his last assignments. The rescue operation was in Stepney, a borough of the Tower Hamlets of London, two and a half miles east of St. Paul's Cathedral. Rex bolted through a doorway into a block of bombed-out flats that stubbornly remained standing. This wasn't the location he had been brought in to search, so his handler retrieved Rex and took him to a different spot where casualties were expected to be found.

But Rex had ideas of his own, breaking free again and racing back to the original spot. Sure enough, he gave rescuers a definite indication, and bodies were found.

At the time of Rex's Dickin Medal ceremony, the *Wembley News* told readers that Rex had been instrumental in locating sixteen casualties in three hours. Four of these were eventually reached by digging through several feet of solid clay.[35]

"At another incident," a second paper reported, "his indications led to the recovery of nine."[36] No one knows exactly how many casualties Rex helped save or recover, but various accounts put the figure in the sixties.[37]

An official report summarized just how extraordinary Rex was at his job: "He has ignored fire hoses spraying quantities of water around him, and has not hesitated to climb over loose and dangerous rubble in his efforts to follow up a scent which may have led him to a trapped casualty. He has very often given clear indications of the exact whereabouts of missing persons, thereby enabling rescue or search work to be carried out at those precise places, saving an enormous amount of time and labor in the clearing up of the incidents."[38]

Rex accepted his Dickin Medal at Wembley Stadium on April 25, 1945, sharing the limelight that day with fellow Dickin honoree Thorn.

FUNDRAISING FIEND

After the war, Rex proved a popular draw at public events. He was also a persuasive fundraiser for the PDSA and other charities. In fact, he inspired so many donations that in November 1949, the PDSA presented him an inscribed harness complete with a replica of his Dickin Medal. The so-called "Award of Animal Service with Crown" honored Rex for having raised more than 450 English pounds for various charities during the previous two years. Nearly half of the contributions went to the PDSA.

Each June, Rex was a star attraction at Newcastle's celebrated annual fair at Town Moor. Visitors to the PDSA exhibit found the decorated war dog "...standing by a battered bucket in which an ever-growing heap of coins testified to the animal-loving nature of Newcastle's residents."[39] Over the years, Rex generated nearly a thousand pounds in PDSA donations. His personal one-year money-raising record at the fair was 107 pounds, 10 shillings.

Rex's labors ended June 17, 1954, shortly before that year's fair, where he was sorely missed. "His memory still lives on," reported the August 1954 issue of the *The Animals' Magazine*, "in the kindly hearts of those who visit there. So many visitors called the PDSA Mobile Dispensary to offer sympathy and give donations to his memory."[40] Because of the huge public outpouring of affection for Rex—and the additional donations his death inspired—the fair arranged a public display of Rex's Dickin Medal and ribbon, inscribed harness, and the many certificates awarded him over the course of a full and heroic life.

Like so many Dickin dogs, he was buried at Ilford Animal Cemetery.

PETER
SCOTCH COLLIE—WAR DOG NO. 2664/9288
DATE OF DICKIN MEDAL: NOVEMBER 29, 1945 (D.M. 33)

"For locating victims trapped under blitzed buildings while serving with the MAP attached to Civil Defence of London."

As a puppy, Peter—a beautiful Scotch collie born in 1941—was purchased for twenty-five shillings by Mrs. Audrey Stables of Birmingham, England. His path to glory was a surprising one.

When he was little, Peter "behaved like a four-legged gangster." He frequently disobeyed commands, fought with other dogs and destroyed anything in the Stables' household he could clamp his teeth onto.[41] When the government call went out for dogs in June 1944, Mrs. Stables offered the rude and spirited three-year-old to the Ministry of Aircraft Production. Peter became War Dog No. 2664/9288 and teamed with handler Archie Knight. MAP was where the unruly collie acquired disciplined habits—and found his calling.

Peter's speed, accuracy, and devotion to finding victims saved rescuers countless hours of searching. Once he worked a bomb site for nine hours straight, only reluctantly taking a six-hour rest break before returning for two more hours of work. As a MAP official noted, "There is no question that the prompt and accurate information he gave to his handler resulted in at least three persons being rescued alive by the rescue squads."[42] Overall, field reports indicate Peter saved the lives of at least six people.

Sometimes the sniffing and digging produced surprises. For example, once while Peter was poking through debris, a voice was heard from below—swearing like a sailor.

Realizing they had a "live" one, Knight called out, "It's all right, we're coming!" and sent for medical reinforcements. Peter picked up the pace of his digging. When rescue workers followed suit, they were surprised to come upon a smashed birdcage. "Sitting amid the wreckage," according to a news account, "vigorously reviling the universe, was a large and very irate parrot."[43]

But laughs were rare in the grim and grueling business of search-and-rescue.

On March 23, 1945, Peter located two adult bodies in the rubble. While Knight considered that a relatively modest total, he still felt the day had produced some of Peter's finest work. He wrote about it in a wartime diary: "We were called twenty hours after the incident and after several hours of heavy rain. Three bodies were missing and he very quickly indicated in a most unlikely spot, but he was right, and they uncovered a man and a woman both on the same spot. The next day we were called to another job. There were so many calls for Peter...."

"I worked him ten hours and he never once refused to give all he had. All his marks revealed casualties. The next day we returned, and he worked like a hero again, until after six hours, I refused to ask any more of him. I hated to work him like this but I also hated to refuse the rescue parties who were asking for him; he was really played out but he worked like a Trojan."[44]

Two months later, Peter saved a boy buried in the rubble left by one of the last V-2 bombings in England. Peter searched the area and indicated where to dig, and within minutes the boy was freed, safe and sound.

ON STRIKE!

Peter refused to work on only a single occasion. It happened at the very end of the war after one of the final rockets landed.

Peter and Knight were teamed with a dog named Taylor and his handler, W. T. Rowe. At the site, both dogs sat down and did...nothing. The handlers tried like the dickens (so to speak) to get them interested, but Peter and Taylor were having none of it. Nothing the men tried did any good. It occurred to the handlers that the dogs must be sick, and they pulled them out of the immediate spot. But neither showed any signs of illness.

Finally Rowe had an epiphany: Every night, the dogs were fed on three pounds of horsemeat and two pounds of biscuits. But for three days the war had interrupted meat deliveries, leaving the dogs with only the biscuits to eat. Peter and Taylor, Rowe realized, had gone on strike. ("No meat, no work!"[45])

When meat deliveries resumed, the strikers forgave management and returned to work. Ultimately the work stoppage was an isolated incident.

POSTWAR PETE

On June 10, 1945, a month after VE Day, Peter's devotion to duty was recognized when he and Irma were invited to march in the Civil Defence Services Stand-Down Parade in Hyde Park.

Irma and Peter at the Stand-Down Parade. June 10, 1945. *PDSA Archives*

At the event, Peter "led the parade and was presented to Their Majesties."[46] Word on the street was that he took a real liking to the Queen. Her daughter, Princess Elizabeth (later Queen Elizabeth II), also admired Peter and gave him a little pat. Irma's owner, Mrs. Cleaver, said of the scrappy Dickin medalist: "Peter was much admired by Her Majesty—who, as a Scot, has I expect a very soft spot in her heart for the collie."

Archie Knight offered his own amusing take on the royal meet-up: "Peter had the great honour of meeting the king and queen and of leading the parade in the march past the Civil Defence Services. The queen was very attracted by him. Peter was not a bit awed by the occasion. Her Majesty asked me many questions about him and praised him for what she called his 'wonderful work'....

"Peter seemed to think the whole thing was for his benefit and answered the applause of the crowds with excited barks." [47]

Another account noted that Peter actually seemed more interested in Her Majesty's fox fur than in the queen herself. An observer reported that Peter's interest in the fur prompted King George VI to remark, "He must think it's a rabbit, my dear."[48]

Jet admiring the Queen's fur as a young Princess Elizabeth looks on. June 10, 1945. *PDSA Archives*

Mrs. Stables learned that her war hero hound would receive the Dickin Medal later that month at the Grosvenor House Hotel in Park Lane. On the big day in November 1945, Sir James Ross, KBE, CB, head of S4 Central Secretariat Branch of the Air Ministry, did the honors. Irma was there to offer a paw in congratulations.

Afterward, the *Birmingham Mail* summarized the Scotch collie's tumultuous life to that point: "[Peter] is only four years of age and yet, in that short space of time he has saved the lives of six people; shaken 'hands' with His Majesty the King; 'kissed' Her Majesty the Queen; had his handsome head patted by Princess Elizabeth; and has now been awarded the People's Dispensary for Sick Animals' Dickin Medal for gallantry."[49]

Peter died at the Nottingham PDSA sanctuary in November 1952. Like so many of Great Britain's heroic war dogs, he was laid to rest at Ilford Animal Cemetery.

Not a bad life for a "four-legged gangster."

8

Judy

"A remarkable canine...a gallant old girl who, with a wagging tail, gave more in companionship than she ever received...and was in her short lifetime an inspiration of courage, hope and a will to live, to many who would have given up in their time of trial had it not been for her example and fortitude."[1]

—FRANK WILLIAMS

PEDIGREE ENGLISH POINTER—PRISONER OF WAR #81A-MEDAN
DATE OF DICKEN MEDAL: MAY 2, 1946 (D.M. 37)

"For magnificent courage and endurance in Japanese prison camps, which helped to maintain morale among her fellow prisoners, and also for saving many lives through her intelligence and watchfulness."

Apurebred with liver and white coloring, the striking English pointer received the exotic name *Shudi* at Shanghai Dog Kennels, where she was born in February 1936. Records from that shelter in Shanghai's British settlement listed her dam as "Kelly of Sussex" (Kelly's owners hailed from the County of Sussex in southeastern England).[2] The Shanghai kennel was run by an Englishwoman known simply as "Miss Jones" with help from a local woman named Lee Sung and her daughter Lee Ming.

Young Ming especially loved puppies, and Shudi, as Ming called her, stood out among Kelly's litter of seven as the entertainingly curious one. While her six siblings clung to mama, Shudi

207

pushed at the boundaries of their enclosure, as if planning an escape. Indeed, at the ripe old age of three weeks, she did just that.

How this little peanut managed to survive cold, famine-stricken Shanghai on her own—and at such a tender age—was a wonder. Shudi, utterly on her own, was foraging for food when she turned up near the back door of a general store run by a Chinese man known as Soo. The storekeeper was taking out the trash one night when he heard the whimpering cries of a little pup. When he found the young runaway gazing up at him with "huge watery brown eyes," his heart melted.

Soo set up a cardboard box as shelter from the cold winds and gave the starving little ragamuffin any scraps of food he could find. But the makeshift doghouse would be Shudi's home for only a few months.

In May 1936, Japanese soldiers destroyed whatever stability Shudi had found in Soo's care. A roving band of drunken Japanese sailors, on liberty from their gunboat anchored on the Yangtze, were stopping at every pub they passed in old Shanghai. When they reached Soo's store, words were exchanged, tempers flared, and the sailors beat the storekeeper and trashed his shop. Terrified by the noise, Shudi heard the cries of her benefactor and slowly inched her way inside. Big mistake. The sailors turned on her. One grabbed the orphan puppy by the neck, walked outside, and—ignoring her cries of fear and pain—literally punted her like a football across the street into a pile of trash. The sailors then disappeared down the street to continue their cruel drunken revelry.

Ironically, the violence actually turned out to be fortuitous. The pitiful, lonely Shudi was too scared, hungry, and hurt to get very far. Quietly whimpering, she collapsed in an abandoned doorway, where she prepared to spend the night.

"Shudi! Oh, Shudi!" cried a voice in the darkness. "Where you been?" It was young Lee Ming from the kennel. She couldn't believe her good luck in stumbling upon the lost, wounded little pointer. Weak from her ordeal, Shudi struggled to wag her tail in recognition of the kind, familiar voice calling her name. Ming scooped up the dog, quickly tucked Shudi inside her coat, and raced back to the kennel a few blocks away.

"Look, I find Shudi!" Ming cried as she rushed to Miss Jones's side. Ming opened her coat to reveal the sleeping pup. Miss Jones, not believing her eyes, took the dog, looked her over—and smiled.

WHAT'S IN A NAME?

"It *is* her. It really is the one that ran away," cried the kennel overseer. "I think we should give her a bath and a good dinner, don't you?" She handed Shudi back to Ming, who whisked her away for some TLC.

Shudi must have felt safe being back home again; she remained calm and relaxed while Ming and Miss Jones cleaned and fed her. Ming wrapped Shudi in a blanket and the innocent pup fell into a deep sleep. "Why do you call her Shudi?" Miss Jones asked.

"Shudi means peaceful—and that is how she looks, doesn't she?"

Miss Jones looked down at the dog asleep in Ming's arms. "Yes, Lee Ming, she does, and that shall be her name: *Judy*."[3]

ALL PAWS ON DECK

Judy's plucky recovery from her early brush with the brutish Japanese sailors was a testament to the dog's spirit and drive to survive.

That September two members of the Royal Navy arrived at the Shanghai Dog Kennels seeking a mascot for their gunboat, the HMS *Gnat*. The men were the skipper, Lieutenant Commander J. M. G. Waldegrave, and his Chief Petty Officer Charles

Jeffrey. When they spotted Judy, it was, hokey as it sounds, love at first sight, especially when she "leapt into Jeffrey's arms when he whistled a hello in her direction."[4]

Before the two men left with their new crewmember, Miss Jones "gave the sailors some background about their new and remarkable dog." Judy was formally adopted by the entire Royal Navy rather than any single service member. British naval archives list her by the rather aristocratic-sounding "Judy of Sussex."[5]

Writing in his diary shortly after Judy's arrival on board, Jeffrey described the *Gnat*'s newest mate: "Judy of Sussex. . .is the most loveable creature. As the captain and I had been the ones to buy her for the ship's company, he decided I should keep her forward so that she would not get too familiar with the men and so spoil our chances to train her for the gun."

Despite that patrician-sounding name, the popular Judy of Sussex quickly became everybody's dog and had the crew eating out of her paw. "The ship's company love and treat Judy as a pet," Jeffrey wrote later, "and I am delighted that the men share her. But of course our chances of making her a trained gun dog are very small."[6]

Like every human member of the Royal Navy, Judy was assigned her own identification number. Able Seaman Jan "Tankey" Cooper, named "Keeper of the Ship's Dog," helped Judy settle in. An empty ammunition crate and ship's blanket placed near the ship's bridge comprised her new sleeping quarters. But Judy soon preferred to curl up in the bunk of one of the men.

It didn't take long for her presence aboard ship to provide a huge morale boost.

DOG OVERBOARD!

Judy's life on the *Gnat* was smooth sailing—until November, when she somehow slipped on deck and plunged off the gunboat into the Yangtze River. Jeffrey witnessed the mishap and screamed "Dog overboard!" The captain ordered the ship to reverse course, and the crew quickly launched a lifeboat into the Yangtze's notoriously dangerous currents. When Judy was pulled safely into the small boat, her gleeful rescuers raised semaphore flags with this message to the main ship: "Christening Complete."

If not for the crew's quick actions, Judy would quickly have been lost. The derring-do was recorded in the ship's log as "Exercised Man Overboard and Away Lifeboat's Crew." The fact that the entry reported the rescue of a "Man Overboard" demonstrated just how much her shipmates valued Judy—she was one of the crew.

Judy became essential to the ship, in great part because of her keen senses of smell and hearing. These helped the pedigreed English pointer develop an "early warning signal" when something seemed amiss. One night she alerted her shipmates to pirates preparing to raid the *Gnat*. The invaders were the ones surprised when they tried climbing aboard.

Another time Judy's frantic barking warned of the presence of a "cess ship"—one carrying human waste—heading down the Yangtze. If the stench had been allowed to drift inside the *Gnat* it would have lingered for days. Judy's heads-up gave her crewmates just enough time to batten down hatches and close portholes. The men marveled at how Judy seemed more person than pet. "She seems to develop a human brain as she gets older," the captain wrote in his log. "She seems to understand every word."[7]

TIME IS CHANGE

In 1938, routine reassignments separated Judy from many of her friends, including the Royal Navy officers who had adopted her from the Shanghai kennel. Then in June 1939 the *Gnat*, launched in 1915 and rapidly aging, was replaced by the

HMS *Grasshopper*, a larger, more efficient vessel. When some of the *Gnat*'s crew moved over, Judy went with them. When Britain formally entered the war on September 3, the HMS *Grasshopper* set sail for Singapore.

Judy on the deck of the HMS *Grasshopper*. *Imperial War Museum*

For a while duty in Singapore was pretty carefree, since the city-state was far from battle zones. The *Grasshopper*'s petty officer George White was assigned to look after Judy. A year later, on September 21, 1940, Commander Jack Hoffman became the *Grasshopper*'s new skipper. Hoffman would later—indirectly—save Judy's life.

The war went global fifteen months after that, following the Japanese attack on Pearl Harbor. And after the devastating assault on the American naval base on Oahu, Japanese forces went after Hong Kong and the Philippines. They also landed troops on Malaya and targeted Singapore for invasion.

ESCAPE FROM SINGAPORE

Under cover of darkness, the *Grasshopper* slipped out of Singapore on February 13, 1942, two days before the city fell to the Japanese. Along with her sister ship the HMS *Dragonfly*, the *Grasshopper*, stuffed to the brim with seventy-five crew and more than two hundred passengers (including women and children) joined three other smaller ships carrying civilian evacuees. All set out for Batavia, the capital of the Dutch East Indies.[8]

Judy made a point of welcoming every passenger. "She seemed to sense the gravity of the situation," according to one account, "and so extended the comforting muzzle of her moist nose where she could."[9] She especially took care of the children, showing them around the ship, playing, and even sleeping with them. She treated the kids as her own and sought to ease their fears.

Japanese airpower ruled the Pacific skies at the time. So instead of taking their usual route, escaping ships tried hiding out at the small islands of the Lingga Archipelago, south of Singapore.

Judy remained quiet over one fitful night and then, just past 9:00 in the morning, she sat up, visibly tense, ears pricked forward on full alert. She bolted for the *Grasshopper*'s bridge, barking frantically with each step. The fears she communicated to the commander and crew were borne out by a Japanese seaplane that appeared in the distance.

While it was a smaller plane, it still carried two bombs. It aimed one at the *Grasshopper*, but missed. The second, aimed at the *Dragonfly*, exploded near the latter's bow. The aircraft was driven off by gunfire, but it was obviously just a matter of time before the next wave of enemy planes appeared.

At last, around 11:30, the two ships spotted land. But as they approached it, Judy again began barking fiercely, and this time she wouldn't stop. No wonder: more than a hundred bombers, flying in five separate formations, bore down on the flotilla. The ships were clearly sitting ducks. "Battle stations!" Commander Hoffman cried.

When the bombs began falling, Judy ran below deck.

The three smaller boats were hit first. All three vanished. Next came the *Dragonfly*, and finally the *Grasshopper*. Dozens were killed in the raid, but luckily Hoffman was able to drive the ship towards the island of Posic, where it became stuck on a sandbar about a hundred yards from shore. The survivors made their way to land in lifeboats and floaters as the Japanese planes strafed both ships with machine-gun fire.

But Judy was nowhere to be found.

FINDING REFUGE

The surviving shipwrecked crew members set up camp near the jungle, where their casualties were treated and the dead were set aside to be buried. Scouting parties set out across the island in search of food, water, and other inhabitants. But when word came back that it was uninhabited, with little food and no fresh water, the situation was obviously dire.

And Judy was still missing.

Commander Hoffman ordered Petty Officer White back to the stricken *Grasshopper* to collect any useful materials he could find. White arrived to find the devastated ship not only taking on water and in danger of sinking but also still burning. Scrambling onto the stricken ship, White soon discovered a bounty of supplies—water, food packed in tins, medical supplies, clothing, bedding, pots and pans, cutlery, even an intact bottle of whisky. "Medicinal purposes only," he murmured to himself as he packed it safely away.[10] But most important, he found Judy! She had been pinned beneath a row of lockers toppled during the bombing. Had Hoffman not sent White back for supplies, the *Grasshopper* surely would have become her watery grave.

The excited petty officer freed Judy. "You silly bitch," he said, "Why didn't you bark?" He carried her up on deck, intending to check her injuries. Instead, she surprised the worried rescuer when she got up, shook herself off, "leaped to the right and left like a playful lamb, and sat down in front of him and licked his hand."[11] White didn't know whether to laugh or cry. But he did know one thing: when Judy licked his hand, her own sense of relief was "palpable."[12]

White, elated, crossed the deck to the bow and shouted back to the beach, "Hey, I found Judy! She's alive!"[13] The sound of cheers floated back to him over the waters.

JUDY SAVES THE DAY

Once back on shore with the supplies—and Judy—the hunt resumed for more fresh water. The crew enlisted Judy's help, but at first she didn't seem to understand what they were asking of her. As the tide receded, she sniffed the sand, ran back and forth to the water's edge and began splashing. At first she seemed just to be playing, or trying to cool off. Yet curiously, she always returned to one particular spot on the shore.

All at once, she began acting strangely—pawing at the ground, whining, barking, all the usual canine ploys for attention. It worked too, especially when one of the Royal Marines called to White, "What's up with your dog, Chief? Can she see something out there that we can't?"

White knelt beside Judy, sensing that she was agitated and offering comfort: "What's up then, old girl?"

But Judy whined again and began digging urgently. The surprised petty officer joined in—stopping when water began to bubble up from the bottom of the hole. White scooped a handful of the liquid and tasted, discovering a clear and fresh taste.

"Water!" he called out to the others. "Judy's found water!"[14]

The men scrambled to collect as much of the water as possible, using pots and pans recovered from the ship. After rationing, there still remained enough water to make rice and cocoa for dinner.

At that evening meal White stood, raised his cup of cocoa, and toasted: "To Judy!" Upon hearing her name, "Judy looked around, wagged her tail, then snuggled down between the two children, shut her eyes and went to sleep."[15]

THE JOURNEY BEGINS

As dinner was ending, a few survivors from the *Dragonfly* arrived on a small whaling ship. They explained that after the bombing they had wound up on an adjacent atoll. Now they were out doing reconnaissance, seeking other survivors. Judy recognized at least one of the men: leading Stoker Les Searle, whom Judy had met weeks earlier at an infirmary in Singapore.

Next, the *Dragonfly's* whaler sailed south; it would succeed in finding help on the larger island of Singkep. Five days after the bombing, the survivors were rescued and brought to Singkep.

Once there, word came that British and Australian naval vessels were waiting to transport people to freedom. But first the survivors had to reach the port city of Padang on Sumatra's western coast—via a hot, humid, arduous three-hundred-plus mile trek across tropical Sumatra.

(At that moment, half a world away in Hollywood, Warner Bros. producer Hal Wallis was about to shoot a wartime action-romance. The film's story involved desperate wartime refugees beating a path to an exotic city where there was hope for safe passage to Portugal—and eventually, "the freedom of the Americas."

The film and very real city shared a name. It was *Casablanca*, which later won the Academy Award as Best Picture of 1943.)

But that was a made-up story. In the real world of 1942, the flotilla survivors would attempt a different route to freedom. First they would board a vessel bound for Sumatra. Next they would sail up the Indragiri River, which bisected Sumatra, to Rengat, a village located about eighty miles inland. From there, vehicles would transport everyone to a railway station in Sawah-lunto, fifty-five miles from Padang. Finally, a train would take them the rest of the way. At least that was the plan.

Before she left, Judy had to say goodbye to friends Commander Hoffman and Chief Petty Officer White.[16] "She seemed to understand all that was going on and licked my hand before I turned away," White said.[17] Now her favorite companions would be Les Searle and his Royal Navy buddies.

THE BEST-LAID PLANS

On February 21, Judy and fifteen Navy men boarded a junk headed for Sumatra. It was fairly smooth sailing to Sumatra and then Rengat. But their plans went awry at Rengat. The promised vehicles weren't available, forcing the men to embark on a horrific 175-mile trek on foot, through some of the thickest jungle imaginable. The route was riddled with poisonous spiders, leeches, snakes, crocodiles, pythons, tigers, and the rare Sumatran tiger.

Judy led the march and, according to Searle, behaved as if the group was in her exclusive care: "She was tireless in the jungle, loping from front to back, sniffing madly, testing the soundness of the terrain, ears perked up for any crashing sounds rumbling out of the darkness."[18]

On the second day, while protecting her sailors, Judy was nearly killed by an attacking crocodile. When she made the mistake of trying to chase the slithering creature upstream, the enormous beast lunged at her. Caught off balance and twisting to escape the croc's clutches, Judy was clawed across the shoulder. Luckily, the resulting six-inch cut wasn't deep enough to be truly dangerous. She was patched up with some of the few medical supplies on hand.

At another point on the trek, according to Searle, Judy's barking saved him from being savagely attacked by a Sumatran tiger.

Three weeks later, on March 15, the men finally emerged from the jungle at Sawahlunto—and caught the overnight train for the final fifty-mile leg to Padang. The anticipation must have been huge. But on arrival the collective joy and hope dissolved into "dispondency and despair." They had missed the evacuation by more than a week, the last ship having sailed March 6.[19] The survivors discovered to their horror that Padang had just been captured by the Japanese. As Searle noted, "Judy seemed to sense the depression that hovered over her friends."[20] Judy and the sailors were taken into custody and officially declared prisoners of war on March 18, 1942.

PRISONERS IN PADANG

As the prisoners trudged through town to the Dutch Army barracks, Judy stayed close to Les Searle. Since she wasn't entitled to an official food ration, Judy had little choice but to forage for food. Searle pleaded with authorities, arguing that as a member of the Royal Navy Judy was, in fact, entitled to meals. But his pleas were dismissed out of hand. So Judy's diet necessarily became rats, snakes, birds, lizards—anything she could kill. The other prisoners feared Judy herself would end up shot and served up as dinner—either by the locals or by the Japanese invaders.

Many nights Judy sneaked out of a barracks window to search for food. One evening, she was busted while climbing back through the window, her jaws closed tight around a half-eaten chicken. Judy's mistake: tripping and landing atop her friend, Petty Officer "Punch" Puncheon. This scared the officer half to death, but adding insult to injury, as she face-planted Judy also accidentally dropped the chicken on him.

After that, the men tied Judy up at night. "Not as punishment," Puncheon insisted to the woebegone war dog, "but because we don't want you to be eaten."[21]

Months passed. Finally came word that the men were to be moved. On June 27, 1942, the POWs were transported to Belawan in northern Sumatra for a few days, then ultimately to Gloegoer, outside Medan.[22]

The men stashed Judy beneath rice sacks, then sneaked her onto one of the trucks that carried them to the next prison camp. They would remember Padang as a paradise compared to their next destination.

THE HORROR OF GLOEGOER

At Gloegoer, the guards were more hostile and the food in shorter supply. To her dismay, Judy watched helplessly while her friends grew weaker by the day. She too had lost weight and a lot of energy. The eager-to-serve canine had to rely more and more on her fierce will to survive.

After three weeks of "enforced captivity" as "punishment for fighting the Imperial Japanese Forces," the prisoners were assigned to forced labor groups.

It was easy to sense how much Judy disliked the Japanese guards. "Inside the camp itself she moved around quite freely and openly," Searle remembered, "giving the Japanese or Korean guards a wide berth. She always loped with her eyes on the guard and her lip curled upwards in a silent snarl, and her obvious hatred put her life in constant danger from a rifle bullet."[23]

One day in August, Judy's life changed forever with the arrival in camp of a new prisoner, twenty-two-year-old RAF Leading Aircraftman Frank Williams. For the first few days he studied Judy from afar and marveled at how the scraggly, emaciated dog foraged for food and survived the rigors of Gloegoer. The airman recognized her intelligence—and the fact that she didn't seem to belong to anyone.

"Something wobbled in [Frank's] soul," says author Robert Weintraub. "He was in a terrible situation and it was all he could do just to survive himself. He could die or be killed at any time.

"But the sight of this dog wasting away, without help from any of the human friends she clearly relied upon, was intolerable to him."[24]

Frank Williams later recalled, "I remember thinking, 'What on earth is a beautiful English pointer like this doing here with no one to care for her?' I realized that even though she was thin, she was a survivor."[25]

Twice a day the men received a small tin filled with "pap"— watery boiled rice. If they wanted to survive the camp, every morsel of food was crucial sustenance, no matter how disgusting. No one shared his food portions; the necessity for survival dictated otherwise.

But as Frank sat down one day to eat, he sensed someone staring at him. When he looked up, it was right into Judy's sad, empathic eyes. The ragged pup approached tentatively, never breaking eye contact with Frank. The leading aircraftman poured some of his precious rice into his hand and held it out to her. "'Come on, Judy,' he encouraged. 'This is yours.'"[26] She didn't move, but instead let out a faint whine. He knew this meant she needed reassurance his gesture was a friendly and kind one, not a cruel trick. In camp, Judy had already learned to be suspicious— to be wary of people until they proved themselves trustworthy.

Frank Williams reached over, gently patted her head, and scratched her ears. "Okay, okay. Make yourself at home," he told Judy while placing his food tin in front of her. [27] The imprisoned pointer relaxed and scarfed down the offerings from both Frank's hand and food tin. When Judy finished, she stretched out at his feet and stayed put.

Judy had finally found "her person." Life for both would never be the same.

LET THE BONDING BEGIN

This was, to borrow a classic movie phrase, the beginning of a beautiful friendship.[28] Frank taught Judy to obey hand signals and whispered speech. These skills proved vital when she was lying low or hiding from guards. As a thank you for his protection, Judy would return from her nighttime foraging with food for Frank.

Judy was an inspiration to the other POWs, providing hope and boosting morale. She was also quite protective of Frank and her other human friends. Among her typical acts of loyalty: Judy alerted the men whenever dangerous spiders and poisonous snakes were afoot.

She also protected her friends as best as she could from the Japanese guards. Her hatred of the guards only grew, and she barked and lunged at them when they came to beat the prisoners. Once during an inspection the guards were about to discover a large bag of stolen rice hidden in Searle's hut. "'Judy certainly sensed the danger in that room,' Searle [recalled], 'and she also knew what to do about it. She also knew, as we all did, that the

[Japanese] had a deep fear, almost horror, of skeletons, graves, almost any evidence of death."

Searle panicked as the guards approached his blanket where the rice was hidden. Cue Judy, who raced in, "like a mad beast, her ears back, eyes glowing redly" with a human skull clenched in her jaws![29] The gothic sight spooked the guards, who "began to scream crazily at the dog and to yell at each other in alarm.... their cries rose to ones of sheer panic."[30] They rushed out just moments before they would have uncovered the stash.

AN INGENIOUS PLAN

"The [Japanese] often threatened to shoot Judy," Frank Williams said, "but we always managed to beg her off, even at the cost of being beaten up."[31] Still Frank became increasingly worried the guards would follow through on the threat—then feed her to the prisoners. He was desperate to protect her.

And in a classic case of the worst possible timing, Frank realized Judy was pregnant. This was a shock because everyone assumed that all of the local dogs had long ago been shot and eaten. "There were bets," according to one account, "that she would give birth to a litter of tiger cubs or goats."[32]

But Frank Williams was a man with a plan. After Judy delivered, he would offer one of the puppies to the camp commandant, Lieutenant Colonel Hirateru Banno, as a gift for his girlfriend, who loved Judy. Whenever she spotted the canine POW, the girlfriend called, "Judy, come" in her limited English, and she was always trying to pet her. Judy played along, even allowing her ears to be nuzzled—so long as Banno wasn't around. Frank's puppy offer would come with a price: a hands-off-Judy policy.

When his troops were present, Colonel Banno appeared to hate Judy. He even drew his sword and seemed to threaten her, provoking growls and snarls from the four-legged prisoner. But it was all for show; the camp commandant was a secret dog lover.[33]

That would help keep Judy alive.

Judy finally had her litter—nine puppies, five of whom survived. They were named Kish, Rokok, Sheikje, Blackie, and Punch. Kish was the pick of the litter, but all proved themselves great morale boosters for the prisoners.

One night when the commandant was drinking alone Frank seized the moment. "'He was very drunk and seemed to forget that he was talking to one of the prisoners,' Frank remembered later. 'I had heard that alcohol put this normally very aggressive man in a good mood, and given enough to drink, he was likely to agree to anything.'"[34]

It was a situation worthy of *Hogan's Heroes*, the 1960s TV sitcom in which the sneaky title character, an American prisoner, repeatedly tricks the gullible commandant of a World War II POW camp.

Frank Williams brushed aside the risks, boldly took Kish under his arm, and dared to enter the commandant's quarters. Normally, this was an executable offense. But between the liquor and Kish's extreme cuteness, the tipsy colonel was caught up in the moment. Kish helped by waddling across Banno's desk before stopping to lick the commandant's outstretched hand.

Frank said Kish was a gift for Banno's lady friend. The commandant was actually moved by the gesture. Frank risked a death sentence by revealing his real reason for being there: he wanted the colonel to officially register Judy as a prisoner of war. This would protect Judy from the guards' wrath.

Before the colonel could answer, Frank deftly refilled his sake glass.

Banno was not opposed to the idea. But he had to refuse—how could he ever justify to superiors the sudden appearance of an additional number on the prisoner list? Frank anticipated the objection and suggested a solution: add the letter "A" to his own prisoner number: Hachi-ju-ichi, no. 81. That way Judy could claim official status without raising undue suspicion up the chain of command.

Banno played with little Kish, rolling him around in his hands while mulling over Frank's scheme. At last he reached for an official writing pad and began scribbling out the order. As he did Frank panicked—watching helplessly as Kish relieved himself on the colonel's desk! The puddle began spreading towards the oblivious commandant's elbow. Frank could only pray that Banno finished scrawling out the order before it was noticed.

Fate smiled on Frank Williams that day: Banno handed him the order, then simply dismissed him. Frank bowed, obsequiously thanked the commandant—and scrammed.

No one knows how Colonel Banno reacted when he finally noticed the desktop puddle. All Frank knew was that the next morning Judy's collar displayed a new metal tag etched with her official status, "81A-Medan." She was the first—and only—official animal POW.

MEET THE NEW BOSS

In June 1944, the camp at Gloegoer got a new commandant, Capt. Nishi.[35] Conditions worsened under the new regime. When he first spotted a dog in camp, Nishi was ready to unleash on Judy. Frank Williams intervened frantically, pulling Colonel Banno's signed order from the pocket of his tattered shorts. Because Banno outranked Nishi, the order stood.

The reprieve would be brief. Three days after Nishi's arrival, all prisoners were ordered shipped to Singapore. Nishi appeared at the barracks to personally inform Frank Williams that under no circumstances would Judy be allowed to go—she was to remain at Gloegoer.

Shaken and desperate, Frank decided to try smuggling Judy onto the prisoners' ship—though being caught in the attempt would mean certain death for both. He spent the night teaching Judy a new trick: with a snap of his fingers, Judy quickly climbed into (or out of) a sack he was holding. She also learned to keep silent and still until Frank released her.

By morning she had the trick down cold. Now all they could do was hope.

Frank left Judy tied to a post with a slipknot. "Now you stay right here, girl," he said louder than usual, in a show for the guards.[36]

Frank stuffed his sack with a blanket so that it appeared full. All prisoners' sacks were checked and rechecked. With the order to move out, seven hundred prisoners walked through the gates and boarded a train bound for the docks. When it was safe, Frank blew a faint whistle for Judy. When he didn't see her at first, Frank panicked, fearing he had tied the knot too tight. But just before he was to board the train, he finally caught sight of Judy hiding under a wagon.

Frank knelt down, pretending to tie his shoe as other prisoners formed a circle around him. He snapped his fingers and on cue Judy jumped into the sack. In one quick action, he slung the bag of dog over his shoulder, and they climbed aboard the train.

When they arrived at the docks, Frank freed Judy from the sack. Captors conducted another inspection of the men and their possessions while they waited to board the SS *Van Warwyck*, a Dutch ship that the Japanese had captured, renamed *Harukiku Maru*, and put into service.

With the inspection complete and the coast clear, Frank again whistled for Judy. The crafty canine adroitly wove and darted between prisoners. The men carefully made room for the scurrying Judy without giving her away. She jumped into the sack again, and Frank again hoisted her over his shoulder. Then he stood for nearly three hours just waiting to board the vessel.

Those hours in the hot sun took their toll on Frank, who became light-headed and began to shake. In yet another case of the worst possible timing, Captain Nishi appeared, seemingly out of nowhere. "Ino murrasini noka?" ("Dog not come?") he asked Frank quite snidely. Nishi had seen Judy tied to the post at camp and no doubt presumed that, per his orders, the dog had been left behind. He had also been there when Frank's bag was inspected.

The smug Nishi just wanted to rub it in. Frank mustered his most pained, crestfallen expression, in a performance made easier by the weight of a heavy dog digging into his bony shoulder. He looked down and shook his head sadly. Satisfied, Nishi grinned and moved on. When Frank's number was finally called, he boarded the ship without incident.

The plan had worked! Conditions aboard the ship were absolutely deplorable, but the POWs were relieved to be together.

Just a few hours later, that relief would give way to new alarms.

"SWIM FOR IT!"

When the first of two British torpedoes from the submarine HMS *Truculent* hit the ship, Les Searle had just been called to the deck to help empty the Japanese latrines into the sea. He witnessed the horrifying sight of white tracks produced by the speeding torpedoes as they beat an insidious path directly for the *Van Warwyck*. There was no way the British sub's commander, Lieutenant Robert L. Alexander, could know that the target actually carried British and Allied POWs.

Searle barely had time to call out a warning. When the shells hit, Frank Williams was momentarily stunned, then felt Judy's nose on his leg. As the panicked prisoners fought to use the only escape hatch, Frank had a quick decision to make. "In a glimpse of an eye, I could see that it was impossible to carry the animal through the mess," he later said.[37]

They were trapped. He managed to open the closest porthole and lift Judy up. "Out you go, old girl," he told his four-legged pal. "Swim for it."[38] He pushed her through the hole, and Judy fell fifteen feet into the sea.

The torpedoes ripped apart the *Van Warwyck*. Miraculously, Frank and the others made it out of the twisted hull and into the sea. But Frank couldn't spot Judy anywhere.

For two hours he treaded water, desperately scanning for Judy while trying to stay alive. "She remained without a trace," Frank recalled. "A Dutchman that held on to a rubber bale told me he had seen Judy swimming about. At that moment I knew she still had life in her."[39]

The survivors were finally rescued by a Japanese tanker. Once onboard, Frank heard more eyewitness accounts of Judy swimming amongst the wreckage. Yet she was still missing. With the apparent loss of his dearest friend, Frank felt he'd hit his lowest point ever.

Two days later, they reached the River Valley prison in Singapore. It was Frank Williams's third prison camp in two-and-a-half years. By then, the grieving Frank "was headed for the end hut," as friend Jock Devani put it.[40]

In other words, Frank Williams was rapidly losing the will to go on.

NEVER SAY DIE

Frank felt numb—in a fugue state of despair, really—as he climbed down from the truck that brought him and other prisoners to the River Valley camp. The men were scuffling along, being herded toward some ramshackle huts, when Frank was shoved suddenly and forcefully from behind. He face-planted in the dirt, momentarily assuming that another prisoner had accidentally collided with him.

But then he heard it. No, he thought. Can't be. But that low, continuous whine was unmistakable. JUDY! "I couldn't believe my eyes," Frank said later. "As I entered the camp, a scraggy dog hit me square between the shoulders and knocked me over. I'd never been so glad to see the old girl. And I think she felt the same."[41]

Judy was covered in bunker oil, and her eyes were tired and red. She didn't care one bit. Judy flung herself at Frank "in a frenzy of wild joy."[42] Frank rolled over on his back and embraced her tightly. It was a miracle. Frank's heart burst in electric ecstasy. But he also ached for Judy as his hands traced her bony ribs and haunches and felt her matted fur encrusted with oil and soot.

"He sensed too how desperate she'd been to find him," author Damien Lewis wrote.[43] At that moment, none of the hardships mattered.

Frank staggered to his feet and scooped Judy up in his arms. "Come on, old girl, and stop acting so daft," he said through tears in his eyes at odds with his usual English reserve.[44]

They were together; that's all that mattered. "[Frank's] shoulders seemed to re-set," Searle said.[45] Hope was bountiful, even in that horrific place—Frank Williams had regained his reason to live. Man and his best friend were determined never to be separated again.

DOGGED DETERMINATION

As they settled in, Searle and others filled Frank in on Judy's heroism in the water. For hours, they reported, she had swum about, helping save many men from drowning by letting them clutch her back as she swam them to safety. "Each time she approached one of the vessels, hands reached out to pull her from the water," according to author Robert Weintraub. "Each time she pulled away from them, to stay in the ocean and continue her rescue efforts."[46] If Judy was too exhausted to ferry someone to safety, she brought debris over to keep them afloat. Gerard McLeod was among those she saved: "I shall always remember her with her forepaws over a spar, to which three of us clung for four hours until we were picked up."[47]

Only when the last man was safe did Judy allow herself to be rescued. "'She was more dead than alive,' recalled one of the men who witnessed her come aboard. 'She had totally given herself to the drowning men.'"[48]

But they couldn't celebrate Judy's latest act of heroism. The prisoners still needed to hide her, then devise a new scheme to smuggle her off the boat. This time, there was no sack in which she could hide. Judy would be out in the open, in full view of the guards.

As the men were herded off the boat, Judy scooted alongside. She somehow managed to stay unseen—until Searle lifted her into the waiting truck. A shriek of abject rage froze Searle in his tracks. Captain Nishi was on the scene! And he had spotted Judy.

The cruel commandant charged over, and two guards stepped forward, guns drawn, cocked and pointed at Judy. All the heroically scraggy war dog could do was muster a weak snarl, revealing her stained, yellow teeth. But there was little mistaking the meaning in Judy's red-rimmed eyes, which burned with hatred for the camp overseer. When the guards moved to carry out their grisly orders, a louder more commanding voice pierced the air. "Nishi!"[49] Everyone stopped and turned.

It was none other than Colonel Banno! Now stationed in Singapore, he had come to the docks to check on the survivors he had lorded over at Gloegoer and to oversee their transfer to River Valley. Upon hearing Nishi's tirade about prisoner 81A-Medan, Banno tore into the man who had succeeded him at Gloegoer. He demanded the dog not be harmed—reminding Nishi that Judy was an official prisoner of war whose protection he had personally ordered. Why, thundered Banno, was Nishi disobeying those orders?

The sadistic commandant had little choice but to back down.

Searle seized the moment. He hurled Judy into the back of the truck, climbed in behind her, and banged on the front cab. The truck jerked away, bound for the next prison camp, as Banno continued tearing into Nishi.

Talk about a close call.

When Searle settled into his hut at River Valley, Judy refused to stay. Instead she went hunting for Frank Williams, searching every square inch of the camp. Only when the pedigreed pointer was certain Frank wasn't there did she finally adjust to the new surroundings. Sort of. Judy still insisted on standing watch at the front gate, hidden from obvious view, head resting on her forepaws, peering through sad, burning eyes to scan every truck rolling through the gate. For two days she kept up the vigil, never deterred, never ceding hope. Judy just knew Frank would show up.

DEATH RAILWAY

River Valley was nobody's last stop. On July 27, 1944, after just four weeks, the POWs—including Judy—were shipped off to Pakan Baroe, the capital settlement of Central Sumatra. The men were told that they were being sent on a "special mission" to work on a fruit plantation. It was a terrible lie.

At Pakan Baroe, the worst was yet to come for Frank, Judy, and the others. Their new home was a slave labor camp. For a year the POWs cut through dense Sumatran jungle while laying down hundreds of miles of "The Death Railway." The work was brutal, the heat searing, and disease ran rampant. Food was a daily handful of grotesque, maggoty tapioca. Ironically, the maggots provided much-needed protein. Frank shared the noxious tapioca with Judy. But she supplemented their diet by scrounging, bringing snakes, rats, lizards—and fruit left by mourners on local graves—for Frank and their friends.[50]

"Every day I thanked God for Judy," Frank said. "She saved my life in so many ways. The greatest way of all was giving me a reason to live. All I had to do was look at her, and into those weary, bloodshot eyes, and I would ask myself, 'What would happen to her if I died?' I had to keep going. Even if it meant waiting for a miracle."[51]

Frank and the other men worked up to sixteen hours a day. The hard labor conditions were so bad that prisoners literally died building the tracks. The sadistic guards made things worse by beating the men when progress slowed. Judy did her best to divert the guards' attention. She grew more aggressive towards their Japanese captors, sometimes snarling, barking, and charging them. She was also known to create diversions—running into the jungle barking, as if some animal were in there, one the guards could kill and eat.

The Japanese hated Judy, which put her life in frequent and extreme danger.

And the dog's personality began to change—life had taken its toll on her spirit. "Judy was no longer a dog that anyone in his right mind would recommend as a suitable household pet," recalled Tom Scott, a POW who slept across from Frank and Judy. "Thin, half-starved, always on the prowl, her eyes only softened when Frank touched her or spoke to her, or when she looked up at him."[52]

Frank Williams himself described her as "a skinny animal that kept herself alive through cunning and instinct."[53]

But Frank took care of Judy as best he could, and they shared an enviable rapport and the ability to communicate non-verbally. As he put it, "I only needed to click with a thumb and middle finger or whistle softly....

"It was our language of understanding which she understood perfectly and without hesitation obeyed. The simple instruction 'go away' was enough for Judy to disappear....

"She calmly remained waiting, sometimes even for hours on end, until she received my signal to reappear. This didn't save her life once—it saved her many times from certain death."[54]

Their bond was so close, Tom Scott observed, that if anything happened to Frank, Judy would most certainly die of a broken heart: "Judy was scraggy and bony. Frank was down to about half his weight—just as we all were. They were both, however, mentally strong and alert. They were both steel-tough and courageous, and between them was a complete understanding and an unbreakable bond of affection."[55] Every day, Frank and Judy clung to a common purpose: just keep the other alive. But bare survival became increasingly difficult.

Still, when there seemed no reason to keep up the effort, Judy's presence, spirit, and uncanny survival instincts inspired everyone in camp. "Through everything we endured in the prison camps," Gerard McLeod recalled, "Judy followed us, a constant example of what even a dog can endure far from the native heath of her ancestors. She became a vital inspiration to us to carry on, and in the darkest days, one often heard the expression, 'While Judy can take it, so can I.'

"I do not exaggerate when I say that this dog, with her example of her courage to live, saved many of us who would surely have died."[56]

PRAYERS ANSWERED

One morning in late August 1945, Judy began barking in the middle of camp and wouldn't stop.[57] This was not the prisoners' usual wake-up call. The sun was high in the sky. Something was wrong. Something different was happening.

Frank hurried out of his hut and tried to quiet her down as the men staggered out to watch the excited Judy follow two strangers wearing red berets across the grounds. They were from the Royal Air Force Parachute Regiment and their presence was something to celebrate.

The men's prayers for a miracle had finally been answered: the war was over.

The liberators of the Pakan Baroe described it as the worst POW camp they had ever seen. "It was a sight almost too horrible to describe," reported G. E .W. Harriott of the Sydney *Morning Herald*.[58]

Lady Edwina Mountbatten, Superintendent-in-Chief of the Nursing Corps Divisions (and wife of England's legendary Lord Mountbatten) visited on September 15. In a written account of her visit she noted that, "there is no doubt that had the war gone on a few more weeks, there would have been no prisoners of war in these areas left alive at all."[59]

Frank Williams and Judy were taken to a POW hospital compound, where they remained for a month while Frank recovered from a recurring case of malaria.

ONE FINAL RUSE

At last, Frank's embarkation papers arrived. He'd be heading home aboard the troopship HMS *Antenor*. Excitedly poring over his orders, Frank's heart sank momentarily when he read, "The following regulations will be strictly enforced. *No* dogs, birds or pets of any kind to be taken on board."[60]

He looked down at Judy and smiled. "No dogs allowed, old girl. Only ex-prisoners of war, and that, of course, means you."[61] Frank knew he'd have to plan one final freedom caper for his four-legged friend.

Frank again enlisted the help of Les Searle and a few others. This time Judy hid on the jetty near the gangplank and waited for a signal while Frank took up a strategic position on deck. As Frank waited, Searle and the others boarded, deliberately trying to distract the guards' attention away from the gangplank. When the coast was clear, Frank's whistle cued the liver-and-white-colored phantom, who scooted up the plank and ducked out of sight on board.

Frank and Judy were finally heading home.

A DIFFERENT KIND OF PRISON

It took six weeks for the *Antenor* to reach Liverpool, providing Frank and the others additional time to recover both physically and mentally. Judy wisely made friends with the ship's cook, who took her under his wing and into his galley for the long voyage home. She began to fatten up.

Three days before landing: a dangerous hitch. The captain finally learned of Judy's existence on the boat and was irate. But once Frank explained the situation, he softened. Still, upon landing in England, certain regulations still had to be obeyed—and this time neither Frank Williams nor Judy could finagle a way around them.

Docking at Liverpool on October 29, 1945, was bittersweet for Frank and Judy. Frank convinced authorities to let Judy come ashore, but he couldn't get them to waive the mandatory six-month animal quarantine. Worse, Judy had to face the sentence alone. She walked down the gangplank, only to be delivered to an official from the Ministry of Agriculture. Bewildered and upset, Judy was summarily hauled off to Hackbridge Quarantine Kennels, nine miles southeast of London. It was the first time that she and Frank had been separated since the sinking of the *Van Warwyck*.

Yet this "prison" turned out to be quite different from the others. Hackbridge gave Judy the royal treatment, including, on her arrival, a full medical exam and complete grooming. The staff pampered the plucky pup, especially after Frank Williams briefed them on her remarkable feats.

Despite her heroic service to the Crown, however, Judy's quarantine was no free ride. Frank was charged the equivalent of fifty U.S. dollars for her boarding—about six hundred dollars in today's currency values.

To help, the nonprofit Tailwaggers Club ran a notice in its December 1945 newsletter about a fundraising drive "to defray the cost of Judy's stay in quarantine."

"Should there be any surplus, it will be paid to Judy's owner as a help toward her future maintenance."[62] The next issue reported that donations of eighteen pounds, eighteen shillings and eight pence—more than $1,000 today—had come in from sixty-one donors. Contributions continued arriving over the next few months.

Despite the staff's loving, appreciative treatment, Judy fretted at the loss of the freedom she had been accustomed to since puppyhood. Even though Frank visited regularly, as did many of Judy's POW and Navy friends, these were six very long months for them both.

"GUNBOAT JUDY" CELEBRATED AS HEROINE

During her confinement, word spread of Judy's exploits. By the time of her own D-(for Dog) Liberation Day, Judy was already a national sensation. Her big reunion with Frank on April 29, 1946, was a camera-ready media event. In his RAF uniform, Frank Williams cut a dashing figure that day, and Judy was impeccably groomed. Both anxiously awaited her release after the enforced vacation that, in one respect, actually turned out well for Judy. Her half-year of resting, eating, pampering, and playing with other dogs had proven restorative.

Frank lovingly grooms Judy. 1946. Fred Morley/Fox Photos/Hulton Archive/
Getty Images

Try to imagine the joy and affection when Judy was freed and the two reunited for good. Frank's own description was elegantly simple: "She was all legs and tongue."[63]

Also that day, Arthur Croxton Smith, chairman of the British Kennel Club, presented Judy with the organization's "For Valor" medal. He then handed Frank Williams a check from the Tailwaggers Club in the amount of twenty-two pounds, one shilling, and four pence—ninety 1946 U.S. dollars and more than $1,100 today. The check represented the bountiful surplus of the Tailwaggers' fundraising campaign. The next day's headline in the *Daily Mail* trumpeted: "Gunboat Judy Saves Lives—Wins Medal and Life Pension."

Two days later, Judy and Frank Williams made even bigger headlines.

HEAVY MEDAL

On May 2, 1946, a crowd gathered in West London's Cadogan Square to witness Judy receive her prestigious Dickin Medal from the PDSA. No less than Maria Dickin herself, then seventy-six, looked on as the impressive medallion was pinned to Judy's collar by Major Viscount Tarbat, chairman of the Returned British POW Association. The medal read:

> *For magnificent courage and endurance in Japanese prison camps, which helped to maintain morale among her fellow prisoners and also for saving many lives through her intelligence and watchfulness.*

Judy's medal presentation. Major Viscount Tarbat reads Judy's citation. *PDSA Archives*

Tarbat wasn't finished. He then presented Frank Williams with the White Cross of Saint Giles medal and an accompanying certificate that acknowledged Frank's amazing devotion to Judy. The Giles is the highest PDSA award presented to humans showing love and devotion to animals.

Flowery inscriptions aside, one newspaper account described Judy's valor in starker terms: "'A dog's life' has meant to Judy being bombed, shelled, torpedoed, shipwrecked, smuggled, starved, sentenced to death, and cast ashore on a desert island."[64]

But at long last, those days were behind her.

The gala ceremony wasn't over. Judy then was declared an official member of the Returned British POW Association in London—the only dog ever so honored. She also was named an official mascot of the Royal Air Force, the prize for which was her own flying jacket, embroidered with the RAF crest.

Judy and her Dickin. May 2, 1946. *PDSA Archives*

Five weeks later, on June 8, Judy was part of a massive Victory Day celebration that featured an appearance by King George. Frank and Judy were also invited to participate in the BBC program *In Town Tonight*, alongside servicemen from every theater of the war. Host Roy Rich prompted Judy to bark loudly for the radio audience. "This happy barking echoed in a lot of houses all over the world," Frank said. "Even in Singapore, people could hear this dog 'talking.'"[65] Later that day, Judy repeated the performance for BBC television's *Picture Page*.

Chinese astrology declared 1946 the Year of the Dog, something Britons no doubt regarded as entirely appropriate.

LIFE IN LIBERTY

Over the next year, Frank and Judy visited grieving relatives of POWs who never made it out of the Sumatran jungles. "Judy always seemed to cushion the news we carried," Frank said later. "Her presence was a comfort."[66]

Judy especially loved visiting children's hospitals. She and Frank Williams continually rode in parades and pitched in at fundraisers for the PDSA, other animal rights groups, and even the London Federation of Boys' Clubs. (Some donations went to postwar recovery bonds.) Judy and Frank also turned up at dog shows around the country, sometimes joined by Rob, Irma, Jet, Rifleman Kahn, and other Dickin medalists.

Chelsea Show 1946: Judy with her pals Irma and Rob. September 7, 1946.
PDSA Archives

In her extensive postwar travels, Judy rubbed noses with and charmed many stage and film notables. Upon meeting the Dickin Award recipient, future Academy Award winner David Niven reportedly called her "the loveliest bitch he had ever clapped eyes on."[67] He meant it in a nice way.

The Tailwaggers Club wasn't done, either. The animal charity presented Frank with a large check, its amount undisclosed, to ensure Judy would never want for anything again. She never did.

NEW ADVENTURES IN AFRICA

After gaining permission in 1948 to fly once again, Frank and Judy left for Africa. Frank Williams went to work there on the UK government-funded Groundnut Scheme, an ultimately failed plan to offset food shortages by planting peanuts in Tanganyika (now Tanzania).

Judy says good-bye to an unidentified woman before leaving for Africa. May 10, 1948. *PDSA Archives*

For two years they worked the land and shared many adventures. Judy loved being out in nature, where she could explore and just soak up the freedom. In 1949, she bore her last litter, of seven pups, in Africa. Life was good.

But on January 26, 1950, Judy went missing out in the African bush. The panicked Frank searched frantically for ten days, even offering a reward of 500 shillings to anyone who found her.[68]

At last, Judy was spotted in a small village a few hours away. Frank jumped in a jeep and rushed to her side. He found her suffering from malnutrition and dehydration. The excitement of seeing Frank brought Judy to her feet, but just as quickly she collapsed in a whine. There was no way of telling how she had wound up there.

Once Judy was home again, Frank spent hours bathing his friend and removing the cattle ticks from her coat. He fed her chicken and milk for the protein she badly needed. After dinner and finally feeling safe, Judy fell into a deep sleep lasting twelve hours. Within a few days she seemed to be just fine. Anyway, that's what Frank believed.

But on February 16, Judy woke in the middle of the night and cried until morning. The pain was so bad that she couldn't walk. Frank carried her to the Nachingwea Veterinary Hospital, where she was seen by an English vet, Dr. Jenkins.

The doctor traced Judy's pain to a mammary tumor, which he surgically removed. But a few hours later tetanus set in, bringing more pain. There was little Dr. Jenkins could do to relieve the dog's suffering.

He went to Frank in the waiting room with a simple but profoundly painful recommendation: "Let me end it, Frank."

Tears rolled down his cheeks as Frank nodded and turned away.

Following Dr. Jenkins inside, Frank held his beloved dog in a final demonstration of love and comfort as the doctor put Judy to sleep.

PAYING RESPECTS

Judy of Sussex crossed the Rainbow Bridge on February 17, 1950. She was fourteen years old, nearly to the day. Clad in her RAF jacket, Judy was placed in a simple wooden coffin and laid to rest not far from the home she and Frank had shared in Nachingwea. Pinned to her jacket were several of her wartime medals, including the Pacific Star campaign medal, the 1939–45 Star, and the Defense Medal—the same honors awarded the men with whom she served, many of whose lives she had saved.

Frank covered the grave with stones to keep disruptive hyenas away. He spent the next few months building a dramatic marble marker, a "worthy monument for an exceptionally brave dog who was an example of friendship, brave and courageous in all, even the most difficult, circumstances and who meant so much for so many when they lost courage."[69]

The bronze plaque recounted Judy's background and the campaigns, disasters, and hardships she had survived:

> *In memory of Judy D.M. Canine V.C.*
> *Breed English Pointer*
> *Born Shanghai February 1936 died February 1950.*
> *Wounded 14 February 1942*
> *Bombed and sunk HMS Grasshopper*
> *Lingga Archipelago 14 February 1942.*
> *Torpedoed SS Van Warwyck*
> *Malacca Straits 26 June 1943.*
> *Japanese Prisoner of War March 1942–August 1945.*
> *China Ceylon Java England Egypt Burma*
> *Singapore Malaya Sumatra E Africa.*
> *They Also Served.*

But to truly capture Judy's spirit, Frank felt the monument needed something more. So he composed an additional tribute: "A remarkable canine. . .a gallant old girl who, with a wagging tail, gave more in companionship than she ever received. . .and was in her short lifetime an inspiration of courage, hope and a will to live, to many who would have given up in their time of trial had it not been for her example and fortitude."[70]

There has never been—nor ever will be again—another dog like *Shudi*.

Frank Williams lived to age eighty-four. He never owned another dog.

Judy and Frank. May 10, 1948. © *TopFoto/The Image Works*

WAR BIRDS

"Pigeons…can win battles. The Blitzkrieg succeeds only when it cuts communications and spreads uncertainty and confusion. It will fail when it meets a defense that can maintain contact, know where its own forces are, where the enemy is and what movements are under way. That's where the pigeons come in. The enemy can jam radio, cut phone lines, capture couriers. But if you have the right birds, properly trained, 95 per cent of your pigeon messages will get through."[1]

—MAJOR JOHN K. SHAWVAN, U.S. Army Pigeon Service

9

Winged Warriors

*"Warfare becomes total indeed when even
the birds are called to the colors."*[1]

—*NEW YORK TIMES,* January 13, 1941

On January 5, 1941, the U.S. Army mandated that all domestic homing pigeon breeders (or "fanciers") begin registering their lofts with Army headquarters in Washington D.C., "to facilitate the conscription of the birds in a national emergency."[2] Nearly a year before Pearl Harbor, America was already preparing for war.

At the time, there were an estimated forty thousand pigeon lofts in America. A week after the announcement, the *New York Times* offered insight as to why registration was so important: "Pigeons, one of the oldest auxiliaries of fighting armies and beleaguered cities, provide a certain means of communication when all else fails. Not so swift as a radio beam, they nevertheless can fly a mile a minute. They carry their own power plant and travel in darkness or storm straight to their destination. When planes have been driven from the sky, when telephone lines are down, when radio stations are bombed out, the meek pigeon comes into his own."[3]

It should be no surprise that the humble homing pigeon has long played a significant role in assisting humans to wage war. After all, the pigeon has a long and intriguing history of helping humanity in general, one that harkens back to antiquity. Indeed, the Bible claims that Noah used a pigeon as a messenger after the Flood.

Verifying a biblical account is never easy. But what is well established is that the domestic pigeon has been selectively bred (from the rock pigeon) to take advantage of an amazing, inborn gift: the bird can navigate its way home over very long distances.

Homing pigeons have lent us a wing in myriad ways. In 2004, pigeon exploits were chronicled at a Parisian postal museum exhibit. Among the fun facts:

- The Greeks used pigeons to announce victories[4]
- At Roman chariot races, the birds were used to inform owners of how their entries had finished
- Genghis Khan set up pigeon relay posts in Asia and Eastern Europe
- The Rothschilds made a financial killing after a homing pigeon brought word of Napoleon's defeat at Waterloo
- Two Napoleons later, during the Franco-Prussian War, pigeons flew for the French during the Siege of Paris. Ultimately the birds couldn't save Napoleon III. But even in defeat, the French remained so grateful that they commissioned a bronze monument to honor the birds. The sculpture was created by Frédéric-Auguste Bartholdi, designer of the Statue of Liberty
- In World War I, both the French and Germans established numerous pigeon lofts. By war's end,

France had assembled an impressive air force of thirty thousand pigeons. These avian messengers were so valued that anyone caught interfering with them faced a death sentence[5]

WHAT MAKES A HOMER FLY HOME?

The jury is still out as to just how homing pigeons find their way home over hundreds of miles.[6] Some believe the sun guides them, although their ability to navigate at night and through bad weather (especially fog)—both of which they hate—makes this theory questionable. (While pigeons never lose their initial fear of flying in the dark, they can be trained to overcome it.)[7]

Others believe the Earth's magnetic pull is involved.

A third school of thought holds that pigeons use identifiable landmarks to navigate. But how is that possible if a pigeon is returning home over the English Channel from a drop point behind enemy lines that it has never seen before?

Some chalk up homing skills to the birds' sheer intelligence. Master Sergeant Clifford Poutré, who was among the U.S. military's foremost pigeon experts, addressed that issue: "We breed for intelligence first of all," Poutré said. "Intelligence and stamina. Speed is not important. They're all fast on the wing....

"What we want is a bird that will get back, one that won't get flustered, one that is intelligent enough to be self-reliant.

"Now and then we get dumbbells, of course."[8]

The homer is determined, bordering on obsessive, in its quest to get home. It also has a great sense of self-preservation, sometimes flying hundreds of miles out of the way just to avoid a storm.[9]

Pigeon physiology is unique. While a homing pigeon's head is small, its brain is a quarter size larger than that of other pigeons. Its small ears are situated below and behind its eyes and covered with feathers, so they can't be seen unless you literally lift up the feathers. The homer has a third eyelid that works like a windshield wiper, protecting the eyes from wind, dust, rain and other elements. "When looking at a distant object, the pigeon is unable to focus both eyes to the front" wrote Wendell Levi, author of the influential book *The Pigeon.* "The bird will cock the head to one side or the other for better vision."[10]

HOME SWEET HOME

Once released, three main factors determine a pigeon's willingness and ability to fly home. First is its "will to home," followed by the ability to find the way. Finally, it needs the physical strength to complete the trip.[11] Early training is key to optimally developing these factors, and of course flying conditions will tremendously affect the speed home.

Of these factors, the strongest is the "will to home," to navigate toward familiar surroundings. "It is the Homer's love of home which brings it coursing back over hill and stream at breakneck pace," Levi wrote. "A bird that is afraid of its home or of the treatment in it will never make a good homer."[12] Beyond its native instincts, a pigeon's incentives include a nice clean loft, a good nesting spot for each bird, and a dependable food supply.

The steely will to home is highlighted in stories of birds injured on their way home—but found, weeks later, actually *walking* home to their lofts!

Now that's determination!

Pigeons are social creatures. They love being with others and are generally unhappy if left alone. They definitely take comfort in the presence of a *human* companion.

Food and a human companion. What more comfort does a bird need? May 27, 1942/September 24, 1942. *U.S. Army Signal Corps/National Archives*

But most important, pigeons are surprisingly romantic. Foremost in the bird's mind, Levi wrote, is its "love of mate, of young, of eggs, and racing breeders have utilized this affection in obtaining quick returns."[13]

So has the military. Sometimes in battle, handlers have employed a little trick to motivate male homing pigeons to fly home quickly. Before a male is plucked from his loft and tucked into a parachuting basket, another male is placed in his loft. The newcomer's presence inflames the first bird's naturally jealous heart; he fears the newly introduced bird will put the moves, so to speak, on his female companion. The jealousy is so intense that as soon as he is released, the first bird will race home like the wind, presumably to the waiting wings of his beloved.

Hunger is also a good motivator, but sexual jealousy is hands down the bigger influence.

When a pigeon mates, it does so for life. "As in any well-run household," Marion Cothren wrote in her classic book, *Pigeon Heroes*, "both the hen and cock have their own jobs to attend to and they never shirk them. When nesting time comes along...both father and mother take turns sitting on [the eggs] for eighteen days, the hen at night and the cock by day."[14] They are a true team.

GOING THE DISTANCE

Long-distance homing racers were especially important to the military during World War II because of the extended distances the birds had to fly, over both land and sea, to return to their home lofts in England. The ability to find their way over long distances has more to do with breeding than training. It's an innate ability. But as with humans, strength and physical condition "are results of daily care and intelligent training," Levi wrote. It takes a lot of work to train these pigeons, and instruction begins as young as four weeks of age, when they are first beginning to fly.

The mobile loft. April 8, 1942. *National Archives*

At that tender age the young "squeaker" is placed in a mobile loft, which then is moved daily for the next two or three weeks, allowing the bird to make short daytime flights to get its bearings. Most important, it is taught to "trap," or enter the loft immediately upon returning, rather than simply landing on the roof.

Food is a powerful incentive, so as soon as a bird returns to his loft, it is fed. The young homer soon associates food with its residence, an important lesson during early training. Curiously, the health of a pigeon depends more upon drinking water than any other factor. The homer doesn't drink water like other birds. Instead, it dips its bill in the water and takes a long, deep draft, like a horse.[15]

Feeding time. September 3, 1942. *National Archives*

But pigeons need water for more than hydration. They love to bathe, perhaps more than any other fowl except ducks.[16]

At four months, the young squeaker can be trusted to fly a mile's distance home. That increases to five, ten, twenty-five miles, then still farther. "At one year a pigeon can fly about eighty miles at a stretch," Cothren wrote, "at two years he is good for two hundred and fifty and the third year he can make a non-stop flight of five hundred miles—but only exceptional birds are in the five hundred mile class."[17]

Considering how fragile the pigeon actually is, it's remarkable how much it sacrifices and how it survives long-distance deliveries despite being battered, beaten, and even shot. If a wing feather gets broken, the flight home is slowed up. If a tail feather goes missing, the poor bird is thrown completely off course. A homer's breastbone has deep muscles that help provide strength in flight. If those muscles are injured, the poor creature really struggles and flies in demonstrable pain. When a bird is wounded, you can really sense its heart, soul, and guts.

Case in point: Cher Ami, America's most heroic bird of the Great War.

WORLD WAR I-DER

The U.S. Army Signal Corps, responsible for, among other things, coordinating all message and communication systems for air, land, and sea forces, established its pigeon service in 1917 at the behest of General John J. Pershing, commander of the American Expeditionary Forces in World War I. In France alone, more than six hundred pigeons were used, most of them donated by British pigeon breeders.

America's most famous flier at the time was a registered blue checker hen with the romantic moniker Cher Ami ("Dear Friend").[18] Although she boasted a French name, Cher was actually British, registered with the National Union of Racing Pigeons (NURP No. 615) and trained by American expert pigeoneers.

Cher Ami was attached to the U.S. 77th Infantry Division, which fought in the Meuse-Argonne Offensive, part of the final

Allied offensive of the war, in early October 1918.[19] The operation, with 1.2 million American soldiers, was the largest Allied offensive of World War I. In fact, it was the largest offensive in U.S. military history, and it is second only to the Battle of Normandy (D-Day) as the deadliest foreign battle in American history, with 26,277 American lives lost. (The battle took an equal number of German lives and an unknown number of French ones.)

Before the Meuse-Argonne, Cher Ami had flown twelve missions from the front lines at Verdun to her loft at Rampont. The flights averaged eighteen miles in twenty-four minutes. Each involved transmission of an important message—and Cher Ami managed to escape unscathed on every flight. The final one would be different.

On October 4, 1918, Cher Ami would take to the air carrying her most important message. She nearly died trying to deliver it. She was serving that day with the First Battalion of the 308th Infantry Regiment. The unit, also known as the "Lost Battalion," included 554 men, mostly New Yorkers, under the command of Major Charles Whittlesay, a lawyer from—where else?—New York.

The battalion had broken through enemy lines only to be pinned down by German forces near Grandpre in the Ardennes. Human error put the men in dire danger when inaccurate coordinates of the battalion's position were given to Command. The result: the unit found itself shelled by friendly fire from its own artillery.

With communication lines out, pigeons were released. The first two were quickly shot dead. Only one remained: Cher Ami. The men attached a message to her leg:

FROM 1st BN 308th INFANTRY

WE ARE ALONG THE ROAD PARALELL 276.4.
OUR AR[T]ILLERY IS DROPPING A BARRAGE
DIRECTLY ON US. FOR HEAVENS SAKE STOP
IT.
WHITTLESAY
MAJ 308th[20]

As soon as she was released, Cher Ami, too, was almost immediately shot down by the Germans. The men were crushed to see their last hope plummet to the earth. Yet, amazingly, she was able to pick herself up, dust herself off, and start all over again (as Rogers and Astaire might have sung). Cher Ami flew twenty-five miles in as many minutes, returning safely to Allied headquarters. On arrival she was found to have been shot in the breast. The trajectory of the bullet had severely injured one eye. Her right leg, which carried the capsule bearing the critical message, had also been hit; it was hanging by a tendon.

Thanks to Cher Ami's sacrifice, the message was received, the shelling stopped, and the men eventually fought their way to safety.

Of 554 members of the "Lost Battalion," 194 walked away relatively unharmed. The rest were either killed, wounded, missing, or taken prisoner. If not for the unbelievable heart, determination, and sheer guts of one small bird, casualties certainly would have been far higher.[21]

Cher Ami was blinded in one eye and lost her right leg. When she was well enough to travel, the brave pigeon sailed to America on the transport *Ohioan* on April 16, 1919. General Pershing himself paid his respects by seeing her off at the docks. Heralded a heroine on arrival in the U.S., Cher Ami was presented the Croix de Guerre with Palm, France's prestigious medal for heroism and bravery in combat.

Cher Ami survived the war, but not by much. Less than two months after arriving in the U.S., the British-born bird succumbed to her wounds at Fort Monmouth, New Jersey. She was stuffed, mounted, and placed on display at the Smithsonian's National Museum of American History in Washington D.C. She remains there today, a reminder to visitors that valor and dedication are traits not strictly limited to human beings.

SPIES IN THE SKIES

Pigeons have also proven to be effective aerial spies. As early as 1907, German pigeon fancier Julius Neubronner fashioned a small automatic camera that he strapped to a bird's belly.

Julius Neubronner and his pigeon camera. 1914. *Wikimedia Commons*

He wanted to examine the routes his birds took from their release locations back to their home lofts. The invention paved the way for the first aerial photography and, in wartime, the first air reconnaissance photos.

While it is not clear how much avian aerial reconnaissance was used during World War II, the method and the means certainly were there.

Later, during the Cold War, the American Central Intelligence Agency developed its own small pigeon camera—a precursor to today's drone, but with feathers and wings. Here's how the CIA's website describes the role of its pigeon spies:

> *With the camera running, the bird would fly over a target on its return home. Being a common species, the pigeon concealed its role as an intelligence collection platform among the activities of thousands of other birds. Pigeon imagery was taken within hundreds of feet of the target, so it was much more detailed than imagery from other collection platforms. (Aircraft took photos from tens of thousands of feet and satellites from hundreds of miles above the target.) The camera could be set to begin taking photographs after release or after a pre-set delay. The camera took a series of still images at a set interval. A tiny, battery-powered motor advanced the film and cocked the shutter.*

It is not known exactly when or how often the birds have been used in this manner because, as the agency website acknowledges, "Details of pigeon missions are still classified."[22]

THE U.S. ARMY PIGEON SERVICE TAKES FLIGHT

In 1938, before war was declared in Europe, the U.S. Army Signal Corps set up its new pigeon center at the Army's Fort Monmouth in New Jersey. Twenty new lofts were completed under the command of Master Sergeant (eventually Colonel) Clifford Poutré. This became the nerve center for the U.S. Army Pigeon Service, also called the Signal Pigeon Corps. It served as the breeding and training center until August 1942, when the program was transferred to Camp Crowder in Missouri. Poutré also transferred to Camp Crowder, where he took command. At its peak, the center dominated American pigeon operations and was home to twelve thousand of the trained war birds.

On January 5, 1941, the Army put out a call for fanciers to register all domestic homers. At the time, the Army was particularly seeking (homing in on, you could say) champion homing pigeons of both sexes. The only stipulation: birds had to have flown a distance of at least two hundred miles. The War Department offered to purchase them at five dollars each—about half the average market price—but the brass really hoped fanciers would simply donate or lend their birds to the cause.

Once again, as with Dogs for Defense and its call for war dogs, pigeon fanciers responded by donating thousands of valuable birds to the Signal Corps. In New York City, one shipment alone contained nearly fifty-two hundred birds.

On March 19, newspapers reported that Great Britain had requested three thousand young U.S. birds for its war efforts, including two hundred needed for shipment just two days later.

Other U.S. pigeon bases were set up at Camp Claiborne, Louisiana; Fort Sam Houston, Texas (where about five thousand pigeons were maintained); Fort Benning, Georgia (five thousand); Fort Meade, Maryland (forty-five hundred pigeons maintained for the 281th Signal Pigeon Company and another six thousand for the 828th Signal Pigeon Replacement Company); and Fort Jackson, South Carolina, where the 281th Signal Company transferred, bringing its pigeons along.

PIGEON PEAK

At its peak, the Signal Pigeon Corps consisted of three thousand enlisted men, 150 officers, and 54,000 pigeons, two-thirds (36,000) of which were deployed overseas. As the *New York Times* reported at the time, "Homing pigeons, the 'Tom Thumb Air Corps,' are giving the walkie-talkie stiff competition. To date 36,000 have been put to use overseas, with 18,000 more in reserve in this country as replacements."[23] Those numbers didn't include pigeons donated to the U.S. Signal Corps in England by British fanciers.

Both birds and men needed training before they could be assigned to companies and sent to the different theaters of the war.[24]

In 1943, Major Otto Meyer assumed command of the Signal Pigeon Corps. Meyer ran the worldwide pigeon breeding and training program and supervised the writing of the pigeon bible— Army Technical Manual No. 11-410, *The Homing Pigeon*, as well as Field Manual 11-80, *Pigeons for Combat Use*.

Major Otto Meyer releases a pigeon. February 25, 1948. *National Archives*

The Pigeon Service took off quickly, so to speak, and enjoyed quick success. Few messages (less than one percent) were coded because the pigeons were so dependable at reaching their lofts. Various sources assert that more than 90 percent of messages borne by pigeons were received, an astonishing record considering how many birds were lost during the war. Those who served with the pigeons appreciated the flappers' importance to their teams. "Our men gave first consideration to the birds," reported Lieutenant Charles A. Koestar. "In Africa, if there was but one cup of water available, the birds drank before the men. That's the way it works."[25]

As the war raged on, the Army found more ways to utilize these flying forces of nature, especially in airborne operations. Pigeons became standard issue on many American bombers.

A pigeon is released from a bomber. *U.S. Army Signal Corps/National Archives*

The Army also introduced a special piece of protective gear for the birds. Maidenform, a leading maker of women's brassieres, designed a unique vest for the birds. Once strapped to a paratrooper's chest, the vest protected the bird during the descent to earth. The birds could remain in it up to six hours. According to the Smithsonian Institute's website, "On December 22, 1944, Maidenform agreed to make 28,500 pigeon vests for the U.S. government, switching, as many companies did, from peacetime production to producing necessary supplies for the war."[26]

Oh—and Maidenform also manufactured parachutes. Who knew?

THE RIGORS OF WAR

It wasn't easy being a homing pigeon in wartime. Home lofts were frequently moved around, confusing the birds. Sometimes a pigeon returned to a previous location before finding its way to the latest loft. Of course this would delay message deliveries. New birds had to be available to replace old ones, who were then used for breeding.

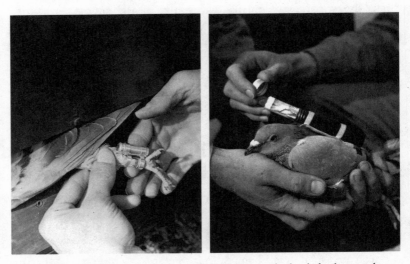

Two types of capsules: one for the leg, the other on the back for larger photos or maps on the back. April 30, 1942/April 28, 1942. *National Archives*

Because pigeons were the communications mode of last resort, they usually flew in the worst conditions. As mentioned, bad weather, night flying (again, they hated both), plus long-distance homing over water from the Continent to England were the easy obstacles. More difficult was dodging bullets and other enemy fire over battlefields. Pigeons could become sitting ducks; if they were spotted, the enemy took direct aim at them, knowing the birds carried significant messages. And friendly fire also threatened the birds, who had to evade shrapnel while flying through areas of bombardment.

The Germans used snipers to shoot the winged warriors out of the sky. Eventually, in critical operations up to a dozen birds were released simultaneously, carrying identical messages, in the hope just one might make it through alive. The Germans sometimes taunted their American enemies over the plethora of pigeons. "In the winter of 1944," reports America in *WWII Magazine*, "the operatically named Lucia di Lammermoor was carried to a forward position. Released with important information, she got delayed in flight. That night she returned with a new message:

> To the American Troops: Herewith we return a pigeon to you. We have enough to eat.
> —the German Troops[27]

The Germans also trained hawks and falcons to attack Allied birds, many of whom were struck over Pas-de-Calais on the French coastline as they made their way home from France to England. Some survived, but many did not.

Those who returned home safely had some stories. These are only a few of the true tales of these great American pigeon patriots.

GI JOE
AMERICA'S MOST CELEBRATED WWII WAR BIRD
BLUE CHECKER SPLASHED COCK—USA43SC6390
DATE OF DICKIN MEDAL: AUGUST 1946 (D.M. 40)

"This bird is credited with making the most outstanding flight by a USA Army Pigeon in World War 2. Making the twenty mile flight from British 10th Army HQ, in the same number of minutes, it brought a message which arrived just in time to save the lives of at least one-hundred Allied soldiers from being bombed by their own planes."

With a name like GI Joe, how could this bird be anything but the most heroic and decorated pigeon of World War II?

Joe was a blue checker cock hailing from the exotic land of the celebrated Casbah. Hatched in Algiers on March 24, 1943, he was merely five weeks old when American forces took him to the Tunisian front. But "due to [GI Joe] being a bit young and due to the fact that the campaign ended, he was unable to be used on many missions," according to Lieutenant Winton T. Prater, commanding officer of the 6681st Signal Pigeon Company (Provisional) APO 464.[28]

GI Joe. *U.S. Army Signal Corps/National Archives*

After the Tunisia campaign, Joe was moved first to Bizerte, Tunisia, then joined his unit on the Italian Front on October 6, 1943. And a dozen days later, GI Joe made a name for himself. According to Lieutenant Prater, the British 56th (London) Infantry Division had "made a request for air support to aid in the breaking of the German defense line at the heavily fortified village of Colvi Vecchia, Italy, the morning of 18 October 1943."

But when the Germans suddenly retreated before the town was scheduled to be bombed, events took a dangerous turn.

"The British 169th Infantry Brigade, of the 56th Infantry Division, had captured the village of Colvi Vecchia at 10:45 hours just a few minutes before a unit of the Allied XII Air Support Command was due to bomb the town," Lieutenant Prater explained.

The now ill-timed bombing mission was scheduled for 11:10 that morning. Radio attempts had failed to get the word out to cancel the attack. With time running out and the situation increasingly desperate, GI Joe was dispatched with the vital message to abort the bombing.

Joe flew twenty miles—from the British 10th Corps Headquarters to U.S. Air Support Command base—in just twenty minutes. The message arrived just as the bombers were on the tarmac, about to take off on the mission. Joe saved the lives of at least one hundred Allied soldiers that day. "Had the message arrived five minutes later," Prater wrote in his recommendation for GI Joe's Dickin Medal, "it might have been a completely different story."[29]

After the war, GI Joe returned home a bona fide hero. He was housed at the Churchill Loft, also known as the U.S. Army's "Hall of Fame" at Fort Monmouth, along with twenty-four other pigeon heroes.[30]

HAIL THE CONQUERING HERO

In August 1946, GI Joe was named the fortieth recipient of the Dickin Medal for Gallantry. He was the first American recipient of this prestigious medal, and at that time the only American so honored—a distinction he held for fifty-five years.

In late October 1946, Joe was flown from Fort Monmouth via Paris to London to accept the award in person. According to Dorothea St. Hill Bourne of the PDSA's Allied Forces Mascot

Club, the pigeon's traveling papers "included a letter from the French Consul in Washington, recommending 'le pigeon voyageur' to the authorities in Paris, asking all help in speeding his journey, and mentioning his valuable war services."[31]

Overnight, Joe went from GI Joe, War Bird to GI Joe, Rock Star. Landing in London, Joe was met by American and British military officials, then spent the night as an honored guest at the International Congress of Pigeon Fanciers.

After some time for rest, Joe's big day came on November 4, 1946.

The Tower of London was chosen for the "investiture." Among the officials greeting Joe were the Constable of the Tower, Field Marshal Lord Chetwode; U.S. Military and Air Attaché Major General Clayton L. Bissell; and the tower's resident governor, Colonel Carkeet James.

"The Tudor uniforms of the Yeoman Warders made a splash of colour," St. Hill Bourne wrote, "the Tower ravens hopped happily about, and from almost every doorway round the green a cat emerged as if to see what all the fuss over a mere pigeon was all about."[32]

Yeoman Warders (aka Beefeaters) display Joe at the Tower of London. November 4, 1946. *PDSA Archives*

As the *Daily Graphic* reported, "An array of generals, American and British, were waiting on the lawn of the Tower with a battery of photographers and radio commentators to greet him."[33]

Dickin Medal Ceremony (L). (PDSA Archives) Wing Commander Lea Raynor holds Joe as Major General Clayton L. Bissell, U.S. Military and Air Attaché, looks on (R). November 4, 1946. *PDSA Archives*

Major General Sir Charles Keightley, who had commanded the 5th Corps in Italy, hosted the hoopla. "It's a very great pleasure and privilege to give the Dickin Medal to this American pigeon for the brilliant exploit he carried out in Italy," the general intoned as GI Joe, held firmly by Wing Commander Lea Rayner, looked on. "His flight, performed under extremely trying conditions, resulted in the saving of some hundreds of British soldiers' lives and the winning of a most critical battle."

The general slipped the medal around Joe's neck. "Well done, GI Joe!" [34]

GI Joe proudly displays his Dickin Medal. November 4, 1946. *PDSA Archives*

Pictures taken that day are crystal clear. No other bird of war ever received such a dramatic day of honor and celebration as did GI Joe.

TIME MARCHES ON

When the Churchill Loft closed in March 1957, GI Joe and some of his friends found a new home at the Detroit Zoological Gardens. Joe lived out his days there as a hero-in-residence until his passing on June 3, 1961 at the impressive age of eighteen years.

GI Joe was stuffed, mounted, and returned to Fort Monmouth, where he remained on display in the Historical Center in Meyer Hall until the Army installation closed its doors in 2011. Last we checked, he was waiting in a box at Ft. Belvoir, Virginia, for the completion of the U.S. Army Museum.

BLACKIE HALLIGAN
BLACK CHECKER COCK—USA42FTM2615

Dark-feathered Blackie Harrington, hatched at Fort Monmouth in early 1942, underwent basic training at Camp Claiborne, Louisiana, and served with the 280th Signal Pigeon Company.

Blackie was shipped first to the Fiji Islands and then to New Caledonia and the famed Americal (23rd Infantry) Division training in the capital of Noumea.

He flew many short missions for the 132nd Infantry Regiment.[35] But it wasn't until the unit shipped off to Guadalcanal that Blackie truly distinguished himself. On January 3, 1943, he was with a patrol near an area known as the "Catcher's Mitt." Blackie was sent flapping back to headquarters with details of the position of three hundred Japanese troops. But en route Blackie was felled by shrapnel that left him bleeding and seriously wounded. Somehow he was able to take flight again. This time, a trip that normally would have taken him twenty minutes required five hours. But Blackie got his message through.

He was awarded a medal for bravery under fire by Americal Division Commander Major General Alexander M. Patch Jr. Afterward, Patch and Blackie posed for pictures.

In October 1945, the valiant bird returned to the United States by special courier after having served forty months in the Pacific. He passed away in February 1949.

BURMA QUEEN
BLUE CHECKER HEN—USA44SC19071

Burma Queen saw service in, well, Burma at just five months of age.[36] The blue checker hen delivered messages during some of the heaviest fighting along the Thailand-Burma border.

The Queen's greatest moment came when she was dropped by parachute from a B-25 Mitchell bomber near Allied forces isolated from their main unit after retreating from an attack "by an overwhelming force of Japanese troops."[37] The isolation was exacerbated by the necessary destruction of the unit's radios and codes for fear of being captured.

Burma Queen, released at 6:00 in the morning, covered three hundred twenty miles in nine hours over some of Burma's highest mountains. She arrived at her home loft at 3:00 that afternoon. "This flight was made all the greater," according to a published 1946 account, "by the fact that she was released 120 miles off the course she was trained to fly. The pigeoneers themselves deemed this feat impossible."[38]

Her message to headquarters described the Allied troops' stranded circumstances and detailed their position. Thanks to Burma Queen, they were soon rescued.

CAPTAIN FULTON

BLUE CHECKER COCK—USA958

Captain Fulton was the first pigeon to deliver the message from Major General Harmon to the Commanding General, II Corps, Major General Omar Bradley, on May 9, 1943, that the German Tenth and Fifteenth Panzer Divisions had surrendered after Bizerte and Tunisia had fallen. He flew sixty-five miles in eighty-two minutes from Bizerte to Beja and arrived almost two hours earlier than any other pigeon that returned.

Captain Fulton. December 16, 1943. *National Archives*

CAPTAIN LEDERMAN

BLUE CHECKER COCK—USA44SC18957

Hatched in Burma in September 1944, Captain Lederman served with the Office of Strategic Services (OSS), the precursor to postwar America's Central Intelligence Agency. The blue checker cock operated with agents behind Japanese lines in Burma commanded by, of all people, Captain Morris Y. Lederman. (Coincidence? *Nah!*)

Captain Lederman (the pigeon, not the commander) carried his first message at age three months while on a patrol mission on the Burmese front, a hundred and twenty miles behind Japanese lines.

Between January and March 1945, the Captain was variously dropped by parachute or carried inside bamboo jump containers behind patrolled enemy lines. Each message that he carried included vital intel on, among other things, troop movements, gun placements, and supplies.

On four trips, he delivered over distances varying from 175 to 320 miles. The terrain on these flights included some of Burma's deepest jungles and highest mountains, but the Captain completed each flight the same day and in impressive time.

JUNGLE JOE

BRONZE T-PATTERN COCK—USA44SC19008

Like Captain Lederman, Jungle Joe also served with the OSS in Burma. On his first flight, at the age of four months, Jungle Joe was dropped behind Japanese lines with an Allied airborne patrol. Reports indicated that Joe "brought through some of the most important news carried by a pigeon during the Burma campaign."[39]

The radio operator went missing on the jump, and contact with the patrol's rear headquarters was lost. Jungle Joe was kept confined in his cramped 14" x4" x4" bamboo jump container for seven days while the team gathered information on the Japanese position, movements, and gun locations. On the eighth day he was finally released to deliver an "urgent" and "secret" message.

Joe flew 225 miles over Burma's steepest mountains, through varying temperatures and difficult wind currents. Thanks to his successful delivery of the critical intel, "a large section of Burma was opened up to occupation by the Allied troops."[40] Joe's message must also have conveyed news of the missing radio man, because a replacement was dropped in and radio contact to rear headquarters was restored.

Lady Astor (L) with Yank in their loft in North Africa. March 19, 1943. *National Archives*

Jungle Joe died in 1953. His remains were stuffed and mounted and remained on display at Fort Monmouth, along with those of GI Joe, until it closed in 2011.

———

LADY ASTOR

BLUE CHECKER HEN

A New York City native, Lady Astor was trained by an Army sergeant and New Jersey fancier, then presented to the Signal Corps. Lady A landed in North Africa and saw duty in French Morocco where she made a memorable flight on May 6, 1943.

Although severely wounded, Lady Astor flew ninety miles to her loft, bringing with her early details of the Allied breakthrough in Tebourba, Tunisia. The message was delivered to the Second Army Corps (or II Corps) and played a major role in the next day's capture of Tunis.

She completed the trip despite three gaping wounds—to her wing, breast, and leg. "Once home, she alighted onto the roof of the loft and immediately collapsed, having delivered her message safely," according to author Toni M. Kiser in *Loyal Forces: The American Animals of World War II*.[41]

When her owner, Sergeant Adam Samson, heard of her heroics, he said with pride, "If there were only medals for birds, Lady Astor would get the highest decoration."[42]

———

YANK

MEALY COCK—USA42 4THCA873

Ironically, the cock called Yank was actually a Reb, a Georgia peach of a pigeon hatched at Fort Benning. Like Lady Astor,

Yank's heroics came in French Morocco and the Tunisian Campaign. According to author Wendell Levi, "Six hundred and
fifty-seven birds were used in this campaign. Two hundred and
fifteen urgent and secret messages were carried with one hundred
per cent delivery."[43] Yank contributed to that remarkable record.

Yank. March 19, 1943. *National Archives*

On March 17, 1943, during Operation Wop, the U.S. 1st
Infantry Division captured the Tunisian town of Gafsa. Yank
was first to reach company headquarters ninety miles away with
the news, a flight completed in one hour and fifty-five minutes.

Yank's second great flight took place on April Fools' Day,
1943, during the Battle of El Guettar, south of Gafsa. He was
sent soaring by no less than Old Blood and Guts himself, Lieutenant General George S. Patton. Horrible weather conditions and
extremely heavy fighting had knocked out communications,
making Yank the only hope. The mealy cock flew ninety miles
in a hundred minutes to deliver the message.[44]

Famous pigeons: Major Otto Meyer holds General Clark, with Yank, Blackie Halligan and GI Joe (left to right). February 27, 1948. *National Archives*

THEY ALSO FLEW

Now a quick mention of a few lesser-known but no less valorous American war birds.

JULIUS CAESAR
BLUE CHECKER GAILY SPLASHED COCK—USA44SC8272

He carried forty-four messages in the North Africa campaign in very good time. But Julius Caesar wasn't finished. As the Allies readied their invasion of Italy, Julius parachuted into an area north of Rome and was later released in southern Italy with information vital to the invasion of Salerno. The flight was remarkable in that three hundred miles of it took place over (for pigeons, hated and unnerving) water—in this case, the Mediterranean—before he arrived safe and sound at his loft in Tunisia.[45]

LILES BOY
SILVER COCK—USA43 7THSC2242

Liles Boy served in Italy, where he carried forty-six messages from the front lines during combat operations. He was officially credited with "carrying more messages than any American pigeon in either World War 1 or World War 2."[46]

After he died, Liles Boy was stuffed and mounted. His remains are on display today at the Army Signal Corps Regimental Museum at Fort Gordon, Georgia.[47]

―――――

WISCONSIN BOY
BLUE CHECKER COCK—783

Hatched in an American loft in Casablanca, Wisconsin Boy was only twelve weeks old when called to service in Tunisia. In his authoritative *The Pigeon*, author Wendell Levi wrote that Wisconsin Boy "carried an important message from Cunningham, War Correspondent with the U.S. 1st Infantry Division, advising of the enemy's evacuation of Tebourba and its flight toward Tunis."

Wisconsin Boy flew forty miles in as many minutes from Tebourba, Tunisia, to his loft in Beja. The message he delivered "paved the way for Allied victories and occupation of Bizerte and Tunis."[48]

U.S. 1169

Sadly, many records on these pigeon heroes are incomplete or unavailable; it would be nice to honor many more of them, especially those whose accomplishments are mostly lost to history. Like, for example, U.S. 1169.

According to *Pigeon Heroes* author Marion Cothren, 1169 was an Army bird lent early in the war to the Coast Guard. Cothren maintained that 1169 had the distinction of being "the first bird to be cited for bravery in World War 2." The incident in question occurred off America's eastern seaboard.

U.S. 1169 was aboard a Coast Guard schooner in the Atlantic when a storm almost sank the ship. With the radio out, 1169 represented the crew's last hope of survival. They attached a message to his leg with the coordinates of their stranded ship. The crewmen released 1169 "in a northeast gale which seemed too strong for his wings."

Undaunted, 1169 made it to shore and saved the day.

Later, when the men learned that the general of the Chesapeake Bay Sector "had especially honored U.S. 1169, they shouted, 'Keep 'em flying! Keep 'em flying!'"[49]

10

Britain's Bird Brigade

"I'm standing here today because of a pigeon."
—RONALD WILLIAM GEORGE VAUGHN, RAF PILOT

From 1939 to the end of World War II, nearly 216,000 young pigeons were offered to the armed services by Britain's racing-pigeon fanciers. Among the birds were many of the era's top racing pigeons. His Majesty King George VI even donated his birds from the Royal lofts in Sandringham in Norfolk.

Many civilian pigeon fanciers became volunteers who joined the National Pigeon Service (NPS). One requirement of membership: every fancier had to maintain a loft of at least twenty pigeons of quality. More than twenty-seven thousand fanciers met the call.

The NPS was established in 1939 by Major W. H. Osman, whose family knew a little about pigeons in war. During World War I, his father, Lieutenant Colonel A. H. Osman, had formed the Army Pigeon Service, which supplied birds for British forces. And during that war the son had secured no less than three military commissions associated with pigeons—with the Navy,

Royal Air Force, and Army. The Osmans understood better than most people the strategic importance of pigeons in wartime.

For eleven years, through 1934, Major General Sir John Sharman Fowler ran Britain's Royal Corps of Signals. Like the Osmans, Fowler worked with pigeons during the Great War. He described their vital role with eloquence:

> If it became necessary immediately to discard every line and method of communications used on the front line except one, and it were left to me to select that one method, I should unhesitatingly choose the pigeon. It is the pigeon on which we must and do depend when every other method fails.
>
> During quiet periods we can rely on the telephone, telegraph, flag signals, our dogs and various other ways in use on the front with the British Army. But when the battle rages and everything gives way to barrage and machine-gun fire, to say nothing of gas attacks and bombing, it is to the pigeon that we go for succor.
>
> When the troops are lost or surrounded in the mazes on the front, or are advancing and yet beyond the known localities, then we depend absolutely on the pigeon for our communications. Regular methods in such cases are worthless and it is just at such times that we need most messengers that we can rely on.
>
> In pigeons we have them. I am glad to say that they have never failed us.[1]

In World War II the NPS provided birds to all service branches. "Fanciers had the opportunity to become RAF or

Army pigeon keepers, subject to a proficiency test," according to John "Pepys" Tucker, a pigeon fancier whose birds flew for the Royal Air Force.[2]

The Royal Air Force Pigeon Service (RAFPS) was responsible for managing pigeons acquired from the NPS and other sources. Headed by Wing Commander W. D. Lea Rayner, MBE, the RAF's pigeon program also oversaw a comparable one at the Coastal Command. The RAFPS relied on the appointed avian experts for technical advice. It demanded a high degree of long-range reliability among its birds because they would be flying in difficult conditions.

Two pigeons became standard crewmembers on all bomber and reconnaissance planes. "Only birds of the best racing strain are used by the RAF," the *New York Times* reported at the time, "with the result that 80 per cent of messages sent while planes are on operational flights reach their destinations."[3] Britain's Air Ministry oversaw the Royal Air Force and its pigeon service. The birds also became standard on Coastal Command flights and ships—and proved especially useful when there was radio silence during U-boat surveillance.

The Army Pigeon Service started flying in late 1939. Its birds, who flew for both the Army and British intelligence services, accompanied agents parachuting behind enemy lines to gather intelligence, especially about enemy troop locations and installations. They also accompanied Allied forces into battle.

The vaguely named "Special Section of the Army Pigeon Service" was, in fact, the birds' very own Secret Service. The spy birds parachuted alone, one to a cage, behind enemy lines. Inside their container was enough food and water to last ten days, a questionnaire, and instructions for the finder. Many of these birds were never found, or found too late, or found by the enemy.

In the three and a half years this program was in effect, 16,554 pigeons were dropped, with only 1,842 returning back to their lofts in Great Britain. That's only 11 percent who made it back home. But those that did return brought valuable information that furthered Allied efforts.

Each war bird had an identification number, and when possible records were kept of their flights and achievements. In general, ID numbers indicated whether a bird originated from an individual NPS member or was registered with a group that had donated birds to the National Pigeon Service. Some of these organizations include the National Union of Racing Pigeons (NURP), Royal Pigeon Racing Association (RPRA), National Homing Union (NHU), North of England Homing Union (NEHU) and Middle Eastern Pigeon Service (MEPS).

Incredibly, these groups furnished more than 46,500 birds to personnel of the U.S. Army Signal Corps based in England. The Signal Corps was happy to have the birds. "We well recognize that this abundant supply of carrier pigeons," the Corps' commander, Brigadier General F. S. Strong Jr., wrote in a letter to the NPS, "would not have been possible without the splendid assistance of the many civilian breeders of your organization who, without cost to us, kept our needs constantly supplied."[4]

The true tales of these brave birds inspire a genuine appreciation for the heart and soul of the homing pigeon. The powerful stories show why these pigeons earned their own version of the "Victoria Cross," the prestigious PDSA Dickin Medal.

THE START OF IT ALL

On December 2, 1943, Maria Dickin realized a dream when the organization she had founded, the People's Dispensary for Sick Animals, bestowed its first-ever Dickin Medals honoring the valor, gallantry, and heroic exploits of wartime animals. The inaugural recipients were three distinguished war pigeons: Winkie, Tyke (a.k.a. George), and White Vision.

At the formal ceremony the following March, Maria Dickin personally presented the three medallions. Looking on was Wing Commander Lea Rayner, chief of the Air Ministry Pigeon Service, who would present medallions to many subsequent Dickin recipients.

Number 1: Winkie receives his medal from Maria Dickin. The medal that started it all. December 2, 1943. *PDSA Archives*

Overall, the PDSA has bestowed the Dickin on thirty-two pigeons, all for service during World War II. Some of their stories may be familiar to moviegoers. In 2005, Disney subsidiary Buena Vista Pictures handled the American distribution of *Valiant*, an animated British film about these so-called "featherweight heroes." Many characters in the film were based on their real-life feathered counterparts. Although it was a British production, by the end of *Valiant* you'd swear it was a Disney movie because (spoiler alert!) the title character receives a Dickin Medal *and* gets the girl.

Let's meet some of these Dickin honorees.

DICKIN DARLINGS

WINKIE

Blue Checker Hen—NEHU.40.NS.1
Date of Dickin Medal: December 2, 1943 (D.M. 1)

"For delivering a message under exceptionally difficult conditions and so contributing to the rescue of an Air Crew while serving with the RAF in February, 1942."

She was among the most famous pigeons of the war. You couldn't discern that, however, by the bureaucratic name with which she was saddled: NEHU.40.NS.1. How she became "Winkie" is quite a tale.

Trained by the National Pigeon Service, Winkie was part of No. 42 Squadron RAF, commanded by Squadron Leader W. Hedley Cliff. Based at RAF base Leuchars in Fife on the east coast of Scotland, the squadron had flown north to RAF base Sumburgh on the southern tip of the Shetland Islands when on February 23, 1942, the men received new orders.

Their mission: intercept a German capital ship off the coast of Norway thought to be joining the German battleship *Tirpitz* farther north in the Trondheim Fiord.[5] Six British Bristol Beauforts (twin-engine torpedo bombers) were dispatched at staggered times to monitor different sections of the 120-mile Norwegian coastline. Their task was simple: just find the ship. To reduce the risk of being spotted by the enemy, each plane was assigned a twenty-mile section of coastline to observe—a ten-minute reconnaissance run. Then each plane was to return to RAF Leuchars.

Squadron Leader Cliff, along with a crew of three and two birds—Winkie and another pigeon—had the longest distance to fly. They took off first, at 2:00 in the afternoon, and completed the 350-mile afternoon flight to the Norwegian coast in well under two hours. When they found no ship in their designated area, at 4:05 Cliff set a course for Leuchars.

About thirty minutes out over the North Sea, Cliff plugged in "George," the automatic pilot, and relaxed a bit for the trip home. His navigator, Flying Officer McDonald, had a flask of hot tea, which he shared with the men.

But it was the wrong time to relax. The Beaufort began experiencing engine trouble and— seemingly in the blink of an eye—the plane went down in the North Sea and broke apart about 120 miles from land.

"It happened with stupefying suddenness," author Ralph Barker wrote. "One moment they were sipping their tea. Thirty seconds later, they were in the water."[6]

In the frigid sea, the men struggled to climb into a dinghy. Both pigeons had been in their containers, but at the moment of impact Winkie's cage broke open, and she was thrown into the oily waters. The goo clung to her wings, making it difficult for the bird to flap herself free, but at last she managed to shake off enough oil to take flight, leaving her mates as sitting ducks, so to speak. Winkie headed home—for once without any message attached to her leg.

The second pigeon remained trapped in its locked cage. The crew took it out and blotted the oil from its wings. At last they attached a message that revealed their position. The crew released the bird around 5:00, but with darkness approaching and being so far from land, the bird never made it home.[7]

The crew had managed to get an SOS out just before the plane crashed. But the signal was so faint that gaining a fix on the aircraft's location was impossible. An air search for survivors was dispatched. It covered seventy square miles in the area where rescuers believed the signal might have been sent.

But no trace of the crew was found.

In the meantime, Winkie successfully flew an estimated 140 miles home to Broughty Ferry, a suburb of Dundee, Scotland. Her owner, George Ross, discovered the exhausted and bedraggled pigeon at 8:20 the following morning. Her feathers were still so clogged with oil that it was a wonder she could fly at all. Ross didn't even recognize her and took Winkie for a stray. There was nothing in the leg capsule, which disappointed Ross, but from the leg ring he knew it was his bird. Ross alerted the airbase at RAF Leuchars.

As we have seen, pigeons dislike and fear flying in darkness, especially over water. This made Winkie's flight all the more impressive.[8]

When authorities considered Winkie's condition and her arrival time home, they realized that rescuers had been searching for the lost crew in the wrong place. RAF officers recalculated the plane's position using variables including the exact time of the SOS signal, Winkie's arrival time home, the wind direction, and even the wind drag factor of her oily plumage.

The RAF's revised math pushed the search-and-rescue mission further south, and the dinghy was discovered in just fifteen minutes by men from the 320 Squadron RAF of the Royal Netherlands Naval Air Service. Commander Cliff and his crew were found floating 129 miles from the base. All owed their lives to Winkie's heroic flight in pigeon-perilous conditions.

The crew was feted at a dinner, and Winkie was the guest of honor. That evening, the men noticed that she was constantly blinking an eye, a sign of exhaustion and strain from the flight.

That was the night that war bird NEHU.40.NS.1 acquired the name Winkie.

Winkie and her medal. *PDSA Archives*

Winkie died in August 1953. George Ross took her to the taxidermist, then donated the stuffed Winkie (and her Dickin Medal) to the McManus Art Gallery and Museums in Dundee, Scotland, where today she remains on public display.

WHITE VISION

WHITE HEN—SURP.41.L.3089
DATE OF DICKIN MEDAL: DECEMBER 2, 1943 (D.M. 3)

"For delivering a message under exceptionally difficult conditions and so contributing to the rescue of an air crew while serving with the RAF in October 1943."

On a Friday evening in the fall of 1998, Jim Carlo was standing in line at a fish-and-chips restaurant in Pilley, a small village in Boldre Parish in Hampshire. While waiting he chatted amiably with an older gentleman behind him who remarked, "I'm standing here today because of a pigeon."

Thus began a twelve-year friendship between Carlo and Ronald Vaughn, a wartime RAF pilot who crashed into the ocean. Struck by Vaughn's powerful true story, Carlo was inspired to write *Three "Cats," a Pigeon, and the 27 Brave Men of Coastal Command*. While researching the 2012 book, Carlo found that many World War II veterans could make the same claim: they owed their lives to a pigeon.

White Vision, a beautiful pure white hen, was born in 1941 in Motherwell, Scotland. Her owners, brothers George and Peter Fleming, were miners and pigeon hobbyists. They lent the bird to the National Pigeon Service, where she was trained and "homed" at RAF Sullom Voe in the Shetland Islands.

White Vision. *PDSA Archives*

The flying boat base Sullom Voe was home to the RAF's Coastal Command, comparable to the U.S. Coast Guard. Its boats cruised coastlines looking for German U-boats and other enemy threats.

At 10:50 in the morning on October 10, 1943, the flight crew of the RAF's Catalina V No. FP/280U set out for the eastern approaches of the North Atlantic on an anti-submarine patrol. Captained by twenty-two-year-old Flying Officer Ronald W. G. Vaughn, this ten-man unit, along with two pigeons, settled into the mission's twenty-plus-hours surveillance patrol.[9]

Because of its long-range fuel tanks, the Catalina aircraft allowed patrols lasting as long as twenty-two hours. The patrol plane was also equipped with plenty of firepower—Browning machine guns and up to two thousand pounds of bombs—making it a versatile aircraft.

For thirteen and a half hours, the patrol proved uneventful. But just past midnight, at 12:30 in the morning on October 11, a radio message from base revealed that because of poor weather and heavy fog, the plane was being redirected to Invergordon on the Scottish mainland. Vaughn set a new course homeward. But a few hours later, at 4:25, thick fog cut visibility to almost nothing. Vaughn and the crew tried to climb above the haze, without success.

An hour later, another change in plans. The plane was again diverted because of weather, this time to Bowmore on the Isle of Islay, west of mainland Scotland.[10] By then the crew had been in the air for almost eighteen and a half hours. With only two hundred gallons of fuel left, the men were becoming concerned. At 6:10 that morning, they informed the base of the fuel problem.

Vaughn feared they wouldn't make it to Bowmore and decided to try landing at their original destination, Sullom Voe, but approaching it from a different direction. At 7:45 the

Catalina aircraft descended through the dense fog. But when it reached a mere twenty feet above the sea—in an attempt to fly under the fog—trouble stared the crew down. "Suddenly, islands appeared on the radar screen dead ahead, one to two miles away," Vaughn later recounted.[11] At that point, Vaughn decided to ditch the aircraft into the sea.

Twenty minutes later, at 8:10, the Catalina skidded onto the surface of the stormy North Atlantic. The crew had no clue of their exact location and worse, the radio was out. Vaughn managed to keep the engines running while two escape dinghies were hurriedly prepared. But ultimately the men decided to stay with the plane.

Vaughn and the crew of the Catalina V No. FP/280U had two secret weapons: White Vision and a second pigeon.

Ten minutes later, at 8:20, both pigeons were released, each carrying the same SOS message:

0820 A/C DITCHED SAFELY N.W. RONAS HEAVY
SWELL TAXYING S.E. NO CASUALTIES[12]

Once airborne, the birds battled not only the thick fog but also rain and buffeting headwinds of about twenty-five miles per hour. With conditions so ominous, the men knew the pigeons likely represented their only real hope of survival.

As seabound search-and-rescue efforts were being organized, air rescue operations were being grounded by the weather. The men faced a long wait—ultimately eighteen hours—before help arrived.

At 5:00 that afternoon, an exhausted and battered White Vision arrived at her loft. She had covered more than sixty miles in eight hours and forty minutes under terrible conditions. White Vision was weather-tested—with blank patches where feathers once had been—to prove it. "Visibility was only a hundred yards at the place of release," author Dorothea St. Hill Bourne wrote, "and three hundred yards at the place of arrival.

"Of such stuff are pigeons made!"[13]

The second pigeon was never seen again.

When the skies cleared, the search began for the plane. Finally at 11:05 that night, the aircraft was sighted by a Royal Navy High Speed Launch. Just in time, too; the plane was so battered by the sea that it had begun taking on water.

The actual rescue wasn't fully completed for another three hours.

Finally, at 2:10 the following morning, Vaughn ordered the crew to abandon ship. One dinghy was accidentally released with just two crewmen in it, leaving the other eight men to cram into the second boat—something that was not feasible, especially in extreme storm conditions. Instead, the eight airmen-turned-sailors stood atop the roof of the pilot's compartment and they were pulled onto the rescue launch from there, one by one.

The timing couldn't have been better. Just as the last man stepped off the aircraft, Catalina FP/280U sank—it really was that close. The two crewmen in the first dinghy were rescued by a team from Aith Lifeboat Rescue in the Shetland Islands.

The ordeal was finally over after a tumultuous forty hours from takeoff to rescue.

When the men arrived back at Sullom Voe, the heroic hen White Vision was aptly renamed. Now she was Saviour.

After becoming a Dickin medalist, White Vision enjoyed a nice life in retirement, even participating in a few exhibitions. She lived until 1953.

———

GUSTAV

GRIZZLE COCK—NPS.42.31066

DATE OF DICKIN MEDAL: SEPTEMBER 1, 1944 (D.M. 6)

"For delivering the first message from the Normandy Beaches from a ship off the beach-head while serving with the RAF on 6 June 1944."

The tag team of Gustav and Paddy participated in Operation Overlord, the D-Day invasion on Normandy's beaches. Each distinguished himself, although with different units, and they received their Dickin medallions on the same day.

In two years of service to the RAF, Gustav had built a solid reputation for reliability. He was bred by National Pigeon Service member Frederick E. Jackson of Cosham, near Portsmouth, England. Gustav received training at RAF Thorney Island.

Gustav and his feeding bowl. *PDSA Archives*

On early missions, the grizzle cock carried Resistance messages out of occupied Belgium. But he really made his reputation as the first bird to arrive with details of Operation Overlord.

Gustav was one of six RAF birds assigned to work with Reuters correspondent Montague Taylor.[14] They were transported in wicker baskets, then released at various times to deliver information back to mainland Britain on how the D-Day landings were progressing. Working under strict radio silence, Taylor dispatched Gustav and his D-Day message from a craft standing off the beach during the first landings.

Like White Vision, Gustav was released into miserably overcast skies. Headwinds were estimated at up to thirty miles per hour, and there was no sun to guide him. Yet Gustav made it safely home to his loft at Thorney Island, 150 miles away, in five hours and sixteen minutes.

Gustav's handler, Sergeant Harry Halsey, retrieved the message:

> We are just twenty miles or so off the beaches. First assault troops landed 0750. Signal says no interference from enemy gunfire on beach.... Steaming steadily in formation. Lightnings, typhoons, fortresses crossing since 0545. No enemy aircraft seen.[15]

PADDY
DARK CHECKER GAY PIED COCK—NPS.43.9451
DATE OF DICKIN MEDAL: SEPTEMBER 1, 1944 (D.M. 7)

"For the best recorded time with a message from the Normandy Operations, while serving with the RAF in June, 1944."

Paddy was a speed demon. The only Irish carrier pigeon to receive the Dickin, he also had an American connection.

Paddy was bred and owned by a National Pigeon Service member, Captain Andrew S. Hughes, and trained by John McMullen, both of Carnlough, Northern Ireland. He was hatched in 1943, and his service record reports that from May of that year to the following March Paddy worked at Air-and-Sea Rescue Training and Operations at RAF Station Ballykelly, an airfield used by the Coastal Command. On the Ides of March, 1944, Paddy was recruited for D-Day duty and transferred to a south coast station, RAF Hurn in Hampshire, for specialized training. He had "rehomed" and was ready to go in less than a fortnight, on March 28.

Beautiful bird, Paddy. *PDSA Archives*

At his new station, Paddy achieved the third highest testing score of eighty pigeons being trained there. His instructor for the Normandy invasion, Sergeant McLean, called Paddy "a pigeon of exceptional intelligence."[16]

HEY, HE'S WITH U.S.

Two days into Operation Overlord, on June 8, 1944, Paddy was among thirty pigeons delivered by RAF Hurn to operational units of the 1st U.S. Army. They were to be used in connection with a secret task code-named "U2." Four days later, Paddy was the last bird released, at 8:15 in the morning. Yet he was the first to touch down at his loft, safely delivering a coded message.

Of several hundred pigeons used in Operation Overlord, Paddy was the quickest to deliver a written account of the successful Allied advance. He completed the flight despite adverse weather, the chaos and danger of maneuvering over battlefields, and the fear of German falcons in the skies near Calais. Paddy flew 230 miles across the English Channel in just four hours and fifty minutes—the fastest-ever pigeon crossing of the English Channel.

"He was the best of the lot," said Paddy's trainer, John McMullen, "the best of thousands."[17]

DOUBLE DICKIN DELIGHT

On September 1, 1944, five years to the day after Hitler marched into Poland, Gustav and Paddy were named PDSA Dickin medalists for their D-Day exploits. The formal presentation came eleven weeks later, on November 18, at the Allied Forces Mascot Club in London.[18] Mrs. Albert V. Alexander, wife of the then-First Lord of the Admiralty, did the honors. Also on hand: Wing Commander Lea Rayner, chief of the Air Ministry Pigeon Service.

The dynamic duo of the day: Gustav (L) and Paddy. November 18, 1944. *PDSA Archives*

As Mrs. Alexander was introduced to Paddy, Rayner told her, "Paddy made the fastest time of all the birds engaged in this operation. He came from Normandy, well to the south, in four hours fifty minutes. It wasn't on the same day as Gustav, so you mustn't compare the two times. But it was the fastest time of all the hundreds of birds engaged in the operation. And by the way, Paddy, an Irish pigeon, was trained in England with a Scotch assistant, and he carried his Normandy message for the Americans."[19]

Newspaper accounts of the event make fun reading. "Both birds behaved with perfect composure, rather like Hollywood stars during the ceremonial presentation and were not at all disturbed either by batteries of cameras or the fierce light of the arc lamps," gushed the *Nottingham Evening Post*.[20]

Maybe that was because both birds brought their wives with them that day.

PIGEON WIVES MATTER

Gustav's wife, Betty, was also an active member of the National Pigeon Service. According to Dorothea St. Hill Bourne, secretary of the Allied Forces Mascot Club, Betty had "several good flights to her credit. When she was absent 'on ops' Gustav took care of the family."

Mrs. Paddy, however, was a "home-bird," according to St. Hill Bourne. "Her chief reason for continuing in the service was her husband's affection for her and the speed with which he always wished to return to her."[21] The "will to home" in action!

The *Herndon & Finley Times* echoed St. Hill Bourne: "Mrs. Gustav (Betty) is, I hear, an excellent message carrier, but Paddy's wife is only retained in the RAF Pigeon Service because of her husband's fondness for her. Maybe his eagerness to return home could explain his speed."[22]

SADLY TOO SOON

Paddy and Gustav spent part of their postwar retirement years attending PDSA fundraisers. Paddy lived to age eleven and died in 1954. Gustav's demise was sadly ironic. He survived the horrors of war—only to die when he was accidentally stepped on while his loft was being cleaned.

———

KENLEY LASS
DARK BLUE CHECKER HEN—NURP.36.JH.190
DATE OF DICKIN MEDAL: MARCH 1945 (D.M. 13)

"For being the first pigeon to be used with success for secret communications from an Agent in enemy-occupied France while serving with the NPS in October 1940."

Kenley Lass enjoyed the distinction of being the first spy-pigeon to work inside Nazi-occupied France. She began her career in "pigeonage"—pigeon espionage—quite early. She was only five weeks old when her owner, Walter Torkington of the Grange, Poynton Park, donated Kenley for aerial war duty. She was trained by the National Pigeon Service's R. W. Beard, of Kenley, Croydon.

This dark blue checker hen parachuted into France in October 1940 accompanied by her human counterpart, a Frenchman known only as "Philippe." For eleven days Philippe hid her somewhere in his clothes while he walked nine miles at night through occupied France, gathering intelligence. Only then did he release her to deliver important information about the French Resistance. (Actually, Philippe carried two pigeons on the mission, each one tucked into a sock with the toes cut out.)

Finally released at 8:20 in the morning on October 20, Kenley Lass covered three hundred miles with the precious message rolled inside a tube attached to her leg. She arrived six hours and forty minutes later.

The second pigeon, a red checker hen with the bureaucratic name NURP. 34.SVS.402, carried a similar message and arrived a minute later. (This second pigeon later vanished on a similar flight.)

Kenley Lass flew another comparable mission a few months later, on February 16, 1941. This time she was cooped up for only four days (instead of eleven) before flying home. Again, she completed the trip in less than a day.

Kenley Lass receives her medal. April 12, 1945. *PDSA Archives*

Kenley Lass was named a Dickin medalist in March 1945. She was formally presented with the medallion on April 12—coincidentally the day America lost its wartime president, Franklin Roosevelt, to a cerebral hemorrhage. The Dickin ceremony, at London's Dorland Hall, was held in conjunction with an RAF Air/ Sea Rescue exhibition there called "To Victory with the RAF." Rear Admiral Roger M. Bellairs did the honors, and Kenley Lass shared the spotlight with five other pigeon patriots: Commando, Royal Blue, Flying Dutchman, Dutch Coast, and Navy Blue.

COMMANDO

RED CHECKER COCK—NURP.38.EGU.242

DATE OF DICKIN MEDAL: MARCH 1945 (D.M. 14)

"For successfully delivering messages from agents in occupied France on three occasions: twice under exceptionally adverse conditions, while serving with the NPS in 1942."

If any war bird ever deserved the recognition and respect conferred by the Dickin Medal, it was Commando. He flew more than ninety missions, including three notably perilous ones in June, August, and September 1942, bringing home crucial intelligence from agents in France.

Commando was bred and trained by National Pigeon Service member Sid Moon of Hayward's Heath, West Sussex, a pigeon fancier who had served with the Army Pigeon Service in World War I. When the next global conflict began, Moon offered his birds to the cause, including Commando.

BEATING THE ODDS

Each time the red checker cock parachuted into France with an agent, he returned the same day with a tube-borne cargo of wartime intelligence intact. The vital information involved the location of industrial sites, positions of and other information on German troops, and reports on injured British soldiers. His official record highlights Commando's derring-do as a winged spy: "The conditions under which this pigeon had to operate on two occasions were exceptionally adverse."[23]

Commando's flight record is more impressive when you consider that only one of eight pigeons released this way ever returned home. Between the bad weather, the long distances, and the fear of trained German falcons and enemy snipers along the French coastline, it's a wonder any of them made it home. Commando did it three times.

As we have seen, Commando shared the Dickin Medal stage on April 12, 1945, with Kenley Lass and four other Dickin recipients.

Commando with his capsule and his Dickin Medal. *PDSA Archives*

After the war, Commando was quite the celebrity, raising money for the PDSA and participating in exhibitions about wartime homing pigeons.

———

ROYAL BLUE

BLUE COCK—NURP.40.GVIS.453
DATE OF DICKIN MEDAL: MARCH 1945 (D.M. 16)

"For being the first pigeon in this war to deliver a message from a forced landed aircraft on the Continent while serving with the RAF in October 1940."

Royal Blue's claim to wartime fame was simple: he was the first pigeon to carry a message from a plane forced to land on the Continent.

He came by the name honestly; Royal Blue was blue in color, and he had been bred and trained by no less than His Majesty the King, George VI. The patrician pigeon's home was a loft at the royals' country home in Sandringham, Norfolk.

When the war began His Majesty donated his birds to the National Pigeon Service. Royal Blue was just a few months old when he went to work at RAF Bircham Newton, not far from his home in Norfolk.

Unlike Winkie and White Vision, who brought messages from crews forced to ditch their planes in the sea, Royal Blue was the first pigeon to carry a message from a plane forced to land on the Continent. On October 10, 1940, an RAF bomber went down in Holland, roughly 120 miles from base. Royal Blue was released at 7:00 that morning and arrived back at his loft at Sandringham at 11:30 with details about the downed plane and crew.

Royal Blue joined Commando and the others at the Dickin Medal presentation on April 12, 1945.

Royal Blue wears his medal proudly. April 12, 1945. *PDSA Archives*

Later that morning, two of the "King's Messengers" were released outside Dorland Hall by Wing Commander Lea Rayner. They carried a written request to King George VI at Sandringham asking for His Majesty's acceptance of the Dickin award to Royal Blue. A reply arrived at the Air Ministry, also by pigeon. In classic English understatement, it said that His Majesty, "was graciously pleased to accept the award."[24]

Wing Commander Lea Raynor releases one of the "King's messengers." April 12, 1945. *PDSA Archives/Imperial War Museum*

WILLIAM OF ORANGE

MEALY COCK—NPS.42.NS.15125
DATE OF DICKIN MEDAL: MAY 1945 (D.M. 21)

"For delivering a message from the Arnheim Airborne Operation in record time for any single pigeon, while serving with the APS in September 1944."

What do Robert Redford, Sean Connery, and heroic war pigeon William of Orange have in common?

Answer: All played roles in *A Bridge Too Far*.

Well, to be honest, Redford and Connery were in the all-star cast of the 1977 movie, the true story of the Allies' disastrous Operation Market Garden in 1944. William of Orange, however, took part in the actual operation.

Like Kenley Lass, William of Orange joined the National Pigeon Service at the tender age of five weeks. He was placed on loan for war service in 1942 by his owner, W. Proctor Smith of Bexton, Knutsford, and trained by the Army Pigeon Service. William seemed a natural for aerial messenger work; during training, he flew sixty-eight miles in fifty-eight minutes, deeply impressing his trainers.

William was handled by Lieutenant Joseph Hardy of the Signals Platoon, Headquarters Company, 1st Battalion, the Border Regiment. The unit was part of the 1st Airlanding Brigade, 1st Airborne Division, the only glider infantry formation assigned to the 1st Airborne Division.

William served with the airborne troops at Arnhem; he was one of two birds in Hardy's personal equipment.

Operation Market Garden (including the Battle of Arnhem) was fought in the Netherlands and Germany from September 17 to 25, 1944. The operation's ambitious goal was to ensure that Allied forces broke through enemy lines and bulled their way into Germany over the Rhine River. The plan was to surround Germany's industrial heart in the Ruhr Valley and thus help the Allies to victory over the Nazis by Christmas.

A GIGANTIC OPERATION

The massive Market Garden was divided into two sub-operations: "Market" involved airborne forces; "Garden," ground forces. In fact, Market ultimately became the largest airborne operation in history.[25] Forces from the First Allied Airborne Army comprised nearly 35,000 men from Britain's 1st Airborne Division, the Americans' 101st and 82nd Airborne Divisions, and the Polish 1st Independent Parachute Brigade. Initially more than 20,000 troops landed behind enemy lines by parachute; another 14,500 were dropped into the occupied territory of Eindhoven, Nijmegen, and Arnhem in the Netherlands. More troops would follow on days two and three.

The goal was to seize five bridges intact, including the one at Arnhem. Two days later, the airborne troops were to be relieved by British XXX Corps ground forces, who would continue the drive across the Rhine River into Germany.

On September 17, William of Orange landed with Lieutenant Hardy in a glider with the 1st Airlanding Brigade. Their first job: secure drop zones for the various units set to arrive from the 1st Airborne Division over the next two days.

The American 101st Airborne would drop near Eindhoven and secure two bridges northwest of there, at the villages of Son and Veghel. The 82nd would parachute to the northeast, at Nijmegen, to secure the roads and bridges at Grave and Nijmegen. The 1st Airborne, backed by the Polish parachute brigade, intended to land near Arnhem, then secure both sides of the bridge there.

That was the plan, anyway.

The operation began well, and bridges were captured. But the situation soon disintegrated, especially for the British 1st Airborne Division, which landed farther from their target than planned. Supply lines became over-stretched, a key bridge was demolished (causing delays in reinforcements), and enemy resistance proved stronger than expected.

Things went from bad to worse early on, when communications lines with the division and the outside world were lost.

Enter William of Orange.

On Day 3 of Market Garden the 1st Airborne and other units were halted by German forces and forced to fall back. When wireless communications failed, Lieutenant Hardy was ordered to send one of his pigeons back to Air Defence Headquarters, Great Britain with a pressing message (the exact details of which are not known). At 10:30 a.m. on September 19, William of Orange took flight, the message securely fastened to one leg. Again, William displayed impressive speed, covering the 260 miles to his loft in England in four hours and twenty-five minutes. In bad weather (was there ever good weather in Europe during the war?), he flew at an amazing speed of about a mile a minute.[26] One author asserted that his speed "has probably never been equaled in weather conditions which were anything but favourable."[27] The flight was unique in that 135 miles of it was over open sea. William's was also among the few messages that made it through Arnhem.

A fraction of the 1st Airborne Division was able to reach and capture the Arnhem Bridge, then hold one end of it. But the division was heavily outnumbered and outgunned. After four days they were overwhelmed, and on the night of September 25 and into the next morning the 1st Airborne withdrew back across the Rhine, in a nighttime evacuation dubbed Operation Berlin.

Lieutenant Hardy was ordered to set free his other pigeon; bird feed was scarce and this was a chance for it to survive. Besides, ravenous Allied soldiers were starting to eye the poor bird with something other than noble admiration. Hardy asked Major Cousens, acting commander of the 1st Border Regiment, what message he should write for the bird to carry. "Anything you like," Cousens replied. Hardy jotted down something at 7:30 a.m. on September 26, then released the bird at the top of the hour. The message read:

1. *Have to release bird owing to shortage food and water.*
2. *About eight tanks laying about in sub-unit areas, very untidy but not otherwise causing much trouble.*
3. *Now using as many German weapons as we have British. MG 34s most effective when aimed towards Germany.*
4. *Dutch people grand but Dutch tobacco rather stringy.*
5. *Great beard-growing competition on in our unit, but no time to check up on the winner.*
6. *Please repeat to Brig R. H. Bower and REAR HQ HSG.*

—*Lieut. J. Hardy*

The bird managed to find its way to Corps Headquarters, where it "became a nine-day wonder."[28]

HEAVY CASUALTIES

Of the roughly 10,600 men of the 1st Airborne Division and other units fighting north of the Rhine, 14 percent (1,485) were killed. More than 60 percent (6,414) were taken prisoner, a third of them wounded. Approximately 2,400 men (about 22 percent) were safely evacuated from Arnhem.

Of the 788 men in William of Orange's Border Regiment, 15 percent (121) died, 29 percent (235) were evacuated, and a whopping 54 percent (432) went missing and were presumed to be prisoners of war. In the nine days of heavy fighting, the 1st

Airborne had lost over three-quarters of its strength. The Battle of Arnhem shattered the division as a fighting force; it saw no further action in the war.

Alas, the goal of Market Garden—crossing the Rhine into Germany—would have to wait until late March 1945 and Operation Varsity.

Five British servicemen earned the Victoria Cross for their bravery and actions at Arnhem. William of Orange earned his "animal V.C." as well.

William received his Dickin on July 31, 1945, from Wing Commander Lea Rayner of the Air Ministry Pigeon Service. The ceremony at the RAF Exhibition at the Bentall's Department Store in Kingston-on-Thames also honored two other Dickin awardees—Scotch Lass and Ruhr Express.

RUHR EXPRESS
DARK CHECKER COCK—NPS.43.29018
DATE OF DICKIN MEDAL: MAY 1945 (D.M. 22)

"For carrying an important message from the Ruhr Pocket in excellent time, while serving with the RAF in April, 1945."

By April 1945 the war was winding down. The retreating German army faced increasing pressure to surrender, and the Nazis' last stand came in the Ruhr Valley. Sometimes called the "Ruhr Pocket," the region was the heart of Germany's steel and coal production, home to the headquarters of the Krupp steel and arms manufacturing empire.

This was a battle of encirclement in which Allied Forces, mostly American and British, closed in on 350,000 Germans, cutting off Nazi supplies and reinforcements.[29] The big squeeze began in late March, and by April 1, the Allied circle was complete. Allied troops launched their attack three days later, pushing the enemy into the "pocket."

During the first week of April paratroopers glided down from the sky into the pocket. Their assignment was to gather information on German troop movements and assess enemy morale. Ruhr Express, then known as NPS.43.29018, was in on the mission.

NPS.43.29018 was a beautiful dark checker cock with a lovely green and blue sheen around his neck. He was bred and trained at RAF Detling, in County Kent. He was coming off two years of "consistently good work" with the Air-Sea Rescue and emergency intercommunication service.

Ruhr Express. *PDSA Archives*

This brave bird was chosen to jump (in a small wooden cage) with paratroopers behind enemy lines in the Ruhr Valley, more than three hundred miles from his home loft.

Once they had finished gathering intel, the paratroopers attached written details to the bird and released him. Overnight the newly-renamed Ruhr Express made his way across land and sea, delivering what his service record called "very valuable information in the best time recorded in this operation. One of the best performances of its kind on record—13th April, 1945—Ruhr 'pocket.'"[30] The report also boasted that the information delivered by Ruhr Express "had a direct influence on the progress of the war at that critical time."[31]

By April 14, American forces had split the pocket in half while driving towards the city of Hagen in the bullseye of the encirclement. German troops, facing shrinking supplies of ammunition and rations, began surrendering. When it was over, German POWs numbered 317,000, twice what U.S. Army intelligence had estimated. On April 30, just two weeks after the surrender of the Ruhr, Hitler committed suicide. A week after that, Germany threw in the towel and the war in Europe was over.

WHAT THE DICKINS?

On July 31, Ruhr Express joined William of Orange and Scotch Lass as the honored guests at their joint Dickin Medals presentation ceremony at the RAF Exhibition at Bentall's department store.

Then in September, at a PDSA event benefiting the RAF Benevolent Fund and the Allied Forces Animals' War Memorial, Ruhr Express, his Dickin Medal, and a famously speedy hen named Per Ardua were all auctioned off. The bidding reached a record high of £420 for Ruhr Express, and a healthy £360 GBP for Per Ardua.[32] Both were purchased by a pigeon breeder whose birds had set many speed records. From these two new members of his flock, the breeder hoped to develop a new line of long-distance racers.

MARY OF EXETER

BLACK CHECKER HEN—NURP.40.WLE.249[33]
DATE OF DICKIN MEDAL: NOVEMBER 1945 (D.M. 32)

"For outstanding endurance on War Service in spite of wounds."

Mary of Exeter was one-of-a-kind. How many times must a pigeon be wounded or attacked before one cries, "Fowl!"? (Sorry. "Foul!") To say she had "outstanding endurance" is the essence of understatement.

Mary's heart, determination, and will to live should make humans envious. She belonged to a cobbler, Cecil "Charlie" Brewer of Exeter. Mary served with the National Pigeon Service for five years, from 1940 to war's end, crossing the English Channel to deliver messages from French operatives. She was wounded three times and survived two bombings, yet somehow always managed to get the job done.

Mary's first injury came on one of her runs from France. When she didn't return for several days, officials assumed that she had been killed. But four days later Mary touched down on her loft, covered in blood. She had likely been attacked by a German hawk or falcon stationed at Pas-de-Calais. The gruesome wound was a deep gash from the neck to her right breast.

Brewer lovingly stitched up Mary and nursed her back to health. But more drama lay ahead. Two months after she had recovered, Mary vanished again, this time for three weeks. When she finally reappeared one night at her loft, Brewer found three gunshot pellets in Mary's body and part of a wing shot off. The cobbler went to work, and although Mary eventually healed, the injured wing was evermore a tad shorter. But easygoing Mary didn't seem to mind, and her flight speed didn't seem to suffer, either.

Before her recovery was complete, Mary was nearly killed—twice—in twin bombing raids two nights apart during the Exeter blitz in late April 1942.[34] A 1,000-pound bomb exploded near Brewer's home and Mary's loft. Brewer and his beloved birds were evacuated to a temporary home. But on the second night of the blitz, another bomb killed nineteen of Mary's comrades. "Mary, who was in one of the baskets blown to pieces," one paper reported, "was found waiting for her owner at the old loft the next morning. She was suffering from shock."[35]

YOU CAN'T KEEP A GOOD BIRD DOWN

Mary was granted time off for R&R. Then, ten days after returning to duty, Mary left on a new mission—only to vanish once more. She was discovered near death in an Exeter field. Exhausted and rail-thin, Mary suffered from wounds stretching from the crown of her head down to her neck, plus smaller injuries across her body. It wasn't clear if the damage was from shrapnel or the result of another hawk attack.

Brewer took great and gentle care of his prized pigeon. He cleaned and stitched her up once more and fed and watered her by hand. Mary's neck wound was so extensive, and the muscles so damaged, that she couldn't hold her head up. So Brewer fashioned a small leather collar to support her head. When he removed the collar a month later, Mary was good to go.

For her many and varied wartime wounds, Mary received twenty-two stitches in her one-pound body. In a two-hundred-pound man, this would be the equivalent of *four thousand* stitches.

On November 12, 1945, Mary of Exeter was named a Dickin medalist on the same day as "Digging Dog" Peter, the beautiful Scottish collie. Then, on November 29, both received their medallions in a grand ceremony at a charity event in Park Lane, London. Four other winged warriors received their medals that day: Maquis, Broad Arrow, NPS.42.NS.2780, and NPS.42. NS.7524.

Mary of Exeter and her medal. *PDSA Archives*

Mary enjoyed a well-earned quiet life in retirement. She was laid to rest at the PDSA's Ilford Animal Cemetery in September 1950.

TOMMY

BLUE COCK—NURP.41.DHZ56
DATE OF AWARD: FEBRUARY 1946 (D.M. 34)

"*For delivering a valuable message from Holland to Lancashire under difficult conditions, while serving with NPS in July 1942.*"

Tommy, the pride of a blacksmith from Dalton-on-Furness, Lancashire, was already a champion racing pigeon with several wins under his wings when he was offered up to the National Pigeon Service. He was the only pigeon not in active service when he performed his derring-do deed.

Many birds donated to the NPS remained at home with their owners or breeders. They lived under normal conditions in their home lofts until receiving mission orders. In fact, these birds were still exercised and raced—including Tommy.

On July 15, 1942, Tommy was competing in a race from Christchurch, Hampshire to his home loft in Dalton-in-Furness. But he must have been blown wildly off course, because two days later he turned up, exhausted, in a street in Holland, hundreds of miles away.

Talk about a wrong turn.

Accounts vary, but many tell this version of the story. Tommy was found by a Dutch boy...who then gave him to a postman ...who in turn knew of a pigeon fancier who could properly care for the bird. The postman delivered Tommy to Dick Drijver in the village of Santpoort, northwest of Amsterdam.

But Drijver was more than an experienced pigeon handler; he was also active in the Dutch Resistance.[36]

When the Germans seized Holland in May 1940, they ordered all Dutch-owned homing pigeons destroyed. To prove compliance, owners were commanded to turn over their birds' metal identification leg rings—while still attached to the ampu-tated legs! So Drijver had to destroy his flock, but he quietly spared two, the black-and-white cock "Tijger" and a blue hen, "Amsterdammer." He outwitted the enemy by cutting off their rings and attaching them to disembodied legs of birds who had died earlier.

The Dutch Resistance fighter then offered Tijger and Amster-dammer to his Underground compatriots.

TOMMY AND DICK

When Drijver met Tommy, he recognized the bird as British by Tommy's red leg ring. He squirreled the pigeon away, so to speak, and nursed the wounded war bird back to health. After a few weeks, Tommy had healed and regained strength and was ready to fly.

Drijver was in the possession of military information he felt could benefit the British.[37] On August 18, he attached to Tommy's leg a coded message, one which included a request: when the message was safely received, it should be "acknowledged in code on the BBC Dutch radio service."[38]

When he was released into the air, Tommy initially seemed dazed and confused. He perched on a windmill to get his bearings, then took flight. The next day the pigeon "arrived home very distressed," Tommy's blacksmith owner William Brockbank told reporters.[39] Somewhere on the flight path he had been shot in the wing. Despite the wound, he had managed to make it home safely, having flown four hundred miles, mostly over water.

Mr W. Brockbank (R) holds Tommy as Major General J. W. Van Oorschot does the honors. February 26, 1945. *PDSA Archives*

Mr. Brockbank called police when he found a return message coded "in double-Dutch." Officers turned it over to military authorities. Tommy's coded cargo contained what the RAF called, in typical British understatement, "extremely helpful information."

Imagine the smile on Drijver's face when he tuned in to BBC Dutch radio and heard the secret message that Tommy had arrived home safely.

On February 26, 1946, Tommy received his Dickin Medal (no. 34) from Major-General J. W. van Oorschot of the Dutch Army's Intelligence Service.

Proudly looking on was twenty-six-year-old Dick Drijver, flown in by his government for the ceremony. After Drijver's reunion with Tommy, the head of the RAF Pigeon Service, Wing Commander W. D. Lea Rayner, presented Drijver with two pigeons, both RAF war veterans, in recognition of his service.

DD.43.Q.879

BLUE CHECKER COCK—DD.43.Q.879 (AUSTRALIAN ARMY SIGNAL CORPS)
DATE OF DICKIN MEDAL: FEBRUARY 1947 (D.M. 39)

"During an attack by Japanese on a US Marine patrol on Manus Island, pigeons were released to warn headquarters of an impending enemy counter-attack. Two were shot down but DD43 despite heavy fire directed at it reached HQ with the result that enemy concentrations were bombed and the patrol extricated."

It's sad that a war bird of DD.43.Q.879's stature, like numerous feathered Dickin medalists, never acquired a regular name. But the lack of one doesn't make him any less heroic.

A Dickin recipient from Down Under, DD43 was donated to the Australian Army Signal Corps by his owner, Mr. A. J. Flavell. The feathered Aussie aviator served with the 1st Australian Pigeon Section and was attached to U.S. forces on Manus Island, the largest of the Admiralty Islands in northern Papua New Guinea.

On April 5, 1944, however, DD43 happened to be attached to a U.S. Marine Corps patrol when he made a remarkable flight. U.S. forces on Manus were engaged in heavy fighting with the Japanese. A reconnaissance patrol unit of U.S. Marines was sent to the "strategic" village of Drabito, "to investigate the enemy's strength and disposition."[40]

Getting into the village was the easy part. The danger came when the patrol was returning with intelligence of a strong counterattack by about five hundred Japanese in Drabito. The Marines came under heavy assault from a small Japanese unit.

With their radio out of commission, the Americans had but one hope to get word of the Japanese assault to headquarters: pigeon power. They counted on three war birds the Marines had brought with them. Two were released, but both birds were quickly shot down by the enemy.

As the Japanese attack on the Marines heavily intensified, the Marines turned to their third and final bird—DD.43.Q.879. He truly was their last hope.

During a brief lull in the battle, they released DD43. He somehow managed to dodge heavy fire aimed specifically at him. Escaping harm, he covered thirty miles in forty-six minutes over difficult territory, safely reaching headquarters with the reconnaissance intel about Drabito, plus a request for air support.

Because of DD43's heroic efforts, the Allies bombed Drabito heavily, forcing a Japanese retreat and allowing the successful rescue of the Marines and the soldiers from the Australian Pigeon Section.

The Chief Signal Officer of American Forces in the region showed his appreciation in a memo to his Australian counter-part: "The cooperative action taken by your Office in furnishing pigeon communications for the United States troops during recent operations is greatly appreciated. Reports from the field indicate that the value of pigeons, as an auxiliary means of com-munication has been established on a firm basis of successful flights performed. The birds, equipment and personnel furnished from Australian sources have proved of the highest value in this respect."[41]

DD43 received his Dickin Medal on February 26, 1947 in a ceremony at a bomb-damaged London church, St. Dunstan-in-the-East. Actually, Lieutenant R. K. Roseblade of the Australian Corps of Signals accepted on DD43's behalf. An Australian col-league, DD.43.T.139, also received a Dickin that day. Colonel L. H. Carkeet James, the resident Governor of the Tower of Lon-don, read the citations.

Present at the ceremony lending his support was another heroic pigeon (and fellow Dickin medalist), the Duke of Normandy.

Afterward, both medals were sent on to Melbourne, where another ceremony awaited. The presentation at the Victoria Bar-racks was attended by DD43's owner, A. J. Flavell, and George Adams, a pigeon fancier who had donated T139 to the Austra-lian Army. Both men received Dickin medallion replicas.

In a letter dated August 19, 1947, Cyril Chambers, Minister of the Australian Army in Canberra, wrote to the Allied Forces Mascot Club informing them that the medals ceremony had taken place: "In view of the historic national significance attached to this high distinction, it was considered appropriate that the med-als be presented to the Australian War Museum, Canberra, for exhibition with the famous Pigeons in the form of a special dis-play dedicated to the part they played in the Pacific War...."

"It is felt that the medals will now be preserved as an everlasting reminder of the gallant part played by our feathered friends in assisting the cause of humanity."[42]

You can visit DD43 today. Stuffed and mounted, he remains on display at the Australian War Memorial in Canberra, alongside DD.43.T.139, their Dickin Medals, and certificates.

———

DUKE OF NORMANDY
BLUE CHECKER COCK—NURP.41.SBC.219
DATE OF DICKIN MEDAL: JANUARY 8, 1947 (D.M. 45)

"For being the first bird to arrive with a message from Paratroops of 21st Army Group behind enemy lines on D Day 6 June, 1944, while serving with APS."

The Duke, as he was known, was bred and owned by Gaston Noterman of London, and he was trained by the Army Pigeon Service. He was in the thick of the action on D-Day. The blue checker cock accompanied paratroopers from the 21st Army Group who landed behind German lines. The 21st included the British Second Army and the Canadian First Army and was commanded by Field Marshal Bernard Montgomery.[43]

More specifically, the Duke was attached to the 9th (Essex) Parachute Battalion of the 3rd Parachute Brigade of the 6th Airborne Division. For jumps his handler, Lieutenant Jimmy Loring, placed him in a cylindrical cardboard canister and then strapped the canister on under his jump smock.

On D-Day, the 9th (Essex) Parachute Battalion participated in the Battle of Merville Gun Battery. The conflict was part of the larger Operation Tonga, the airborne assault charged with securing the left flank of the Allied invasion during Operation Overlord, the Battle of Normandy.

The 9th was given a seemingly insurmountable challenge: destroy the Merville artillery battery. This was extra risky because the 9th was working at only a fraction of its usual manpower—150 paratroopers instead of the usual 600-plus. In addition, the men were dropped over a very wide area, diluting their potential effectiveness. The men also lacked any heavy weapons or equipment on the ground.

Those landing close to the battery banded together for the assault. Fighting was fierce and casualties heavy, but the paratroopers beat the odds and captured it.

THE DUKE GOES TO WORK

Cooped up in his cage for six days, the Duke was finally liberated at 6:00 in the morning on June 6. His assignment: report back details of the capture of the Merville battery.

One paratrooper with the 9th Parachute Battalion, Sergeant William Thomas Walker, offered his take on what the Duke likely endured:

He had been confined for six days. Then [came] the natural aircraft noise in the flight to Normandy; a possible battering on the landing from the jump, and the fearsome battle noises during the assault when suddenly, his prison cell is opened, a message is attached to his leg and he is thrown into the air.

He then flies away and circles the battery. . .

On his release the battery was being shelled by the enemy; this he negotiated, as also he did the bombing of the RAF and the shelling by the Royal Navy behind the invasion beaches. He also survived and crossed over these beaches safely. His troubles were still not over, the weather in the channel had worsened, but yet again this

brave little pigeon, overcame these elements and made
his way home to England the following day.[44]

Despite all these perils, including gale force winds and heavy
rain, the Duke landed on his loft at 8:50 in the morning on June
7. He was the first bird to return with news of the Normandy
paratroopers. The Duke clocked in at twenty-six-hours, fifty
minutes—the second fastest flight time of any bird working the
Normandy operation.

On January 8, 1947, the Duke was awarded his Dickin
Medal. He was joined by NURP.43.CC.2418, who was awarded
hers posthumously.

The Duke gets his Dickin. January 8, 1947. *PDSA Archives*

Pigeons continued to be used during the Korean War and into
the mid-1950s, yet at no time were they used more than during
World War II. Wing Commander W. D. Lea Rayner of the Air
Ministry perhaps expressed it best: "It remains a curious fact
that, whilst it seemed that each step of progress in telegraphy and
radio from 1900 onwards, must reduce or extinguish the value
of the racing Pigeon in War, the reverse has proved to be the case,

and Pigeons were used more extensively and for a greater variety of tasks in this War than any other in the World's long history of Wars."

Hopefully now, after all this, we will never think of a pigeon as a rat with wings.

WAR HORSES (AND MULES)

"(A) good battle horse must be able to take any kind of noise in his stride. Somehow, he can master most noises of battle more easily than he can band music. This is no discredit to cavalry musicians; it is simply a peculiarity of the horse."[1]

—RICHARD DEMPEWOLFF

11

Heroes With Hooves

"(They) served without a word of complaint or lack of courage. They transported artillery, ammunition, food, and medicine, and under enemy fire transported the wounded. Many of the CBI veterans are here today because a mule stopped a bullet or a piece of shrapnel meant for the GI. Mules fell in battle, mortally wounded, and we shed tears for them."[1]

—TECHNICAL SERGEANT EDWARD ROCK JR. (RETIRED)

When the Second World War erupted in 1939, the U.S. Army anticipated that, in the event America entered the war, as many as two hundred thousand horses would be needed for the fight. But as early as the following year mechanization of the Army already was well underway. By the time America formally entered the war on December 8, 1941—the day after Pearl Harbor—and sent actual forces into battle during Operation Torch on November 8, 1942, the need for horses had been dramatically reduced. This had to be a relief to war planners, as both horses and feed were expensive to ship overseas, and shipping space was in short supply.

The total number of equines purchased by the Quartermaster Corps in 1941 and '42 was 26,399. But from 1943 to war's end two years later, only a mere four additional horses were purchased for battle duty. During the whole span of the war, of the 26,403 horses procured, only forty-nine were shipped to

United States forces overseas. Horses who actually saw combat were either bought or captured in the different war theaters.

HORSES ON THE HOME FRONT

Most of the horses used by American forces in World War II stayed home, serving the Coast Guard to protect the home front by patrolling homeland beaches and coastline. Demand for them peaked in 1943, when the Coast Guard requested three thousand horses for beach patrols on the East, West, and Gulf coasts. Their responsibilities included keeping a vigilant watch for hostile submarines.

"Sailors on horseback." Original photo caption. *National Archives*

By 1944, that danger had passed and the horses were returned to Quartermaster Remount Depots.

BRAYING FOR WAR

A popular series of 1950s service comedies starred Donald O'Connor and a "talking" Army mule named Francis. While the idea of combat mules was played for laughs, the need for them, talking or not, was genuine.

As the Allies' demand for war horses decreased through the war, the need for pack mules actually rose. Pack animals were needed in the rugged terrain of North Africa, Sicily, Italy, and, most extensively, the China-Burma-India campaign. Mules proved especially vital in traversing mountainous and jungle regions where roads were few or nonexistent.

Army troops lead pack mules carrying supplies in Piaggio, Italy. March 17, 1945. *National Archives*

Mules were preferred over horses for several practical reasons. The mule was more sure-footed, less flighty, hardier, and, practically speaking, polished off less food. And mules were easier to care for. Finally, a mule could go where cargo trucks and jeeps could not, namely beyond the trails, where much of the fighting took place. These forlorn-looking animals carried ammunition, water, and food to where they were especially needed: dugouts, foxholes, and gun sites. Sometimes they helped transport heavier weapons to the troops. Also, to some extent mules could be counted on to help evacuate the wounded and dead.

Of the 30,500 wartime mules procured in the U.S., only about one of every four (or 7,800) was sent overseas to U.S. forces. Under the Lend-Lease Act of 1941, 3,500 mules were shipped to British forces.[2]

But the demand by the U.S. Army was much greater than the number of mules actually shipped. So mules were also procured in the various theaters as need arose. Again, as with horses, it was easier and more convenient to purchase or hire mules locally than to ship them from the United States.

A machine gun crew loads a pack mule with a machine gun and ammunition for the long trek up a mountain pass in Venafro, Italy. December 12, 1943. *National World War II Museum Archives*

For instance, in Italy the U.S. Army Quartermaster Remount Service procured nearly 15,000 mules, sharing 11,000 of them with Allied forces fighting there. Many mules were also captured from the enemy, and when the need arose civilians' pack mules were pressed into service, carrying supplies to troops in the mountains.[3]

ENGLISH EQUINES

For four years through 1944, the London Metropolitan Police employed 186 horses, for traffic control and to improve local morale during the Blitz and other bombings. Like war dogs, each horse was assigned an individual officer—a handler, if you will—who was expected to bond with his mount, riding and working with the horse throughout the animal's service life. The work was especially difficult when panic set in, as a horse's natural inclination is to run from chaos, not remain steady in it.

London's police horses also helped civilian equines pull milk carts and other wagons or trailers. This meant negotiating streets littered with broken glass, debris, nails, and jagged metal pieces. Besides crowd and traffic control, mounted policemen also worked to prevent looting, something that worsened over time. Incredibly, nearly half of looting arrests at new bombing sites were of volunteer Civil Defence rescuers who were supposed to be helping bombing victims.[4]

In 1947, three police horses from Yorkshire were awarded the PDSA Dickin Medal. Regal, Olga, and Upstart were selected to represent all their colleagues in a ceremony to honor the entire mounted police force, rather than single out any particular horse, incident, or event.

Regal, Olga, Upstart. *PDSA Archives*

REGAL

BAY GELDING—METROPOLITAN POLICE HORSE NO. 52
DATE OF DICKIN MEDAL: APRIL 11, 1947 (D.M. 50)

"*Was twice in burning stables caused by explosive incendiaries at Muswell Hill. Although receiving minor injuries, being covered by debris and close to the flames, this horse showed no signs of panic.*"

Regal had the distinction of earning a Dickin Medal not for what he did but for what he didn't do. The bay gelding with memorable markings—a white star on his forehead and white socks on his rear legs—did not panic in the heat of enemy attack. On two separate occasions, Regal kept his calm when his stable was hit by enemy bombs.

Regal stands regally. June 17, 1947. *PDSA Archives*

On April 19, 1941, a cluster of bombs struck part of the Muswell Hill Stables in North London, where Regal was billeted. Neither police nor stable hands were on duty, but Regal remained royally unflappable as flames crept dangerously close before he finally was rescued.

Three months later, another bomb exploded, this one sixty feet from his stable. This time, damage was considerable, as the roof also collapsed onto the war horse. Regal was hit with flying debris, suffering minor injuries. "In spite of this," Dorothea St. Hill Bourne wrote, "'he once again lived up to his name'—to quote his citation—'and was not unduly perturbed.'"[5]

Panicking on either occasion would have risked serious harm (or worse) to rescuers, the other horses in the stable, or both.

OLGA

BAY MARE—METROPOLITAN POLICE HORSE NO. 195
DATE OF DICKIN MEDAL: APRIL 11, 1947 (D.M. 51)

"On duty when a flying bomb demolished four houses in Tooting and a plate-glass window crashed immediately in front of her. Olga, after bolting for one hundred yards, returned to the scene of the incident and remained on duty with her rider, controlling traffic and assisting rescue organizations."

Twelve-year-old Olga sported a fashionably narrow white coronet just above her right front hoof.[6] The bay mare, stationed in the South London district of Tooting, worked crowd control and rescue operations.

On July 3, 1944, Olga's usual rider was on other duties. So she and a temporary partner, Police Constable J. E. Thwaites, were patrolling the streets near the rail line at Besley Street SW16. Without warning, the distinctive scream of a V-1 flying bomb pierced the air. The missile exploded about two hundred and fifty feet in front of Olga and Thwaites, killing four people, destroying as many houses, and scattering debris everywhere. When a plate glass window shattered at Olga's feet, the startled horse bolted three hundred feet before Thwaites could get her under control.

But then Thwaites, astride Olga, was the first officer to arrive at the blast site. Olga performed her duties flawlessly, assisting with search-and-rescue, helping control traffic, and keeping onlookers away.

Olga. June 17, 1947. *PDSA Archives*

Fittingly, three years later Olga helped unveil an emergency vehicle designed to treat animal patients in devastating situations such as wartime. On December 17, 1947, Olga and fellow Dickin medalist Ricky, the tousle-haired terrier mine-detection dog, were at Westminster Abbey for the "blessing ceremony" of the PDSA's very first motorized dispensary van. The Reverend Alan Camp-bell Don, the Dean of Westminster, conducted the ceremony. The van, essentially a "hospital on wheels," was presented "as a war memorial in gratitude and memory to the animals and birds which died on active service."[7]

Olga and Ricky supporting the cause. December 17, 1947. *PDSA Archives*

UPSTART
CHESTNUT GELDING—METROPOLITAN POLICE HORSE NO. 78
DATE OF DICKIN MEDAL: APRIL 11, 1947 (D.M. 49)

"While on patrol duty in Bethnal Green a flying bomb exploded within seventy-five yards, showering both horse and rider with broken glass and debris. Upstart was completely unperturbed and remained quietly on duty with his rider controlling traffic, etc., until the incident had been dealt with."

Like Regal, Upstart was blessed with the good sense to keep calm amidst the chaos of bombs and battle. He was a handsome chestnut gelding with a face that boasted a small star, a narrow center stripe ending in a snip—a white marking between the nostrils—and four white socks.

At first Upstart was stationed near anti-aircraft batteries at Hyde Park, but after he survived a bombing raid that damaged his stables, he was moved to new stables in the East End, London. And once again he displayed a Steve McQueen-style cool when another bomb damaged those digs.

On August 22, 1944, Upstart and his handler, District Inspector J. Morley, were patrolling the streets in Bethnal Green when a bomb exploded seventy-five yards in front of them. Glass and shrapnel rained down, but remarkably, neither was hurt. Morley and Upstart instantly went to work, segueing into traffic and crowd control. Their prompt control of the situation allowed arriving rescuers and ambulances easy access to casualties. Without the heroic efforts of Upstart (and, yes, Morley too), more lives would surely have been lost.

Olga (R) and Upstart. June 17, 1947. *PDSA Archives*

GETTING THEIR DUE

Not until 1947 did the PDSA salute heroic equines. "Horses of the Mounted Branch had been in the front line during the whole of the bombing of London," the PDSA declared that year in a statement at the Chelsea (Dog) Show, "and how gallantly they had stood up to the danger and the terror of strange sounds, guns, sirens and bombs, as well as the terror of fire."[8]

Regal, Olga, and Upstart were presented their medals at a June 17, 1947 ceremony held at the Cockpit at Regent's Park, London. Major General Sir John Marriott pinned the medals to their harnesses, assisted by Metropolitan Police Commissioner Sir Harold Scott.

For nearly seventy years, these three remained the only horses awarded the Dickin Medal. Then in 2014, an honorary Dickin Medal was bestowed upon Warrior, a World War I horse that served on the front lines for four years. Dubbed "the horse the Germans couldn't kill" because of his incredible tenacity and bravery, Warrior represents all of the animals who served valiantly in World War I.

Two years later, America's legendary war horse Sergeant Reckless was posthumously honored with a Dickin for her truly remarkable Korean War service with the United States Marine Corps.

AND A WAR . . .
CAT?

―――――

*"Cats are creatures of routine and will not allow outside events
to interfere with their own personal arrangements if they can help it."*[1]

—DOROTHEA ST. HILL BOURNE, Allied Forces Mascot Club

12

The One and Only—Simon

"Simon was a wonderfully soothing friend who took everyone's mind off our predicament."[1]

—LIEUTENANT COMMANDER STEWART HETT, "Cat Officer"

"ABLE SEAMAN" SIMON

TOMCAT

DATE OF DICKIN MEDAL: AUGUST 5, 1949 (D.M. 54)

"Served on HMS Amethyst during the Yangtze Incident, disposing of many rats, though wounded by shell blast. Throughout the incident his behaviour was of the highest order, although the blast was capable of making a hole over a foot in diameter in a steel plate."

What? There are war *cats*? Really?

Yes, really. In fact, cats have been clawing their way into wartime history for a long time. Take for example Crimean Tom, sometimes called Sevastopol Tom. In a Russian port town in 1854, he saved invading French and British troops from starvation by leading them to a secret cache of food.

Then there was Tiddles, who served several Royal Navy ships in World War II, along the way logging more than thirty thousand miles.[2]

During the London blitz in 1940, Faith the Church Cat seemed almost psychic in how she saved her newborn kitten from a German air raid that destroyed their home, St. Augustine's Church.[3]

And as recently as 2004 in Iraq, Private First Class Hammer ingratiated himself to a U.S. Army unit and eradicated the mice that were contaminating their food supplies.[4]

But none of those cats could boast of having a Dickin Medal. This chapter is about the one cat—as of 2018, still the only cat— who indeed earned the prestigious PDSA prize.

His name was simple: Simon.

Like Punch and Judy (see appendix), Simon showed his stuff not on the battlefield but after the war—aboard a British Royal Navy frigate on China's Yangtze River.

PICKED UP ON A PIER

Simon was discovered in March 1948 poking around the docks of Stonecutters Island in Hong Kong. Thought to be about a year old, the scrawny black and white tomcat was scrounging for food when a British sailor spotted him. Seventeen-year-old Ordinary Seaman George Hickinbottom had been killing time while his ship, the HMS *Amethyst*, was docked and loading supplies.[5]

Hickinbottom took a liking to Simon and decided a cat was just what the ship needed to get rid of its rats. The rodent infestation posed risks to onboard foodstuffs—and to the crew's overall health. So George tucked Simon inside his jacket, smuggled him aboard, and hid the tomcat in his cabin.

Simon wasn't the only four-legged sailor on board. There also was Peggy, a small, four-year-old terrier mix who belonged to Petty Officer George Griffiths. While moody, Simon was friendly to Peggy—when he wasn't ignoring her. But with both aboard, morale seemed to improve on the *Amethyst*.[6]

THE CAPTAIN'S CAT

Hickinbottom was "captain of the fo'c'sle," or forecastle, the forward part of a ship where living quarters are located. His job was to ensure "fo'c'sle" conditions stayed shipshape; not coincidentally, Hickinbottom's quarters were near those of the captain. And it wasn't long before Simon, the newest "fo'c'sle" resident, made himself known to everyone, including the Captain, Lieutenant Commander Ian Griffiths.

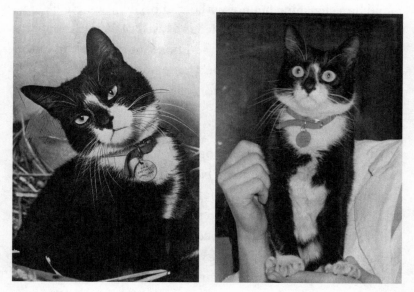

Simon. *PDSA Archives, Getty*

Luckily for Simon and the crew, Griffiths was a cat lover. He owned several back home and had even kept one with him on a previous command. Simon took a real liking to the captain and spent many nights in his cabin, curled up inside the lieutenant commander's upturned white, gold-braided cap. Simon also showed his affection and gratitude by presenting dead "trophies" to Griffiths, thoughtfully placing the gifts at the captain's feet or, sometimes, atop his bunk.

Simon did the same for other friends as well, although the bond with Griffiths was special. All the captain had to do was whistle and Simon came running, no matter where he was or what he was up to. During evening rounds, Simon stayed right at the captain's heels.

In no time, the ship's cat became the "captain's cat."

"Blackie," as some called him, was spoiled by shipmates, who found him charming but not without idiosyncrasies. He liked to fish ice cubes out of a jug of water and loved sitting on the charts while a course was being set. In addition, Simon's table manners were questionable; sometimes he'd jump onto, then cross the laps of the captain's dinner guests, foraging for tidbits.

CHANGE OF MANAGEMENT

In December 1948, Lieutenant Commander Griffiths was reassigned to a new command. He felt that to take the *Amethyst* mascot with him would be unfair to both Simon and the men. So Griffiths and the tomcat said their goodbyes, and Simon pivoted to meet the Captain's successor, Lieutenant Commander Bernard Skinner. Like his predecessor, Skinner was a cat lover. He happily adopted Simon, confirming all the privileges the feline had enjoyed with Griffiths.

But it took some time for Simon to get used to his new boss and cabin mate and settle back into a routine. According to biographer Vera Cooper, Simon took a different attitude toward the new captain: "[Simon] *never again answered to a whistle.* He came when he was ready, and not before. Because he felt in his heart that it would be disloyal to his first master, *he never again followed at the heels of any man,* but walked sedately alone."[7]

Simon walks the gangplank. *Courtesy of Purr 'N Fur*

ATTACK ON THE *AMETHYST*

In April 1949, the *Amethyst* was ordered to sail up the Yangtze River from Shanghai to Nanking, then relieve the HMS *Consort* of her duties. China was in the midst of a bloody civil war between the communist insurgents of Mao Tse Tung's People's Liberation Army (PLA) and the ruling nationalist (or Kuomintang) Party of Chiang Kai-shek, and the *Consort* was long overdue for relief, having guarded the British Embassy for some time in case Mao's army took the city and forced an embassy evacuation.

A cease-fire agreement between the two sides was due to expire at midnight on April 21, with the communists demanding that the nationalists agree to their terms or else fighting would resume. Mao's PLA held the Yangtze's north side and the nationalists controlled the south bank.

Because Britain had not taken a side in the Chinese conflict, no trouble was expected. British officials believed the *Amethyst* could reach Nanking by April 20, twenty-four hours before the cease-fire ended. But because all this was taking place in a war zone, anything could happen.

And it did.

On Tuesday morning, April 19, the *Amethyst* set out from Shanghai for Nanking, about 185 miles away, traveling at a leisurely speed of 11 knots. She displayed the White Ensign and Union Jack flags; the latter was also painted on her hull. Late in the afternoon the *Amethyst* anchored in Kiangyin, about one hundred miles upstream from the city. There she awaited daylight before continuing. Not only was night-time traffic on the river forbidden; the river contained many hazards at night.

At 5:15 the following morning the ship had resumed the trip upstream. About three hours into the journey, at 8:31 in the morning, the communists began shelling the *Amethyst*. But since none of the ordnance landed near the British ship, her crew assumed the shelling was part of regular bombardment of the nationalists. When Skinner sped up, the firing stopped. For a time.

The respite was brief. About an hour later, at around 9:30 a.m., the *Amethyst* was about sixty miles from Nanking when communist fire—heavier this time—resumed from the north shore. Explosions rocked the ship, with the bridge, wheelhouse, and low power room hit first. Captain Skinner was gravely wounded and died later that morning. Other officers on the bridge were severely injured. Skinner's second-in-command, First Lieutenant Geoffrey L. Weston, assumed command even though he, too, was seriously wounded in the chest. Weston sent an SOS just before shells struck the sick bay, the port engine room, and then the generator: "Under heavy fire. Am aground in approx. position 31.10' North 119.50' East. Large number of casualties."[8]

With casualties mounting, confusion on the bridge, and a damaged steering mechanism, the HMS *Amethyst* had run aground on Rose Island, known today as Leigong Dao.

In all, the ship sustained more than fifty hits. Nineteen men, including Captain Skinner, were killed in the April 20 attack; twenty-seven more were wounded.[9]

Sometime between 10:00 and 10:30 that morning, evacuation efforts began. About sixty *Amethyst* crew members, including some of the wounded, reached shore either by swimming or by riding in flat-bottomed Chinese canoes called sampans. They managed to escape despite the continuous intense shelling and machine gun fire all around them. Further evacuations were stopped because of the firing, which finally ended around eleven that morning.

When the HMS *Consort* arrived from Nanking around 3:00 that afternoon to assist her sister ship, she was immediately fired upon. The *Consort* tried several times to tow the *Amethyst* away but came under renewed attack with each attempt. The *Consort* was able to silence a lot of the enemy by returning fire, but by day's end ten sailors were dead, four more were seriously wounded, and the *Consort* was forced to retreat.

Around 2:00 in the morning of April 21, the *Amethyst* had sufficiently lightened its load and was re-floated. She moved upriver, dropping anchor two miles above Rose Island and away from the main communist battery. But she couldn't go farther, as much of her hull had been blown to bits. The men set about making repairs.

Later that morning two more British ships, the frigate HMS *Black Swan* and a heavy cruiser, HMS *London*, hurried to the scene to rescue the *Amethyst*. But they too drew heavy fire and suffered casualties. Thirteen crew members of the *London* were killed and another fifteen wounded; seven *Black Swan* sailors were wounded. The would-be rescuers retreated to Shanghai.

HOUSE CALL

The crew of the stranded *Amethyst* desperately needed medical help, but the ship's doctor had been killed in the attack. In the late afternoon of April 21, a British Sunderland "flying boat" landed on the river under fire to deliver a replacement medical officer. Flight Lieutenant Michael Fearnley brought with him medical supplies, food, and water.

The *Amethyst* took shelter in a creek a little way upstream. On the night of April 21 and into the early morning hours, the ship crept about ten miles upstream and dropped anchor. More of the wounded were evacuated, including Weston, who turned over command of the *Amethyst* to Lieutenant Commander John Kerans, the assistant naval attaché in Nanking.

Negotiations with the communists soon began for the release of the stricken, cornered *Amethyst* and its crew.

THE SEARCH FOR SIMON

Where was Simon during the chaos and carnage? No one knows for sure, but when the shelling began, he likely was in the captain's cabin curled up in his cap. A Chinese shell blasted a huge hole in the nearby bulkhead, and four shards of shrapnel hit the defenseless cat in the back and legs as he bolted or was thrown by the force of the explosion. Simon's face was also burned, and his whiskers and eyebrows singed. The stunned cat apparently crawled into a corner, out of the way, and passed out.

Simon was missing for several days before he staggered on deck and was discovered by Petty Officer George Griffiths, who gingerly picked the cat up and took him to sick bay.

The *Amethyst* mascot was in very bad shape—severely weak, dehydrated, and in pain from his injuries. Medical officer Fearnley went to work. He removed the shrapnel in four places and stitched Simon up before tending to his burned face. There was concern that the cat's hearing might have been damaged by being so close to the deafening blast. Besides all that, Simon's heart was also weak. Fearnley gave Simon only a fair chance of survival at best.

From the start, the ship's new commander, Lieutenant Commander Kerans, made it clear that he didn't like cats and certainly wouldn't share his cabin with one. So Petty Officer Griffiths made a makeshift bed for Simon in his own room. As days passed and negotiations with the Chinese dragged on, Simon grew stronger.

Feline curiosity finally got the better of him. As Simon's strength gradually returned, he began to explore the boat in search of his old friend Captain Skinner. When he couldn't find him, Simon curled up in what he thought was his favorite place, Skinner's cap. Big mistake. It wasn't Skinner's familiar cap; this one belonged to cat-averse Captain Kerans, who was not amused at having Simon in his quarters, much less curled up in a key part of his uniform. A time would come when Simon would win Kerans over. This, however, was not that time.

Out, out went the darned cat, which surprised the living daylights out of Simon.

PURRING PSYCHOLOGIST

Dr. Fearnley suggested that Simon hang out in sick bay to help shore up morale among the remaining young crewmen, many traumatized by the attack, the loss of their crewmates, and the grief of having to witness twenty burials at sea. Because Simon had also endured the horrific attack and its aftermath, he was considered one of them.

In short, he became a *therapy cat*.

The purring psychologist adopted a simple routine: he'd lie on the sailors' bunks or climb onto their chests and "contentedly kneed his paws and purr. His injuries obviously helped the boys to relate to him and they started to welcome his visits, which helped them to get over their own traumas."[10] Simon appeared to feel better too.

ON RAT PATROL

Before long, Simon returned to his onboard specialty: rat removal. During the cat's convalescence, stowaway vermin had multiplied so dramatically that they seriously threatened the ship's already scarce food supplies. Their presence had become much more noticeable once the shelling displaced many from their usual hiding places. Simon began catching at least a rat a day—another boost to crew morale.

One rat in particular made himself a big nuisance. He was huge, smart, and possessed obvious leadership skills. In fact, he commanded an army of smaller rats who followed him around and helped raid the ship's food supplies.

Naturally, the crew named him Mao Tse Tung, after the charismatic leader of the Chinese communist insurgents. During Simon's recuperation, the men had tried setting traps for Mao, without success. In fact, the wily rat eluded all efforts to neutralize him.

When at last Simon was again strong enough, the crew called in their leading rat catcher. When the two met mano-a-mano (cata-a-rata?), it was simply no contest.

For vanquishing Mini-Mao, the triumphant tomcat was rewarded with a promotion to "Able Seaman" Simon—only because "Able Seacat" was a rank not yet recognized by the Royal Navy. (Sadly, it remains unrecognized today.)

I'M GONNA MAKE YOU LOVE ME

Negotiations with the Chinese seemed to be taking forever; no one knew how long the men of the *Amethyst* would remain in limbo. Simon decided the time was right to win over Captain Kerans, and he took matters into his own paws. He swaggered up to Kerans and dropped a dead rat at his feet. The astonished captain didn't quite know what to make of the offering. Griffiths told him it was a gift, that many household cats and dogs did the same thing.

The gesture softened Kerans, who began stroking Simon in thanks. The captain didn't want to hurt the cat's feelings, so he waited until Simon wasn't looking before tossing the dead rat overboard.

Sometime later, Kerans fell ill with a virus and was ordered to bed. Simon, being the good therapy cat, came by for a visit and jumped up onto the captain's bunk. Again, Simon worked his magic by kneading his paws and purring.

This time he wasn't kicked out. From that moment on, the HMS *Amethyst* was Simon's oyster, and once again he had the run of the ship.

MAKING A RUN FOR IT

Conditions aboard the *Amethyst* began to seriously deteriorate. Because of dwindling food and water supplies, rations were cut in half. The crew began to suffer from dehydration and hunger, with the powerful heat and humidity also taking a toll. Simon, meanwhile, continued morale boosting duties by visiting patients in sick bay and showing off his latest trophies. But morale was being chipped away by another enemy: boredom.

Something had to be done—and soon.

It was nearly three months since the original attack. Negotiations were deadlocked, at least in part on account of the communists' demand that the *Amethyst's* men admit they had wrongly invaded national Chinese waters and fired first on Mao's army.

Neither contention was true, of course, and the British would never meet such demands. Between the standoff in talks and the ship's dangerously low fuel supplies, Captain Kerans was increasingly fearful. And his solution was old-fashioned and simple: make a run for it.

On the moonless night of July 30, with the merchant vessel *Kiang Ling Liberation* passing the HMS *Amethyst* and heading down river around 10:00, Kerans seized the moment and dared to attempt a 104-mile run to the open sea under cover of darkness.

The enemy's response from shore was less aggressive than expected; luck certainly seemed to be with the crew of the *Amethyst* that hot summer night. Almost five hours later, the ship rendezvoused with the HMS *Concord* part way up the Huangpu River south of Wusong and was escorted the rest of the way. Kerans sent a message: "Have rejoined the fleet south of Woo Sung. No damage or casualties. God save the King."[11]

After being held hostage for 101 days, the crew's ordeal was over, and the *Amethyst* was cruising to Hong Kong.

SALUTING SIMON

News traveled fast as the *Amethyst* made its way to Hong Kong. Word of the ship's exploits spread, and the entire crew were hailed as heroes—including Simon. The tomcat became an international celebrity overnight, thanks to heavy coverage by the press and movie newsreels. An army of cameras and reporters recorded the ship's arrival in Hong Kong Harbor, and Simon posed for pictures with his shipmates during the celebration.

Simon with his shipmates. *PDSA Archives*

Captain Kerans, now Simon's biggest supporter, replied to a request from the PDSA asking for confirmation of Simon's heroic deeds. His testimonial letter reads, in part:

> For many days Simon felt very sorry for himself, nor could he be located. His whiskers, even now, show signs of the explosion.
>
> Rats, which began to breed rapidly in the damaged portions of the ship, presented a real menace to the health of the ship's company, but Simon nobly rose to the occasion and after two months the rats were much diminished.
>
> Throughout the incident Simon's behaviour was of the highest order. One would not have expected a small cat to survive the blast from an explosion capable of making a hole over a foot in diameter in a steel plate.

Yet after a few days Simon was as friendly as ever. His presence on the ship, together with Peggy, the dog, was a decided factor in maintaining the high level of morale of the ship's company.[12]

Kerans's letter closed the Dickin deal for the topside tomcat. On August 5, the Associated Press broke the news of the PDSA's decision. One newspaper headline over the AP story told the tale: "Amethyst's Cat Gets Dickin Medal for Catching Rats."[13] The PDSA's decision had been unanimous.

Not only was Simon the only feline ever to receive a Dickin, he was also the *only Royal Navy animal* to earn the Dickin distinction.

And the next day, on August 6, 1949, a special presentation of a Campaign Ribbon for service on the *Amethyst* was staged at the British Navy's China Fleet Club in Hong Kong. The ceremony, complete with honor guard, saluted Able Seaman Simon and Guardsman Peggy the terrier.

Once Peggy was given her *Amethyst* Campaign Ribbon, it was Simon's turn.

A young seaman held the war cat as Griffiths read Simon's citation:

> Able Seaman Simon, for distinguished and meritorious service to HMS *Amethyst*, you are hereby awarded the *Amethyst* Campaign Ribbon.
>
> Be it known that on 26 April 1949, though recovering from wounds, when HMS *Amethyst* was standing by off Rose Bay, you did single-handedly and unarmed stalk down and destroy Mao Tse Tung, a rat guilty of raiding food supplies which were critically short.

Be it further known that from 22 April to 1 August
you did rid HMS *Amethyst* of pestilence and vermin
with unrelenting faithfulness.[14]

All of this attention inspired fan mail for Simon—more than
two hundred pieces a day—along with gift cans of food and cat
toys. Lieutenant Stewart Hett, declared "cat officer," was placed on
a unique duty assignment: handling all of Simon's mail and gifts.

THE LAST HURRAH

On November 11, 1949, Simon arrived home in England to
another media frenzy, including *Life* magazine. He was placed
in routine quarantine for six months, like other returning war
animals. Shipmates visited their celebrated cat, among them the
converted cat lover Lieutenant Commander John Kerans, plus
his first master, former petty officer—now a lieutenant commander—George Griffiths. When visitors weren't around,
Simon's kennel maid in quarantine, Joyce Ballack, spent a lot of
time entertaining her clawed charge and ensuring his needs were
met. And Kerans applied to permanently adopt Simon once the
cat left quarantine.

The formal Dickin Medal presentation was set for December
11. Maria Dickin herself, along with the Lord Mayor of London,
planned to attend. It was shaping up to be a grand and glorious
affair.

But it was not meant to be. Two weeks before the presentation, Simon fell ill with a virus. He received treatment, including
injections for a high fever and acute enteritis. But his war wounds
had seriously weakened Simon's heart.

Joyce Ballack stayed with him the entire night of November
27.

Joyce Ballack plays with Simon with a toy mouse. November 17, 1949. *PDSA Archives*

Simon passed away the next day, having crammed a lot of living into his two short years. As one tribute put it, "the spirit of Simon slipped quietly away to sea." Some said he died of a broken heart, that he missed his life aboard ship and the men he loved so much.[15]

Captain Kerans and the crew were heartbroken. Cards and letters arrived at the quarantine shelter "by the truckload." On its obituary page, *Time* magazine featured Simon's picture beneath a simple headline: "In Honored Memory."[16]

"Able Seacat" Simon was buried at Ilford Animal Cemetery. He was placed in a custom casket draped with the Union Jack and received full naval honors at the funeral. His tombstone reads:

> *In memory of "Simon"*
> *Served in H.M.S. Amethyst*
> *May 1948–November 1949*
> *Awarded Dickin Medal August 1949*
> *Died 28th November 1949.*

Throughout the Yangtze Incident
His behaviour was of the highest order

On April 13, 1950, a plaque of Simon by artist Elizabeth Muntz was unveiled at the Plymouth PDSA Hospital. Pulling the tarp to unveil the plaque was Lieutenant Geoffrey Weston, the officer who had assumed command of the *Amethyst* after Captain Skinner was killed and who was interim captain until Lieutenant Commander John Kerans arrived.

Lieutenant Geoffrey Weston holds Simon's Dickin Medal at the plaque ceremony at Plymouth PDSA Hospital. April 13, 1950. *PDSA Archives*

Simon is remembered as the most famous cat in British military history.

Epilogue

2018 marked the seventy-fifth anniversary of the PDSA's Dickin Medal, universally accepted as the most prestigious award for animals.

To start the celebratory year off right, on January 15 a small crowd gathered at the Churchill War Rooms in London. This author was honored to witness, in person, the long-delayed, posthumous Dickin Medal presentation for Chips, America's first canine hero of World War II.

The date and location were neither random nor coincidental. Exactly seventy-five years earlier to the day, Chips had guarded the leaders of the free world, President Roosevelt and Prime Minister Churchill, at the Casablanca Conference war summit. Guests at the 2018 event included Randolph Churchill, Sir Winston's great-grandson.

But of everyone gathered there that day, the occasion may have meant the most to "little" Johnny Wren, a toddler when his family lent Chips to the war effort in the spring of 1942.

Three quarters of a century later, Wren, fit and energetic well into his seventies, flew in from New York to accept the honor on behalf of his family's beloved collie-German-shepherd-husky mix.

Chips became the seventieth recipient (and the twentieth dog from the World War II era) to receive the bronze medallion.

John Wren and Ayron, the military working dog who stood in for Chips (L). U.S. Lieutenant Colonel Alan Throop, who accepted Chips's medal on behalf of the U.S. Army; Staff Sergeant Jeremy Mayerhoffer, Ayron's handler; Ayron; Jan McLoughlin, Director General/PDSA; author Robin Hutton, who nominated Chips for the Dickin; and Chips's owner, John Wren (R, from L to R). January 15, 2018. *PDSA Archives*

Chips's medal and citation will be displayed, quite appropriately, at the National World War II Museum in New Orleans—a fitting place to celebrate such an accomplished World War II hero.

Over the years several dogs in this book have been memorialized: Caesar, captured by artist and sculptor Jocelyn Russell, proudly stands guard at the Timothy T. Day Overlook at the National Museum of the Marine Corps in Triangle, Virginia. By his presence there, Caesar represents all military dogs that have served so valiantly in war.

Caesar as sentry. *(National Museum of the Marine Corps)*

Smoky, recipient of the PDSA Certificate for Animal Bravery or Devotion, has eight—yes, *eight!*—monuments around the world, with two more in the works. Smoky is also credited with renewed interest in the Yorkshire terrier breed.[1]

The legacy of Sinbad also continues to the present day. Sinbad's ship, the USCGC *Campbell* (WPG-32), was used as a training target and summarily sunk in November 1984 after forty-six years of loyal service. Her replacement, also christened the USCGC *Campbell* (WMEC-909), remains active today. In the latter-day *Campbell*'s mess hall stands a statue of Sinbad; even today the men of the *Campbell* believe that as long as Sinbad is aboard the ship, nothing bad will befall her.

In fact, the *Campbell*'s motto is: "Sinbad lives!"

———

I'm happy to announce that a national War Animals Museum is at last in the works. Plans call for the museum to feature animal heroes who, despite having had no say-so over their service, bravely and tirelessly assisted America's Armed Forces. The monument will keep alive their stories of valor and sacrifice—plus those of the brave men and women who served beside them—for generations to come. More information on the museum is available online at WarAnimals.com.

In preparing this book, it has been an honor, privilege, and inspiration to learn about these courageous creatures. Because of them, I learned more about the history of World War II than I thought was possible. Along the way, I also acquired a profound appreciation, respect, and admiration for all the brave men and women who served in that war for the Allies, and for the people of Great Britain, who survived the Blitz.

I hope you feel the same.

With Thanks
and Gratitude

There are so many to thank for helping me along on this remarkable journey.

First, I thank the Lord up above, followed closely by my family, especially sisters Layne Wilson and Amy Hall and my brother, Michael Holzbeierlein. They had my back throughout the project's wonderful, crazy journey. (Which includes putting up with the bad behaviors of a stressed-out writer) I'm especially indebted to Layne, who helped suggest the title. You are an "unsung" hero to me, Sisty!

Next, a huge thank you to my publisher, Regnery History, for backing this book. In particular, thank you, Alex Novak, for suggesting the subject in the first place and for believing in me as a writer. I'm so happy you discovered these stories while I was in England (to pick up the Dickin Medal for Sgt. Reckless) and believed they would make a cool book.

Thank you, Marjory Ross, for again taking a chance on me, and Elizabeth Kantor, for your wonderful heart and spirit in making the manuscript's final edit.

Speaking of editors, my deepest and most heartfelt thanks go to my fabulous editor, Barry M. Grey. Barry, you have a way of taking the story I'm trying to tell and just making it...*better*. In fact, you make it sing! I don't know how you do it, pal, but I especially love your wonderful alliteration, which helps make the book such a fun read.

You always make me look so good.

To John and Sharon Wren, who not only opened up their archives on Chips, but made the trip to London with me for Chips' well-deserved Dickin Medal. What a blast! To Marc Wortman for trusting me with his dad's mementos and personal photos of Jack. And a special heartfelt thanks to William Wynne for our friendship over the years and sharing Smoky's wonderful story and pictures with me. You're the best, Bill!

Special thanks go to my friends at the People's Dispensary for Sick Animals, who enthusiastically supported this book and (quite significantly) opened their rich archives to me. I'm especially grateful to Director General Jan McLoughlin for writing such a beautiful introduction; to Gill Hubbard for tirelessly teaming with Karen Storms and me as we combed the archives; to Karen Hailes for your Dickin Medal work; and to Amy Dickin (whose surname is a fun coincidence, as she's no relation to PDSA founder Maria Dickin), for your great PR and wonderful friendship.

Finally, my greatest love, appreciation, and thanks go out to Karen Storms, my roommate at Ithaca College and bestie for more than forty years. Karen, thank you for visiting England with me three times in eighteen months—to pick up the Dickin Medal for Sgt. Reckless, to conduct research for this book, and to witness with me the Dickin Medal ceremony for Chips. I think it is your hard work in the archives that I appreciate the most. I'd probably still be in there, if not for your steadfast determination, dedication, and especially your amazing organizational skills. Girlfriend, we've been on a wonderful ride together all these years. I'm so blessed to have you in my corner.

To all the friends who have offered their love and support over the years, please know how much I appreciate having you in my life. I'm a better person because of you. I hope you enjoyed reading the book as much as I enjoyed researching and writing it.

But I really don't think that's possible.

Appendix

WE ALSO SERVED—AND FLEW!

These courageous animals were also awarded the Dickin Medal for their service in World War II.

WAR BIRDS

TYKE

Red Checker Cock—M.E.P.S. 43/1263 (Middle East Pigeon Service)
Date of Dickin Medal: December 2, 1943 (D.M. 2)

"For delivering a message under exceptionally difficult conditions and so contributing to the rescue of an Air Crew, while serving with the RAF in the Mediterranean in June, 1943."

A red checker cock of British and South African parentage, Tyke flew for the Middle East Pigeon Service (MEPS), a small organization in the desert outside the Egyptian capital.

BEACHCOMBER

NPS.41.NS.4230

Date of Dickin Medal: March 6, 1944 (D.M. 4)

   "For bringing the first news to this country of the landing at Dieppe, under hazardous conditions in September 1942, while serving with the Canadian Army."

Beachcomber wove his way back to his loft through all the gunfire and mayhem of Operation Jubilee, averaging fifty miles per hour.

FLYING DUTCHMAN

Dark Checker Cock—NPS.42.NS.44802

Date of Dickin Medal: March 1945 (D.M. 15)

   "For successfully delivering messages from agents in Holland on three occasions. Missing on fourth mission, while serving with the RAF in 1944."

According to official records, he had already completed "a great many flights from light naval craft in the North Sea" when he was selected to be dropped by parachute, accompanied by an Allied spy, on the Continent.[1]

DUTCH COAST

Red Cock—NURP.41.A.2164

Date of Dickin Medal: March 1945 (D.M. 17)

   "For delivering an SOS from a ditched Air Crew close to the enemy coast 288 miles distance in 7½ hours, under unfavourable conditions, while serving with the RAF in April 1942."

Dutch Coast flew on RAF bombing missions. His flight was recorded as the best performance to date by a pigeon in the National Pigeon Service.

NAVY BLUE

Blue Cock—NPS.41.NS.2862

Date of Dickin Medal: March 1945 (D.M. 18)

"For delivering an important message from a Raiding Party on the West Coast of France, although injured, while serving with the RAF in June, 1944."

Navy was cherry-picked to join a small reconnaissance party in a seaborne landing on the west coast of France. Mystery still surrounds the mission, and official records indicate only that Navy Blue's message was "of immense value to the Intelligence Branch concerned."[2]

SCOTCH LASS

Blue Checker Hen—NPS.42.21610

Date of Dickin Medal: June 1945 (D.M. 23)

"For bringing thirty-eight microphotographs across the North Sea in good time although injured, while serving with the RAF in Holland in September 1944."

Scotch Lass made forty-three flights from a small naval craft in the North Sea before she and a spy parachuted behind enemy lines in Holland.

BILLY

Blue Cock—NU.41.HQ.4373

Date of Dickin Medal: August 1945 (D.M. 25)

"For delivering a message from a force-landed bomber, while in a state of complete collapse and under exceptionally bad weather conditions, while serving with the RAF in 1942."

Precious little is known about Billy's story, but according to official records, on February 21, 1942, he was aboard an RAF plane when it was forced down in the Netherlands.

COLOGNE
Red Cock—NURP39.NPS.144
Date of Dickin Medal: Unknown (D.M. 26)

"For homing from a crashed aircraft over Cologne although seriously wounded, while serving with the RAF in 1943."

Cologne participated in more than one hundred bombing sorties, homing from various aircraft diverted and forced down over Great Britain and Europe.

MAQUIS
Blue Checker Cock—NPS.42.36392
Date of Dickin Medal: October 1945 (D.M. 28)

"For bringing important messages three times from enemy occupied country, viz: May 1943 (Amiens) February, 1944 (Combined Operations) and June, 1944 (French Maquis) while serving with the Special Service from the Continent."

Maquis was dropped behind enemy lines and returned four times.

NPS.42.NS.2780
Date of Dickin Medal: October 1945 (D.M. 29)

"For bringing important messages three times from enemy occupied country, viz: July 1942, August 1942 and April 1943, while serving with the Special Service from the Continent."

NPS.42.NS.2780 made three flights that earned him the Dickin Medal.

NPS.42.NS.7524
Date of Dickin Medal: October 1945 (D.M. 30)

"For bringing important messages three times from enemy-occupied country, viz: July 1942, May 1943 and July 1943, while serving with the Special Service from the continent."

NPS.42.NS.7524 did espionage work for the Special Section of the Army Pigeon Service.

BROAD ARROW
41.BA.2793
Date of Dickin Medal: October 1945 (D.M. 31)

"For bringing important messages three times from enemy occupied country, viz: May 1943, June 1943 and August 1943, while serving with the Special Service from the Continent."

Broad Arrow made three successful drops into enemy territory and returned home to his loft in Dorchester with important information.

ALL ALONE
Blue Hen—NURP.39.SDS.39
Date of Dickin Medal: February 1946 (D.M. 35)

"For delivering an important message in one day over a distance of four-hundred miles, while serving with the NPS in August, 1943."

All Alone and a British agent were dropped into France, landing twenty miles south of Lyon in the city of Vienne on the Rhône.

PRINCESS
Smoky Blue Hen—42WD593 (Middle East Pigeon Service)
Date of Dickin Medal: May 17, 1946 (D.M. 36)

"Sent on special mission to Crete, this pigeon returned to her loft (RAF Alexandria) having travelled about 500 miles mostly over sea, with most valuable information. One of the finest performances in the war record of the Pigeon Service."

There is virtually nothing written about Princess's flight other than it was a spectacular performance.

MERCURY

Blue Hen—NURP.37.CEN.335

Date of Dickin Medal: August 1946 (D.M. 38)

"For carrying out a special task involving a flight of 480 miles from Northern Denmark while serving with the Special Section Army Pigeon Service in July 1942."

According to one newspaper account Mercury was "considered by the RAF to have made the most outstanding single operational flight of the war."[3]

NURP.38.BPC.6

Date of Dickin Medal: August 1946 (Posthumous) (D.M. 39)

"For three outstanding flights from France while serving with the Special Section, Army Pigeon Service, 11 July 1941, 9 September 1941, and 29 November 1941."

This brave bird made three trips back to its loft from France, where it was dropped behind German lines at the height of the V-1 bombings on England.

DD.43.T.139

Blue Bar Cock—DD.43.T.139 (Australian Army Signal Corps)

Date of Dickin Medal: February 1947 (D.M. 41)

"During a heavy tropical storm, this bird was released from Army Boat 1402 which had foundered on Wadau Beach in the Huon Gulf. Homing forty miles to Madang, it brought a message which enabled a rescue ship to be sent in time to salvage the craft and its valuable cargo of stores and ammunition."

DD.43.T.139 had twenty-three successful flights under his wings, with a total distance flown of more than one thousand miles. A veteran of the Australian Army Signal Corps, T.139 served with Detachment 55 Port Craft Company, Madang, Papua New Guinea.

NURP.43.CC.2418

Blue Checker Hen—NURP.43.CC.2418

Date of Dickin Medal: January 8, 1947 (posthumous) (D.M. 46)

"For the fastest flight with message from 6th Airborne Div. Normandy, 7 June, 1944, while serving with APS."

The pigeon who flew even faster than the speedy Duke of Normandy with news from the D-Day landings was known simply as NURP.43.CC.2418.

WAR DOGS

TICH

Egyptian mongrel—1st Battalion King's Royal Rifle Corps

Date of Dickin Medal: July 1, 1949 (D.M. 53)

"For loyalty, courage and devotion to duty which helped greatly in maintaining morale while serving with the 1st King's Royal Rifle Corps from 1940-45 in Africa and Italy."

Tich, a black Egyptian mongrel—mostly terrier, with a dash of Dachshund—was just another nameless starving stray roaming North Africa when she won the hearts of the 1st Battalion King's Royal Rifle Corps (KRRC), a unit of the famed Eighth Army.

BOB

Labrador/Collie mix—6th Royal West Kent Regiment

Date of Dickin Medal: March 24, 1944 (D.M. 5)

"For constant devotion to duty with special mention of Patrol work at Green Hill, North Africa, while serving with the 6th Battalion Queen's Own Royal West Kent Regt."

Bob has the honor and distinction of being the war's very first dog to receive the Dickin Medal.

PUNCH AND JUDY
Boxers
Date of Dickin Medals: November 1946 (D.M. 43 & 44)

"These dogs saved the lives of two British Officers in Israel by attacking an armed terrorist who was stealing upon them unawares and thus warning them of their danger. Punch sustained 4 bullet wounds and Judy a long graze down her back."

The heroic brother-and-sister boxer team of Punch and Judy came to prominence not in World War II, but just afterward, in terror-torn Palestine.

GANDER
"THE BLACK BEAST"
Newfoundland—Royal Rifles of Canada
Date of Dickin Medal: August 15, 2000 (D.M. 55)

"For saving the lives of Canadian infantrymen during the Battle of Lye Mun on Hong Kong Island in December 1941. On three documented occasions, Gander, the Newfoundland mascot of the Royal Rifles of Canada, engaged the enemy as his regiment joined the Winnipeg Grenadiers, members of Battalion Headquarters 'C' Force and other Commonwealth troops in their courageous defence of the Island. Twice Gander's attacks halted the enemy's advance and protected groups of wounded soldiers. In a final act of bravery the war dog was killed in action gathering a grenade. Without Gander's intervention many more lives would have been lost in the assault."

Gander was awarded his medal posthumously, a whopping fifty-five years after the end of World War II, and on the anniversary of V-J Day.

Bibliography

It would fill a book to list every source consulted in researching this book, but below are some of the key sources used.

BOOKS

Barker, Ralph. *Down in The Drink*. London: Pan Books, 1958.

Behan, John M. *Dogs of War*. New York: Charles Scribner's Sons, 1946.

Bowman, Martin W. *Deep Sea Hunters: RAF Coastal Command and the War Against the U-Boats and the German Navy 1939–1945*. South Yorkshire, England: Pen & Sword Books, 2014.

Carlo, Jim. *Three "Cats," a Pigeon, and 27 Brave Men of Coastal Command*. Kent, England: FVRepro, 2012.

Cawthorne, Nigel. *Canine Commandos: The Heroism, Devotion and Sacrifice of Dogs in War*. Berkeley, CA: Ulysses Press, 2012.

Cooper, Jilly. *Animals at War*. London: Corgi Books, 2000.

Cooper, Vera. *Simon the Cat*. London: Hutchinson & Co. Ltd., 1950.

Cothren, Marion B. *Pigeon Heroes: Birds of War and Messengers of Peace*. New York: Coward-McCann Inc., 1944.

Dempewolff, Richard. *Animal Reveille*. Garden City, New York: Doubleday, Doran & Company, Inc., 1943.

Downey, Fairfax. *Dogs for Defense: American Dogs in the Second World War 1941–45*. New York: Trustees of Dogs for Defense, Inc., 1955.

Eastwood, Stuart, Charles Gray, and Alan Green. *When Dragons Flew: An Illustrated History of the 1st Battalion: The Border Regiment 1939–45*. Rushden, Northamptonshire, England: Silver Link Publishing, 1994.

Foley Jr., George F., *Sinbad of the Coast Guard*. Connecticut: Flat Hammock Press, 2005. Introduction by Michael Walling.

Gardiner, Juliet. *The Animals' War*. London: Portrait, Piatkus Books Ltd., 2006

Garland, Albert N. and Howard McGaw Smyth. *United States Army in World War II: Mediterranean Theater of Operations, Sicily, and the Surrender of Italy*. Washington, DC: Center of Military History, United States Army, 1993.

Going, Clayton G. *Dogs at War*. New York: The Macmillan Company, 1944.

Gray, Earnest A. *Dogs of War*. London: Robert Hale Ltd., 1989.

Hamer, Blythe. *Dogs at War: True Stories of Canine Courage Under Fire*. London: Carlton Publishing Group, 2006.

Hawthorne, Peter. *The Animal Victoria Cross: The Dickin Medal.* Barnsley, South Yorkshire: Pen & Sword Military, 2014.

Kiser, Toni M. and Lindsey F. Barnes. *Loyal Forces: The American Animals in World War II.* Baton Rouge: Louisiana State University Press, 2013.

Kistler, John M. *Animals in the Military: From Hannibal's Elephants to the Dolphins of the US Navy.* Santa Barbara, CA: ABC-CLIO, LLC, 2011.

Le Chene, Evelyn. *Silent Heroes: The Bravery & Devlotion of Animals in War.* London: Souvenir Press, 2009.

Lemish, Michael G. *War Dogs.* Lincoln, NE: Potomac Books, 1999.

Levi, Wendell. *The Pigeon.* Sumter, SC: Levi Publishing Co, 1974.

Levine, Alan J. *Captivity, Flight, and Survival in World War II.* Westport, CT: Praeger Publishers, 2000.

Lewis, Damien. *Judy: A Dog in a Million.* London: Quercus Editions Ltd., 2014.

The Dog Who Could Fly: The Incredible True Story of a WWII Airman and the Four-Legged Hero Who Flew at His Side. New York: Atria Books, Simon & Schuster, 2013.

Lewis, Val. *Ships' Cats in War and Peace.* Middlesex, England: Nauticalia Ltd., 2001.

Long, David. *Animal Heroes: Inspiring True Stories of Courageous Animals.* London: Arrow Books, 2013.

Marder, M. "Real Devil-Dogs," in *Fighting War Dogs of World War II.* New York: U.S. Sales Company, 1944.

McCafferty, Garry. *They Had No Choice: Racing Pigeons at War.* Stroud, Gloucestershire, England: Tempus Publishing, Ltd., 2002.

Osman, W. H. ed. *Pigeons in World War II: The Official Records of the Performances of Racing Pigeons with the Armed Forces.* London: The Racing Pigeon Publishing Co., Ltd., 1950.

Philips, C. E. Lucas. *Escape of the "Amethyst."* London: Pan Books. Ltd., 1958.

Richardson, Anthony. *One Man and His Dog.* New York: Bantam Books, 1967.

Risch, Erna and Chester L. Kieffer. *The Technical Services, The Quartermaster Corps: Organization, Supply, and Services.* Vol. 2. Washington, DC: Office of the Chief of Military History, Department of the Army, 1958.

Ross, Hamish. *Freedom in the Air, A Czech Flyer and his Aircrew Dog.* Barnsley, South Yorkshire, England: Pen & Sword Books, Ltd., 2007.

Ross, William F. and Charles F. Romanus. *The Technical Services: The Quartermaster Corps: Operation in the War Against Germany.* Washington, DC: Office of the Chief of Military History, Department of the Army, 1965.

St. Hill Bourne, Dorothea. *They Also Serve.* London: Winchester Publications Ltd., 1947.

The Homing Pigeon, Technical Manual TM 11-410. Washington, DC: War Department, 1945.

Thurston, Mary Elizabeth. *The Lost History of the Canine Race: Our 15,000-Year Love Affair with Dogs.* Kansas City, KS: Andrews and McMeel, 1996.

Varley, E. *The Judy Story: The Dog with Six Lives*. Glasgow: Fontana/Collins, 1976.

Waller, Anna M. *Dogs and National Defense*. Washington, DC: Department of the Army, Office of the Quartermaster General, 1958.

War Dogs Technical Manual, TM 10-396. Washington, DC: War Department, July 1, 1943.

Weintraub, Robert. *No Better Friend: One Man, One Dog, and Their Extraordinary Story of Courage and Survival in WWII*. New York: Little, Brown & Company, 2015.

Woolhouse, Andrew. *13—Lucky for Some: The History of the 13th (Lancashire) Parachute Battalion*. Amazon Createspace, 2013.

Wynne, William A. *Yorkie Doodle Dandy: A Memoir*. Denver, CO: Top Dog Enterprises, LLC.

ARTICLES

"Aid Dogs for Defense: Artists, Writers, Actors from Committee in Westport," *New York Times*, August 5, 1943.

"Air Raid Rescue Dogs Receive 'Animals' V.C.,'" *Hampstead News*, January 18, 1945.

"Airmen's Friends—Shepherds," *Citizen Glasgow*, July 27, 1945.

Alleyne, Richard. "SAS Reports of Canine Heroics 'Just a Shaggy Dog Story,'" *Daily Telegraph*, July 21, 2006.

"Alsatians' 'Nose for Rescuing' Sets Up Records, 'V.C.' Dog Found Casualty Buried 20 ft. Deep," *Evening Standard Reporter*, March 17, 1945.

"Amethyst's Cat Hero: Full Story," *South Wales Echo*, October 31, 1949.

"Animal Hero—Exploits of a Dog—Prisoner of Japanese," *Otago Daily Times*, September 26, 1949.

Ardman, Harvey. "World War II: German Saboteurs Invade America in 1942," *World War II Magazine*, February 1997.

"Army Dog Is First to Win DSC Award," *New York Times*, January 14, 1944.

"Army Pigeons: Hall of Fame," *Racing Pigeon Digest*, December 1, 1998.

"Army Registering Homing Pigeons for Conscription in an Emergency," *New York Times*, January 6, 1941.

"Award of Soldier Medals to Dogs is Barred by Army After Protest," *New York Times*, February 16, 1944.

Blume, Mary. "The Hallowed History of the Carrier Pigeon," *New York Times*, January 30, 2004.

Brackett, Charmain Zimmerman. "Museum tells Signal Corps story," *Augusta Chronicle*, December 21, 1999.

"Bravery of One Man and His Dog," *Daily Mail*, December 14, 2005.

"But the Army Made Peter a Gentleman," *Sunday Pictorial*, May 5, 1946.

Callahan, Maureen. "The Dog That Went on Air Raids against Nazis and Became a Hero," *New York Post*, June 1, 2014.

"Chips, Dog Hero of the Invasion of Sicily, Receives Big Welcome on Return to Home," *New York Times*, December 12, 1945.

"Coast Guard Cutters to Ram Submarines," *New York Times*, April 6, 1943.

"Dog Heroes, Medals Awarded," *Wembley News*, April 27, 1945.

"Dog Saves Master," *Star*, January 28, 1949.

"Dogs Guard War Plant: 3 Animals Trained for Sentry Duty Reported on Job," *New York Times*, April 24, 1942.

"Dogs 'V.C.' for Alsatian, Gallant Rescue Work," *Palmers Green Gazette*, April 27, 1945.

Downey, Fairfax. "Dogs for Defense," *Popular Dogs*, September 1943.

"Film Newcomer," *Edinburgh Evening News*, June 17, 1947.

"Five Years Ago—Irma Gave a Signal," *Evening Standard*, February 11, 1950.

Fryer, Jane. "Judy, the Dogged POW Who Defied the Japanese," *Daily Mail*, August 12, 2010.

"Gallant Dog, Good Work in Blitz Rewarded, Dickin Medal for Peter," *Birmingham Mail*, December 5, 1945.

George, Isabel. "A Cat's Tale," *The Lady*, May 1993.

"GI Joe (Pigeon) Gets His V.C.," *Daily Graphic*, November 7, 1946.

Hale, Beth. "Who Grrrrs Wins ...but Was SAS War Dog Really a Hero?" *Daily Mail*, July 21, 2009.

Harris, Paul. "Bing, the Dog of War Who Parachuted into France to Become a D-Day Hero," *Daily Mail*, April 17, 2012.

Henderson, Clyde. "Battle Dogs of the Devil Dogs," *The American Magazine*, August 1944.

"Here and There, Dog Hero Passes On," *The Animals' Magazine*, August 1954.

"He Walks Alone," *The Star*, January 1, 1948.

Israels II, Joseph. "Soldiers on Leashes," *Saturday Evening Post*, September 5, 1942.

Jedick, Peter. "Smoky the Wonder Dog," *Cleveland*, October 19, 2007.

"'Jet' Is Dog Hero, Liverpool Alsatian Gets Bravery Medal," *Liverpool Echo*, January 12, 1945.

"Judy—Animal V.C. And Prisoner of War," *Wellington Evening Post*, September 24, 1949.

"Judy—P.o.W. Heroine—Gets Dog 'V.C.' To-Day," *Evening Standard*, May 2, 1946.

"Judy, V.C., Dies after Search," *Daily Express*, March 21, 1950.

Kelly, Kate. "The Government Asked for Pets for Defense in the 1940s," *Huffington Post*, August 3, 2011.

Kilbon, Roland. "Dogs for Defense," *Popular Dogs*, September 1943.

Lewis, Damien. "So Loyal, So Brave, the Dog Who Flew against the Luftwaffe," *Daily Mail*, London, October 31, 2013.

"Lost Pigeon Brought Home Military Secrets, Wins Medal," *Manchester Daily Sketch*, January 1, 1946.

"New Dog Star," *Evening News*, June 6, 1947.

"'Noncombatant' Dogs Get Rank for Fee: Pet Can Become General for $100 & Thus Assist War Fund," *New York Times*, March 12, 1943.

O'Brien, Cyril J. "Bougainville—Then and Now," *Leatherneck*, October 1989.

"World War II: Marine War Dogs, Part I," *Leatherneck*, December 1994.

"Our War Pigeons," *Nottingham Evening Post*, November 22, 1944.

"Pigeons for Defense," *New York Times*, January 13, 1941.

"Pigeons Save Life in RAF, for Planes Forced Down at Sea or Those in Flight They Carry Messages," *New York Times*, July 11, 1943.

"Presentation of The Dickin Medal by Lord Wavell," *The Animals' Magazine*, April 1949.

"Presentation of the Dickin Medal in Australia," *The Animals' Magazine*, October 1947.

Razes, Joe. "Pigeons of War," *America in WWII*, August 2007.

"Rescue Dogs Medals, Pioneers in Life-Saving and Air Raids," *Herndon Times*, January 17, 1945.

"Rescuer Beauty Even Found a Goldfish," *Liverpool Echo*, January 1965.

"Scots Shepherds Save Lives of American Airmen," *Greenock Telegraph*, July 27, 1945.

Simpich, Frederick. "Your Dog Joins Up," *National Geographic*, January 1943.

"Sinbad A.W.O.L. Sentenced at Captain's Mast," *Patrol*, November 1944.

Smith, Steven Trent. "A Few Good Marines: Dogs in Wartime," *World War II*, February 16, 2016.

"Sorry about That, Chips," *Army Digest*, February 1968.

"The Dog Known as 'Rifleman Khan,'" *Evening Standard*, March 31, 1945.

"There's Joy and Sadness When Khan Comes Home from the War!" *Weekly News* (Dundee), January 12, 1946.

"This Film Star Was Really Shot—by Mistake," *Evening News*, January 21, 1948.

"Tibby and a Memory Fly to America," *Shields Evening News*, August 2, 1946.

"Tribute to a Pioneer," *Technical Officer*, November 1950, vol. 3, no. 11.

"USCG at War—Beach Patrol," in *Official History of United States Coast Guard*, vol. 17, 1945.

"VC Dog is Needed by a Baby, It will Teach Her to Walk," *Daily Mail*, February 10, 1945.

"V.C. Dog May Lead Cameronians 'Freedom' Parade, Saved Strathaven Man's Life at Walcheren," *Hamilton Advertiser*, July 19, 1947.

"War Dog and Master Get Medals," *Evening Standard*, March 27, 1945.

"War Dogs in the Marine Corps in World War II," United States Marine Corps, reposted by the United States War Dogs Association, Inc. n.d., http://www.uswardogs.org/war-dogs-in-the-marine-corps-in-world-war-ii/.

"War Equines Vanish; Dogs, Pigeons Join Up," *New York Times*, January 28, 1945.

"Well Done, 'GI Joe'!," *London Calling*, November 14, 1946.

"Well Flown!" *Herndon & Finley Times*, November 28, 1944.

West, Ward. "But the Pigeons Still Get Through," *New York Times*, April 27, 1941.

"We've Not Another Just Like Mary, Romance of an Exeter Pigeon," *Exeter Express & Echo*, November 17, 1945.

Wilcox, Richard. "Sinbad: An Old Sea Dog Has Favorite Bars and Plenty of Girls in Every Port," *Life*, July 19, 1943.

ONLINE SOURCES

303rd Bomb Group, http://www.303rdbg.com/360kyle.html.

"'A Special Creature': Chips the WW II Hero Dog Honoured with Posthumous Medal of Bravery," CBC Radio, January 17, 2018, www.cbc.ca/radio/asithappens/as-it-happens-wednesday-edition-1.4491266/a-special-creature-chips-the-ww-ii-hero-dog-honoured-with-posthumous-medal-of-bravery-1.4491280.

"Aerial Reconnaissance," Central Intelligence Agency, July 23, 2012, https://www.cia.gov/about-cia/cia-museum/experience-the-collection/text-version/collection-by-subject/aerial-reconnaissance.html.

"Amethyst's Cat Gets Dickin Medal for Catching Rats," Associated Press, August 5, 1949, http://www.maritimequest.com/warship_directory/great_britain/pages/sloops/hms_amethyst_u16_able_seacat_simon_page_2.htm.

Backovic, Lazar. "Britain's Luftwoofe: The Heroic Paradogs of World War II," ABC News, December 28, 2013, http://abcnews.go.com/International/britains-luftwoofe-heroic-paradogs-world-war-ii/story?id=21344669.

Blundell, Nigel. "Terror of the Doodlebugs: Sinister V-1 Flying Bomb That Menaced London 70 Years Ago," May 31, 2014, https://www.express.co.uk/news/uk/479386/Terror-of-the-Doodlebugs-Sinister-V-1-flying-bomb-that-menaced-Britain-70-years-ago.

Carter, Suzanne. "Poodles in WWII," www.poodlehistory.org/PoodlesinWWII.HTM.

"Carrier Pigeon 'GI Joe' Wins Medal," World War II Today: Follow the War As It Happened, http://ww2today.com/18th-october-1943-carrier-pigeon-gi-joe-wins-medal.

Churchill, Winston. "Every Man to His Post (1940)," National Churchill Museum, https://www.nationalchurchillmuseum.org/every-man-to-his-post.html.

"D-Day Fliers Decorated (1944)," British Pathe, YouTube, April 13, 2014, https://www.youtube.com/watch?v=msqgZFvQk_E.

Davies, Stephen R. "UK Royal Air Force Police Dog History," K9 History, http://www.k9history.com/uk-royal-air-force-police-dog-history.htm.

"Did Marines, Not German Soldiers, Coin the Phrase 'Devil Dogs'?" Stars and Stripes blog, January 4, 2011, www.stripes.com/blogs-archive/the-rumor-doctor.

Erlanger, Arlene. "The Truth About War Dogs," *The Quartermaster Review*, March-April 1944. Retrieved at www.qmfound.com/dog_truth.htm.

"Foreign News: In Honored Memory," *Time*, December 12, 1949, http://content.time.com/time/magazine/article/0,9171,854035,00.html.

Green, Robert. "Able Seacat Simon, D.M., R.N. (1947–48)," http://www.maritimequest.com/warship_directory/great_ britain/pages/sloops/hms_amethyst_u16_able_seacat_simon. htm.

"Hero Pigeon's WWII Medal on Show," BBC News, June 1, 2005, http://news.bbc.co.uk/2/hi/uk_news/england/ hampshire/4600865.stm.

Hollingham, Richard. "V2: The Nazi Rocket That Launched the Space Age," BBC, September 8, 2014, http://www.bbc. com/future/story/20140905-the-nazis-space-age-rocket.

Heuer, Victoria. "Five Famous Cats of War," Pet MD, https:// www.petmd.com/cat/slideshows/seasonal/five-cats-of-war.

Kerans, J. S. "HMS Amethyst Incident, Yangtse River, April to May 1949," Naval History, February 20, 2016, http://www. naval-history.net/WXLG-Amethyst1949.htm.

Kozaryn, Linda D. "Pfc. Hammer Finds a Home," American Forces Press Service, April 24, 2004, http://archive.defense. gov/news/newsarticle.aspx?id=26813.

Meyer, Otto. "GI Joe," American Racing Pigeon Union, www. pigeon.org/pdf/gijoe.pdf.

Newton, Tom. "WW II Mascots: Dogs and Others," K9 History, http://www.k9history.com/WWII-military-mascots.htm.

Roberts, Patrick. "Faith the London Church Cat," Purr 'n' Fur, http://www.purr-n-fur.org.uk/famous/faith.html.

"Simon, of HMS Amethyst," Purr 'n' Fur, http://www.purr-n- fur.org.uk/famous/simon.html.

"Short History of the Australian Corps of Signals Pigeon Service from 1942," South Australian Homing Pigeon Association archives, http://www.sahpa.asn.au/archives/flyers/dickinmedal.htm.

"The Amazing Paradogs of WWII," Knowledge Nuts, February 13, 2014, http://knowledgenuts.com/2014/02/13/the-amazing-paradogs-of-world-war-ii/.

"The Use of Pigeons by the RAF in WW2: Extract from Military Reports on The United Nations: Number 15, Signal, February 15, 1944," Arcre: Independent Professional Research at the British National Archives (TNA), January 4, 2013, https://www.arcre.com/pigeons/pigeonsraf.

Whitlock, Flint. "The National Pigeon Service: Our Fine Feathered Friends," Warfare History Network, April 4, 2017, http://warfarehistorynetwork.com/daily/wwii/the-national-pigeon-service-our-fine-feathered-friends/.

"World War II: "Semper Fi, Marine Devil Dogs!," K9 History, www.k9history.com/WWII-uscm-devil-dogs.htm.

"World War II: U.S.—Dogs for Defense," K9 History, www.K9history.com/WWII-us-dogs-defense.htm.

"World War II: USQMC War Dog Training," K9 History, www.K9history.com/WWII-usqmc-war-dog-training.htm.

Notes

EPIGRAPH

Dorothea St. Hill Bourne, They Also Serve (London: Winchester
Publications Ltd.,1947), 5.

WAR DOGS

1. Steven Trent Smith, "A Few Good Marines: Dogs in Wartime,"
    World War II Magazine, February 16, 2016.

ONE: LASSIE GOES TO WAR

1. "World War II: U.S.—Dogs for Defense," K9 History, www.
    K9history.com/WWII-us-dogs-defense.htm, 12.
2. Forty dogs had been donated to the army earlier in 1941 after
    the Byrd Antarctic Expedition returned; they were sent to
    Greenland to locate and rescue crashed pilots. Also, a handful
    of dogs were part of a sentry program for the Coast Artillery at
    Camp Haan in California. Michael G. Lemish, War Dogs
    (Lincoln, NE: Potomac Books, 1999), 33.

3. Roland Kilbon, "Dogs for Defense," *Popular Dogs*, September 1943, 162. Roland Kilbon also wrote under the byline Arthur Roland.

4. Fairfax Downey, *Dogs for Defense: American Dogs in the Second World War 1941–45* (New York: Trustees of Dogs for Defense, Inc., 1955), 17.

5. Downey, "Dogs for Defense," *Popular Dogs*, September 1943, 163.

6. Clayton G. Going, *Dogs at War* (New York: The Macmillan Company, 1944), 6–7.

7. Ibid., 6.

8. "Dogs Guard War Plant: 3 Animals Trained for Sentry Duty Reported on Job," *New York Times*, April 24, 1942; Suzanne Carter Isaacson, *Poodles in WWII*, www.poodlehistory.org/PoodlesinWWII.HTM.

9. Downey, *Dogs for Defense*, 18–19; Joseph Israels II, "Soldiers on Leashes," *Saturday Evening Post*, September 5, 1942.

10. Going, *Dogs at War*, 10.

11. "Aid Dogs for Defense: Artists, Writers, Actors from Committee in Westport," *New York Times*, August 5, 1943.

12. Downey, *Dogs for Defense*, 38.

13. Ibid., 65.

14. *War Dogs Technical Manual, TM 10-396* (Washington, DC: War Department, July 1, 1943), 18. Though the *Manual* was written by Arlene Erlanger, her name does not appear in it.

15. Downey, *Dogs for Defense*, 27. The story of Chips in the next chapter illustrates the necessity.

16. Ibid., 31

17. *War Dogs Technical Manual, TM 10-396*, 24.

18. Erna Risch and Chester L. Kieffer, *The Technical Services, The Quartermaster Corps: Organization, Supply, and Services*, vol. 2 (Washington, DC: Office of the Chief of Military History, Department of the Army, 1958), 327.

19. Anna M. Waller, "Dogs and National Defense," Department of the Army, Office of the Quartermaster General, 1958, 52.

20. "USCG at War—Beach Patrol," *Official History of United States Coast Guard* (1945), 3.

21. Harvey Ardman, "World War II: German Saboteurs Invade America in 1942," *World War II*, February 1997, republished June 12, 2006 on HistoryNet, http://www.historynet.com/world-war-ii-german-saboteurs-invade-america-in-1942.htm.

22. By July 27, 1942, just a month after the men were apprehended, the tribunal had finished its work. On August 8, 1942, six of the men were executed as spies in the electric chair at the District Jail in Washington, DC. The seventh received a life sentence at hard labor. The eighth, Dasch, was sentenced to thirty years.

23. "USCG at War—Beach Patrol," 5.

24. Michale G. Lemish, *War Dogs: A History of Loyalty and Heroism* (Lincoln, NE: Potomac Books, 1999), 49.

25. Ibid., 40.

26. Colonel Richardson was considered "the most instrumental figure in the training of war dogs during the early part of the century and a benchmark for measuring future endeavors." (Lemish, *War Dogs*, 261, n. 12). His books include *British War Dogs, Their Training and Psychology* (London: Skeffington and Son, LTD., 1920), *War, Police and Watch Dogs* (London: William Backwood, 1910), and *Watch Dogs: Their Training and Management* (London: Hutchinson & Co., LTD, 1923).

27. Downey, *Dogs for Defense*, 47.

28. Ibid., 49.

29. Kate Kelly, "The Government Asked for Pets for Defense in the 1940s," *Huffington Post*, August 3, 2011.

30. Going, *Dogs at War*, 144.

31. "'Noncombatant Dogs Get Rank for Fee: Pet Can Become General for $100 & Thus Assist War Fund," *New York Times*, March 12, 1943.

32. Downey, *Dogs for Defense*, 50.

33. Going, *Dogs at War*, 148. Some sources, including Going, give the dog's name as Pupschen. But most sources refer to the dog as Boopschen.

34. Ibid., 147.

TWO: YOU'RE IN THE ARMY NOW. COAST GUARD TOO. DON'T FORGET THE NAVY. AND HEY, MARINE CORPS, LOOKIN' GOOD!

1. Josef Israels II, "Soldiers on Leashes," *Saturday Evening Post*, September 5, 1942, 20.
2. "World War II: U.S.—Dogs for Defense," K9 History, www.K9history.com/WWII-us-dogs-defense.htm, 13.
3. "USCG at War—Beach Patrol," *Official History of United States Coast Guard*, vol. 17 (1945), 29.
4. Going, *Dogs at War*, 19.
5. Downey, *Dogs for Defense*, 56.
6. The fault was in the protocol used at the time to train the dogs to sniff out mines. That protocol was later changed, and today military working dogs do a beautiful job of sniffing out IEDs and other explosive devices.
7. "World War II: U.S.—Dogs for Defense," 4; Frederick Simpich, "Your Dog Joins Up," *National Geographic*, January 1943, 111.
8. *War Dogs Technical Manual*, TM 10–396, 100.
9. Ibid., 107.
10. Erlanger, "The Truth About War Dogs," *Quartermaster Review*, March-April 1944, 3, www.qmfound.com/dog_truth.htm.
11. Going, *Dogs at War*, 125.
12. Ibid., 25.
13. *War Dogs Technical Manual*, 123.
14. Going, *Dogs at War*, 26.
15. Downey, *Dogs for Defense*, 38.
16. The Coast Guard required more trained handlers—2,662—than the Army's 2,169, to command sentry and attack dogs. "World War II: USQMC War Dog Training," K9 History, www.K9history.com/WWII-usqmc-war-dog-training.htm. The districts were Boston, New York City, Philadelphia, Norfolk, Charleston, Miami, New Orleans, Long Beach, San Francisco, and Seattle.

17. "USCG at War—Beach Patrol," 31.

18. Lemish, *War Dogs*, 51–53.

THREE: CHIPS

1.   A wholly pastoral and entirely fictional version of the village was the setting for the 1998 fantasy film *Pleasantville*. The real-life Pleasantville, in Westchester County, New York, may be best known as the former home of *Readers Digest* magazine.

2.   "'A Special Creature': Chips the WW II Hero Dog Honoured with Posthumous Medal of Bravery," CBC Radio, January 17, 2018, www.cbc.ca/radio/asithappens/as-it-happens-wednesday-edition-1.4491266/a-special-creature-chips-the-ww-ii-hero-dog-honoured-with-posthumous-medal-of-bravery-1.4491280.

3.   Downey, *Dogs for Defense*, 69. All were German shepherds, either crosses or purebreds.

4.   Ibid., 71.

5.   Ibid.

6.   Going, *Dogs at War*, 32.

7.   Downey, *Dogs for Defense*, 72.

8.   Going, *Dogs at War*, 32.

9.   Mena went on to star in The Westminster Kennel Club Dog Show of 1944. Downey, *Dogs for Defense*, 72.

10. Chips and Rowell were part of the 3rd Infantry Division/2nd Battalion/30th Infantry/Company "I" commanded by Major General Lucian K. Truscott and part of Attack Force JOSS (Joint Task Force Operations Support Systems Force), which formed the left flank of the attacking force.

11. Going, *Dogs at War*, 33–34.

12. Letter from W. H. Bryant Jr., to Mr. Wren, January 29, 1946.

13. There has been some confusion about whether Chips attacked a German or Italian pillbox. Rowell said Italian, but many newspaper accounts incorrectly identified it as German. In fact, the Germans were fighting the 1st Infantry Division at Gela, east of Licata. According to the U.S. Army Center for Military History's report, "Only one Italian coastal division, backed by a few scattered Italian mobile units, stood initially in the 3rd

Division's path. Two Italian mobile divisions—
Assietta and Aosta—and two-thirds of the German 15th Panzer
Grenadier Division, the only effective fighting forces in the XII
Corps sector, were well off to the west near Palermo." Albert
N. Garland and Howard McGaw Smyth, *United States Army
in World War II: The Mediterranean Theater of Operations:
Sicily and the Surrender of Italy* (Washington, DC: Center of
Military History, United States Army, 1993), 125.

14. Going, *Dogs at War*, 34.
15. General Order No. 79, issued by Headquarters, 3rd Infantry
    Division, Reinforced, APO 3, dated 24 October 1943. "Sorry
    about That, Chips," *Army Digest*, February 1968, 35.
16. Going, *Dogs at War*, 35.
17. Personal letter to the Wren family from William H. Bryant Jr.,
    January 29, 1946.
18. Going, *Dogs at War*, 35. There was confusion about which
    award Chips had received. It was heavily publicized that Chips
    had been awarded the Distinguished Service Cross, the second
    highest military decoration for extraordinary heroism in
    combat, yet Army officials at the time "expressed doubt that
    the dog had received the Distinguished Service Cross." (*New
    York Times*, January 15, 1944) As best can be determined, and
    sources confirm, Chips was "cited in orders" to be awarded the
    Distinguished Service Cross (DSC) in Captain Parr's
    recommendation, but instead he was awarded the Silver Star,
    which is the third highest military decoration for extraordinary
    heroism in combat. The DSC was heavily publicized at the time,
    and because the Silver Star was awarded and also heavily
    publicized, it appeared he had received both—but he did not.
    The excitement and over-exuberance of Dogs for Defense in
    promoting both of these awards added to the confusion and
    misinformation. There is, however, no confusion about the fact
    that Chips did in fact receive the Silver Star, only to have it later
    revoked.
19. Ibid.
20. The amendment read, in part: "So much of Section I, General
    Orders 79, this headquarters, dated 24 October 1944, as

pertains to the Award of the Silver Star to Chips, 11-A, U.S. Army Dog, Company I, Thirtieth Infantry, is revoked." (Army Digest #23, February 1968, 36).

21. "Award of Soldier Medals to Dogs is Barred by Army After Protest," *New York Times*, February 16, 1944.
22. Going, *Dogs at War*, 36.
23. Ibid., 38.
24. "Army Dog Is First to Win DSC Award," *New York Times*, January 14, 1944.
25. Personal letter to the Wren family from William H. Bryant Jr.
26. Ibid.
27. Ibid.
28. Ibid.
29. Ibid.
30. "'A Special Creature.'"
31. "Chips, Dog Hero of the Invasion of Sicily, Receives Big Welcome on Return to Home," *New York Times*, December 12, 1945.
32. Interview of John Wren by the author, November 27, 2017.
33. Ibid.
34. Ibid.

FOUR: DEVIL DOGS OF THE MARINE CORPS

1. Going, *Dogs at War*, 79; Downey, *Dogs for Defense*, 89.
2. Cyril J. O'Brien, "World War II: Marine War Dogs, Part I," *Leatherneck*, December 1994, 8.
3. "War Dogs in the Marine Corps in World War II," USMC History Division, Marine Corps University.
4. Terhune was so enthusiastic about her role that she was "retained by the Corps to help initiate the dog training part time." O'Brien, "World War II: Marine War Dogs, Part I."
5. Some sources refer to Jack as a Belgian shepherd. Five-year-old Thor was actually a descendant of the famous movie dog Strongheart, who starred in several films in the 1920s and has a star on the Hollywood Walk of Fame.

6. While it is supposed to have happened after the Battle of Belleau Wood in June 1918, a front-page headline with the term "Devil Dogs" appeared in the *La Crosse Tribune and Leader-Press* on Saturday, April 27, 1918, following a different encounter with the Germans. In addition, according to the National Museum of the Marine Corps, there is no credible proof the term even came from the Germans. See "Did Marines, Not German Soldiers, Coin the Phrase 'Devil Dogs'?" Stars and Stripes blog, January 4, 2011, www.stripes.com/blogs-archive/the-rumor-doctor.

7. By war's end, German shepherds had replaced Doberman pinschers as the preferred breed because Dobies were considered too high strung.

8. Going, *Dogs at War*, 56–57.

9. The USMC routinely referred to these as tattoos, although they differed from the painfully applied artwork that adorns human skin. Military working dogs still receive this kind of branding today.

10. National Archives Record Group 127: Records of the United States Marine Corps, Entry UD-WW 100. Other sources, however, put the number of Marine Corps war dogs at 1,047.

11. Fritz became "honorary captain of the canines" and went on to serve at the Naval Section Base in Eureka, California. National Archives Record Group 127: Records of the United States Marine Corps, Entry, "Fritz, Dog Pioneer Here, Rates High at New Post." Date unknown.

12. Going, *Dogs at War*, 60.

13. Steven Trent Smith, "A Few Good Marines: Dogs in Wartime," *World War II*, February 16, 2017.

14. Once the Marine dogs were tested in battle, it was discovered that there was no need for casualty dogs, "as seldom is a Marine wounded without being seen by a buddy," so they were retrained as scouts. Going, *Dogs at War*, 72–73.

15. Ibid., 72.

16. Clyde Henderson, "Battle Dogs of the Devil Dogs," *The American Magazine*, August 1944, 24.

17. In 1941 the first of more than twenty-seven-hundred identical emergency vessels (dubbed EC2 ships) were hurriedly built from prefabricated sections and launched specifically for use in World War II. Each cost under $2 million. Liberty ship names honored American heroes. The first one launched was the SS *Patrick Henry.*

18. "Semper Fi, Marine Devil Dogs!," K9 History, www.k9history. com/WWII-uscm-devil-dogs.htm, 13.

19. Henderson, "Battle Dogs," 24.

20. Other sources put the number as high as sixty-five-thousand Japanese soldiers. Cyril J. O'Brien, "Bougainville—Then and Now," *Leatherneck*, October 1989.

21. Henderson, "Battle Dogs," 25.

22. Going, *Dogs at War,* 91.

23. Interview of Homer Finley by the author, September 17, 2017.

24. Going, *Dogs at War,* 94.

25. According to the official Journal of the 1st Marine Dog Platoon, it appears that Prince, a scout dog, and Topper, a sentry dog, and their handlers were also part of that patrol, yet Andy and Caesar were the ones put to work. Mayo led Caesar up to the front line and Kleeman stayed back at command to await any messages.

26. Henderson, "Battle Dogs," 25.

27. Ibid., 135.

28. An article in Prologue Magazine, "Buddies: Soldiers and Animals in World War II," by Lisa B. Auel (National Archives publication, Fall 1996, Vol. 28, No. 3) incorrectly states in the caption of this picture, "A Marine Corps German shepherd is comforted by his partner while being x-rayed. Shot by a Japanese sniper on Bougainville, the dog died of his injuries (emphasis mine)." To clarify, this is Caesar being x-rayed for his injuries. Also, two dogs died on Bougainville and both were Doberman Pinschers. Because this came from the National Archives, other sources have also misstated this caption.

(https://www.archives.gov/publications/prologue/1996/fall/
buddies.html).

29. Going, *Dogs at War*, 96.

30. Ibid.

31. In a letter Wortman sent home to his parents. Going, *Dogs at War*, 107.

32. Ibid., 105.

33. Ibid., 106.

34. Ibid., 107.

35. Ibid., 108.

36. Ibid., 110.

37. Davis Junction Marine, "Urge Congressional Medal for Dog Handled by Davis Junction Marine." Publication and date unknown.

38. Going, *Dogs at War*, 109

39. Interview of Homer Findley by the author, September 17, 2017.

40. Going, *Dogs of War*, 111.

41. Interview of Homer Finley by the author, September 17, 2017.

42. Going, *Dogs at War*, 89.

43. Ibid., 82.

44. Ibid.

45. National Archives, Record Group 127, Box 1, Book #71.

46. Henderson, "Battle Dogs," 25.

47. Ibid.

48. Ibid., 136.

49. M. Marder, *"Real Devil Dogs": Fighting War Dogs of World War II* (New York: U.S. Sales Company, 1944), 4.

50. Henderson, "Battle Dogs," 136.

51. Marder, *"Real Devil Dogs,"* 4.

52. Going, *Dogs at War*, 88.

53. Marder, *"Real Devil Dogs,"* 4.

54. Henderson, "Battle Dogs," 136.

55. Yvonne Cahoon, "Devil Dogs Are Born Heroes," USMC Archives. Date and publication unknown. The number of enemy soldiers killed ranges from eight to nineteen, depending on the source.

56. National Archives, Record Group 127, Box 1, Book #71.

57. Going, *Dogs at War*, 120. Rex's citation was given to him by the Commandant of the Marine Corps, General Holcomb.

58. Ibid., 79; Downey, *Dogs for Defense*, 89.

FIVE: MORE THAN MASCOTS

1. Tom Newton, "WW II Mascots: Dogs and Others," K9 History, http://www.k9history.com/WWII-military-mascots. htm.

2. Michael Walling, Introduction to George F. Foley Jr., *Sinbad of the Coast Guard* (Mystic, CT: Flat Hammock Press, 2005), 3.

3. Ibid., 2, quoting Martin Sheridan, *Boston Daily Globe*.

4. A native of Scotland, Campbell had arrived in North Carolina in 1772 as a toddler. He eventually enjoyed a remarkable career in government, serving variously as an associate justice on the U.S. Supreme Court, a congressman and also U.S. senator from Tennessee, ambassador to Russia and, in the Madison Administration, treasury secretary.

5. Sources vary as to who smuggled Sinbad on board, and where he came from. According to a document from USCG archives, Ensign A. A. Rother claims to have obtained Sinbad from a local New York veterinarian and brought him aboard at Patrol Base Pier 18 in New York. ("Sinbad the Pup," As related to J. H. Jebens, Cox, by Ensign A. A. Rother.) A February 23, 1989, letter in the USCG Archives from Oscar C. Peterson who served on deck of the *Campbell* from 1938–40 and claims he was "one of Sinbad's more favored shipmates," confirms that it was "Dutch" Rother who brought him aboard, but says that Rother had help from Boatswain's Mate "Pappy" Green. Peterson claimed that Sinbad was "part of a litter aboard either the CG Tug Manhattan or Roritan."

6. It appears that the captain at the time was H. L. Lucas, but records are a bit sketchy. A "muster" is a daily afternoon roll call and general meeting of enlisted men and their ship's officers.

7. I have not been able to verify the original source of this quotation, which has been repeatedly used to describe Sinbad—including in Michael Walling's introduction to USCG Chief George F. Foley Jr.'s biography *Sinbad of the Coast Guard* (Mystic, CT: Flat Hammock Press, 2005), 2 and has been attributed variously to Martin Sheridan of the *Boston Daily Globe* and to the December 1943 edition of *Life* magazine.

8.   Foley, *Sinbad of the Coast Guard*, 62. A "mast" is a formal hearing held by the captain to discipline any member of the crew.

9. A "wolf pack" is a pack of submarines.

10. Foley, *Sinbad of the Coast Guard*, 98.

11. Ibid., 102.

12. Ibid., 106. See also "Coast Guard Cutters to Ram Submarines," *New York Times*, April 6, 1943.

13. Walling, in introduction to *Sinbad of the Coast Guard*.

14. Foley, *Sinbad of the Coast Guard*, 85.

15. Richard Wilcox, "Sinbad: An Old Sea Dog Has Favorite Bars and Plenty of Girls in Every Port," *Life*, July 19, 1943, 14.

16. Sources vary on the number of times Sinbad was left behind. In *Sinbad of the Coast Guard*, George Foley says that Sinbad never forgot the lesson he learned in Iceland when he jumped in the water and swam after the ship, causing the captain to turn around and get him. News articles tell a different story.

17. "Sinbad A.W.O.L. Sentenced at Captain's Mast," *Patrol*, November 1944, 7. USCG Archives.

18. Ibid., 10.

19. Foley, *Sinbad of the Coast Guard*, 111.

20. Ibid., 112.

21. Ibid., 114.

22. USCG website: http://coastguard.dodlive.mil/category/history/.

23. William Wynne, "Smoky: 'Corporal Smoky': United States Army/Air Corps," Patsy Ann, no date, http://www.patsyann.com/smoky.htm.

24. William A. Wynne, *Yorkie Doodle Dandy* (Hinckley, Ohio: Smoky War Dog, LLC, 2017), 1.

25. Ibid., 2.

26. Ibid., 11.

27. Peter Jedick, "Smoky the Wonder Dog," *Cleveland*, October 19, 2007, 4.

28. Wynne, *Yorkie Doodle Dandy*, 4.

29. Correspondence between the author and William Wynne, August 18, 2011.

30. Jedick, "Smoky the Wonder Dog," 4.

31. Wynne, *Yorkie Doodle Dandy*, 29.

32. Sadly, Topper passed away a few months later from a fast-spreading disease that killed nearly thirty other dog mascots in the squad in only a week.

33. Research confirmed by Animal Planet.

34. Correspondence between the author and William Wynne, August 18, 2011.

35. Ibid.

36. An LST is a tank landing ship. William Wynne, "Smoky."

37. Wynne, *Yorkie Doodle Dandy*, 52.

38. Ibid., 71.

SIX: GREAT BRITAIN'S WAR DOGS

1. Dorothea St. Hill Bourne, *They Also Serve* (London: Winchester Publications Ltd.,1947), 177–78.

2. CBE—Commander of the Most Excellent Order of the British Empire—is Great Britain's third-highest order of chivalry. The CBE "recognizes distinguished service to the arts and sciences, public services outside the Civil Service and work with charitable and welfare organizations of all kinds." See "The Queen and Honours," The Home of the Royal Family, https://www.royal.uk/queen-and-honours.

3. Stephen R. Davies, "UK Royal Air Force Police Dog History," K9 History, http://www.k9history.com/uk-royal-air-force-police-dog-history.htm. In 1944, the school became part of the Royal Air Force and was renamed RAF Police Dog Training School. Lieutenant Colonel Baldwin remained chief training officer, and police dogs became a permanent part of the RAF.

4. Many proved gun-shy and were returned to their owners. Earnest A. Gray, *Dogs of War* (London: Robert Hale Ltd., 1989), 128.

5. William F. Ross and Charles F. Romanus, *The Technical Services: The Quartermaster Corps: Operation in the War Against Germany* (Washington, DC: Office of the Chief of Military History, Department of the Army, 1965), 286.

6. Sheila's PDSA Dickin Medal Citation. These citations will appear under each Dickin Medalist's name throughout the rest of the book; they can be found on the PDSA's website at www.pdsa.org.uk/what-we-do/animal-awards-programme/pdsa-dickin-medal.

7. During World War I, John Dagg was a decorated private who served in the King's Own Scottish Borderers, a line infantry regiment in the Scottish Division of the British Army.

8. Details of the crash are from the 303rd Bomb Group website, http://www.303rdbg.com/360kyle.html.

9. "Bravery of One Man and His Dog," *Daily Mail Reporter*, December 14, 2005.

10. David Long, *Animal Heroes: Inspiring True Stories of Courageous Animals* (London: Arrow Books, 2013), 204.

11. The BEM is awarded for meritorious civil or military service worthy of recognition by the Crown.

12. Some more recent sources report the BEM was awarded that day to Dagg and Moscrop, not in a previous ceremony in June. But at the time, most newspaper accounts of Sheila's Dickin Medal ceremony suggest the medals had been previously presented to the two shepherds. As one story reported, "Mr John Dagg and Mr Frank Moscrop, the two shepherds who found the plane and brought the wounded men to safety, had been previously presented with British Empire medals by the King." "Scots Shepherds Save Lives of American Airmen," *Greenock Telegraph*, July 27, 1945.

13. PDSA Archives, date and source unknown.

14. "Airmen's Friends—Shepherds," *Citizen Glasgow*, July 27, 1945. PDSA Archives.

15. St. Hill Bourne, *They Also Serve*, 20.

16. "Sheila, the Star," PDSA Archives, date and source unknown.

17. Some sources spell it "Tibby."

18. Some sources say it was the RAF that flew Tibbie to America.

19. *Northumberland Gazette*, August 2, 1946. PDSA Archives.

20. "Sheila's Story," from the history of the College Valley website: http://www.college-valley.co.uk/history.htm.

21. "Tibby and a Memory Fly to America," *Shields Evening News*, August 2, 1946. PDSA Archives.

22. Andrew Woolhouse, *13—Lucky for Some: The History of the 13th (Lancashire) Parachute Battalion* (Amazon Createspace, 2013), 42.

23. Ibid.

24. Lazar Backovic, "Britain's Luftwoofe: The Heroic Paradogs of World War II," ABC News, December 28, 2013, http://abcnews.go.com/International/britains-luftwoofe-heroic-paradogs-world-war-ii/story?id=21344669.

25. Woolhouse, *13—Lucky for Some*, 94–95.

26. Some sources say that Bing's handler at the time was Lance Corporal Ken Bailey. But Bailey was in another plane with Ranee at the time. Bailey, as we shall see, took over Bing after Ranee's disappearance.

27. Woolhouse, *13—Lucky for Some*, 174.

28. Paul Harris, "Bing, the Dog of War Who Parachuted into France to Become a D-Day Hero," *Daily Mail*, April 17, 2012, http://www.dailymail.co.uk/news/article-2131034/Bing-World-War-Two-parachuting-dog.html#ixzz36XTzojlY.

29. Woolhouse, *13—Lucky for Some*, 534–35.

30. Ibid., 565.

31. "There's Joy and Sadness When Khan Comes Home from the War!" *Weekly News* (Dundee), January 12, 1946. PDSA Archives.

32. "The Dog Known as Rifleman Khan," *Evening Standard*, March 31, 1945. PDSA Archives.

33. "V.C. Dog May Lead Cameronians 'Freedom' Parade, Saved Strathaven Man's Life at Walcheren," *Hamilton Advertiser*, July 19, 1947. PDSA Archives.

34. Ibid.

35. "There's Joy and Sadness When Khan Comes Home from the War!"

36. Ibid.

37. St. Hill Bourne, *They Also Serve*, 19.

38. "There's Joy and Sadness When Khan Comes Home from the War!"

39. The ten Dickin Medalists joining the festivities were Rifleman Khan, Beauty, Judy, Ricky, Punch, Rob, Jet, Irma, Peter, and Rex. Bob's owner was also on hand to accept Bob's award. PDSA Archives.

40. "War Dogs Parade at Wembley," 8–9. PDSA Archives.

41. "V.C. Dog May Lead Cameronians 'Freedom' Parade, Saved Strathaven Man's Life at Walcheren."

42. Cawthorne, *Canine Commandos*, 67–68.

43. "VC Dog is Needed by a Baby, It will Teach Her to Walk," *Daily Mail*, February 10, 1945. PDSA Archives.

44. Cawthorne, *Canine Commandoes*, 158.

45. "Who Paws Wins," *Pets in Peril*, no date, https://petsinperil. wordpress.com/2015/07/13/who-paws-wins/.

46. Edna Bayne, "Rob—Parachute dog no. 471/322," publication and date unknown. PDSA Archives.

47. St. Hill Bourne, *They Also Serve*, 18.

48. "Robb, Shropshire Cattle Collie, left the Farm to become War Dog 471/322," publication and date unknown, 16–17. PDSA Archives.

49. Beth Hale, "Who Grrrrs Wins … but Was SAS War Dog Really a Hero?" *Daily Mail*, July 21, 2009. PDSA Archives.

50. Richard Alleyne, "SAS Reports of Canine Heroics 'Just a Shaggy Dog Story,'" *Daily Telegraph*, July 21, 2006. PDSA Archives.

51. Long, *Animal Heroes*, 75.

52. Alleyne, "SAS Reports of Canine Heroics."

53. The Home Guard was a defense organization of the British Army in place from 1940 to 1944, comprising 1.5 million local volunteers who were ineligible for military service—those too young or too old to join the services, or those in reserved occupations—but still wanted to serve in some capacity.

54. Some sources spell his name, "Yelding." But the Litchfields, who received letters from Yielding during the war, spell it "Yielding" on Ricky's website. "Ricky Litchfield: Canine War Hero, 1945," no date, http://rickylitchfield.com/rickys-story/.

55. St. Hill Bourne, *They Also Serve*, 185.

56. Damien Lewis, "So Loyal, So Brave, the Dog Who Flew against the Luftwaffe," *Daily Mail*, London, October 31, 2013.

57. Damien Lewis, *The Dog Who Could Fly: The Incredible True Story of a WWII Airman and the Four-Legged Hero Who Flew at His Side* (New York: Atria Books, Simon & Schuster, 2013), 10.

58. Lewis, "So Loyal, So Brave."

59. Hamish Ross, *Freedom in the Air: A Czech Flyer and His Aircrew Dog* (Barnsley, South Yorkshire, England: Pen & Sword Books, Ltd., 2007), 41, quoting an unpublished manuscript written by Robert Bozděch titled *Gentlemen of the Dusk* (Gentlemeni Soumraku).

60. Ross, *Freedom in the Air*, 42, quoting Bozděch, *Gentlemen of the Dusk*.

61. Lewis, *The Dog Who Could Fly*, 143.

62. Ibid., 144.

63. Ibid., 165.

64. Ibid., 169.

65. Ross, *Freedom in the Air*, 55, quoting Bozděch, *Gentlemen of the Dusk*.

66. While some sources report that the Cecilia actually dropped her bombs on Bremen, then fought off a German night fighter Zerstorer while heading home, this doesn't appear to have been the case, according to Bozděch's papers and manuscript.

67. Damien, *The Dog Who Could Fly*, 182.

68. Ibid., 188.
69. Ross, *Freedom in the Air*, 61.
70. Maureen Callahan, "The Dog That Went on Air raids against Nazis and Became a Hero," *New York Post*, June 1, 2014.
71. Ross, *Freedom in the Air*, 64, quoting Bozděch, *Gentlemen of the Dusk*.
72. Cawthorne, *Canine Commandoes*, 86.
73. Lewis, *The Dog Who Could Fly*, 280.
74. "Dog Saves Master," *Star*, January 28, 1949. PDSA Archives.
75. "Presentation of The Dickin Medal by Lord Wavell," *The Animals' Magazine*, April 1949, 9. PDSA Archives.
76. Ross, *Freedom in the Air*, 146.
77. Bozděch wrote his story in the third person and disguised his own identity for political reasons. Although he was living in Britain, Bozděch's family remained in Czechoslovakia, and he feared potential retribution against them by the communist regime.
78. Hamish, *Freedom in the Air*, 146–147, quoting Bozděch, *Gentlemen of the Dusk*. Hamish's book is an excellent source for more details of Antis and Bozděch's adventures during the war and afterward.

SEVEN: HOME FRONT HEROES

1. Aerial bombing attacks of England resumed three years later, on June 14, 1944, shortly after the Allied D-Day landing at Normandy. By resuming them, Hitler hoped to regain lost momentum in the war. This time it was with V-1 flying bombs (Vergeltungswaffe 1, the "Revenge Weapon"), also called doodlebugs or buzz-bombs because of their intermittent buzzing sound. The V-1 was the first cruise missile. The bombing continued until October 1944. At the campaign's peak, Germany launched more than a hundred a day, killing six thousand civilians and injuring three times as many. On September 8, 1944, the first V-2 rocket was launched at London. More than 1,300 were fired at England, killing an estimated

2,754 civilians in London, and injuring another 6,523. Nigel Blundell, "Terror of the Doodlebugs: Sinister V-1 Flying Bomb That Menaced London 70 Years Ago," *Express*, May 31, 2014, https://www.express.co.uk/news/uk/479386/Terror-of-the-Doodlebugs-Sinister-V-1-flying-bomb-that-menaced-Britain-70-years-ago; Richard Hollingham, "V2: The Nazi Rocket That Launched the Space Age," BBC, September 8, 2014, http://www.bbc.com/future/story/20140905-the-nazis-space-age-rocket.

2. David Long, *Animal Heroes: Inspiring True Stories of Courageous Animals* (London: Arrow Books, 2013), 190.
3. Winston Churchill, "Every Man to His Post (1940)," National Churchill Museum, https://www.nationalchurchillmuseum.org/every-man-to-his-post.html. Later in this memorable speech, Churchill declared, "This is a time for everyone to stand together, and hold firm, as they are doing. I express my admiration for the exemplary manner in which all the Air Raid Precautions services of London are being discharged, especially the Fire Brigade, whose work has been so heavy and also dangerous. All the world that is still free marvels at the composure and fortitude with which the citizens of London are facing and surmounting the great ordeal to which they are subjected, the end of which or the severity of which cannot yet be foreseen." Such fortitude. Such spirit. Such courage.
4. "Rescuer Beauty Even Found a Goldfish," *Liverpool Echo*, January (day and month unclear), 1965. PDSA Archives.
5. "Tribute to a Pioneer," *The Technical Officer* vol. 3, no. 11 (November 1950): 115. PDSA Archives.
6. KCB stands for "Knight Commander of the Most Honourable Order of the Bath," a British order of chivalry. The Order of the Bath is the third highest honor of the British Orders of Chivalry. It is awarded to senior civil servants. The DSO is the Distinguished Service Order, a military decoration. The SGM is the "Sea Gallantry Medal."
7. St. Hill Bourne, *They Also Serve*, 158.

8. Ibid.

9. Ibid.

10. Five of the fourteen dogs that were originally trained to do this kind of work from the MAP Guard Dog School went on to win Dickin Medals: Irma, Jet, Rex, Peter, and Thorn.

11. St. Hill Bourne, *They Also Serve*, 158.

12. Jilly Cooper, *Animals in War: Valiant Horses, Courageous Dogs, and Other Unsung Animal Heroes* (London: Corgi Books, 2000), 162. Tommy Brock is the badger in the Beatrix Potter story.

13. "'Jet' is Dog Hero, Liverpool Alsatian Gets Bravery Medal," *Liverpool Echo*, January 12, 1945. PDSA Archives.

14. Cooper, *Animals in War*, 163.

15. "Rescue Dogs Medals, Pioneers in Life-Saving and Air Raids," *Herndon Times*, January 17, 1945. PDSA Archives.

16. *Sunday Pictorial*, June 9, 1946, picture caption. PDSA Archives.

17. Owd Bob is based on the author Alfred Ollivant's 1898 novel *Owd Bob: The Grey Dog of Kenmuir*. The film drama starred Will Fyffe, John Loder, and Margaret Lockwood and was released in the U.S. as *To the Victor*. The novel has been filmed several times since 1924, including a 1998 American remake featuring James Cromwell and Colm Meaney.

18. "Alsatians' 'Nose for Rescuing' Sets Up Records, 'V.C.' Dog Found Casualty Buried 20 ft. Deep," *Evening Standard Reporter*, March 17, 1945. PDSA Archives.

19. Cawthorne, *Canine Commandos*, 98–99. If the reader is interested in learning about other incidents Irma and Psyche performed with their search-and-rescue work in addition to what is presented here, this book is a great reference.

20. St. Hill Bourne, *They Also Serve*, 164.

21. Ibid.

22. "Five Years Ago—Irma Gave a Signal," *Evening Standard*, February 11, 1950. PDSA Archives.

23. St. Hill Bourne, *They Also Serve*, 164.

24. Long, *Animal Heroes*, 192.

25. "War Dog and Master Get Medals," *Evening Standard*, March 27, 1945. PDSA Archives. Also reported by Dorothea St. Hill Bourne in *They Also Serve*, 172. Some later sources report that the bodies recovered from this building were alive, but Russell's description of "casualties" as "later recovered" indicates that there were no survivors.

26. KBE, or Knight Commander of the Most Excellent Order of the British Empire, is another grade within the British orders of chivalry.

27. Some contemporary sources reported that Thorn was a descendant of Rin Tin Tin. It is easy to see how that mistake can have been made. The *Edinburgh Evening News* reported that Thorn came "from a theatrical family"—which was true enough, given his relationship to *Owd Bob* star Storm. See "Film Newcomer," *Edinburgh Evening News*, June 17, 1947. PDSA Archives. Another newspaper called him "The British Rin-Tin-Tin." "This Film Star Was Really Shot—by Mistake," *Evening News*, January 21, 1948. PDSA Archives. So it must have been easy to make the leap to the conclusion that Thorn, a German shepherd like the enormously popular Rin Tin Tin, must have been a descendent.

28. "New Dog Star," *Evening News*, June 6, 1947. PDSA Archives.

29. "He Walks Alone," *Star*, January 1, 1948. PDSA Archives.

30. "This Film Star War Really Shot—By Mistake," *Evening News*, January 21, 1948. PDSA Archives.

31. While it does not appear that Thorn ever acted again, one source reported Thorn also appeared in two other films, *And So to Work* and *The Captive Heart*.

32. For unknown reasons, at some point after 1946 Rex became the property of a new owner, Mr. M. Ramshaw.

33. St. Hill Bourne, *They Also Serve*, 173.

34. Ibid., 174.

35. "Dog Heroes, Medals Awarded," *Wembley News*, April 27, 1945. PDSA Archives.

36. "Dogs 'V.C.' for Alsatian, Gallant Rescue Work," *Palmers Green Gazette*, April 27, 1945. PDSA Archives.

37. Some accounts published from 1949 and later claim that Rex saved anywhere between sixty-three and sixty-nine people, but the exact figures cannot be confirmed. These numbers, which were not published at the time Rex's exploits attracted extensive newspaper coverage across the UK, in 1945, are considered suspect.

38. St. Hill Bourne, *They Also Serve*, 173. The author does not state the name of the "official report."

39. "Here and There, Dog Hero Passes On," *The Animals' Magazine*, August 1954, 13. PDSA Archives.

40. Ibid.

41. St. Hill Bourne, *They Also Serve*, 171.

42. "The P.D.S.A. Allied Forces Mascot Club Bulletin," date unknown, 8. PDSA Archives.

43. Source and date not identified. PDSA Archives; the same incident is described by Dorothea St. Hill Bourne in *They Also Serve*, 166.

44. Peter Hawthorne, *The Animal Victoria Cross: The Dickin Medal* (Barnsley, South Yorkshire: Pen & Sword Military, 2014), 37.

45. St. Hill Bourne, *They Also Serve*, 175.

46. "Gallant Dog, Good Work in Blitz Rewarded, Dickin Medal for Peter," *Birmingham Mail*, December 5, 1945. PDSA Archives.

47. St. Hill Bourne, *They Also Serve*, 171.

48. "But the Army Made Peter a Gentleman," *Sunday Pictorial*, May 5, 1946. PDSA Archives.

49. "Gallant Dog, Good Work in Blitz Rewarded, Dickin Medal for Peter."

EIGHT: JUDY

1. Robert Weintraub, *No Better Friend: One Man, One Dog, and Their Extraordinary Story of Courage and Survival in WWII* (New York: Little, Brown & Company, 2015), 323.

2. Ibid., 15.

3. The story of Judy's early months is from two sources: *No Better Friend: One Man, One Dog, and Their Extraordinary Story of Courage and Survival in WWII* by Robert Weintraub, 8–12; and *The Judy Story: The Dog with Six Lives* by E. Varley (Glasgow: Fontana/Collins, 1976), 5–7.

4. Weintraub, *No Better Friend*, 7.

5. Ibid., 8.

6. Ibid., 16.

7. Varley, *The Judy Story*, 17.

8. Other passengers included British Army and Royal Marine personnel, a few Australian nurses, and Japanese prisoners. Official Report S7900, Naval Historical Branch. Varley, *The Judy Story*, 137. Batavia fell to the Japanese on March 5, 1942. The Dutch formally surrendered to the Japanese occupation forces on March 9, 1942, and rule of the colony was transferred to Japan. The city was renamed Jakarta, and the country, Indonesia.

9. Ibid., 53.

10. Ibid., 63.

11. Ibid., 61.

12. Or, perhaps, "puppable"?

13. Weintraub, *No Better Friend*, 119.

14. Varley, *The Judy Story*, 62.

15. Ibid. 62–63.

16. Commander Jack Hoffman was killed in action a few weeks later, on March 2, 1942. "Jack Sanler Hoffman, Commander," Force 'Z' Survivors, http://www.forcez-survivors.org.uk/biographies/grasshoppercrew/hoffman.html.

17. Weintraub, *No Better Friend*, 141.

18. Ibid., 147.

19. Some sources say they missed the evacuation by just twenty-four hours, but this doesn't appear to be accurate. Alan J. Levine, *Captivity, Flight, and Survival in World War II* (Santa Barbara, CA: Praeger, 2000), 43.

20. Weintraub, *No Better Friend*, 165.

21. Varley, *The Judy Story*, 73.

22. Sources vary on the spelling. Earlier sources, including E. Varley's *The Judy Story*, spell the POW camp name "Gloergoer." The correct spelling appears to be "Gloegoer," without the extra "r."

23. Ibid., 75.

24. Weintraub, *No Better Friend*, 192.

25. Jane Fryer, "Judy, the Dogged POW Who Defied the Japanese," *Daily Mail*, August 12, 2010, http://www.dailymail.co.uk/news/article-1302677/Judy-dogged-PoW-defied-Japanese.html.

26. Weintraub, *No Better Friend*, 193.

27. Varley, *The Judy Story*, 78.

28. Yes, once again, the movie is *Casablanca*.

29. Weintraub, *No Better Friend*, 189.

30. Damien Lewis, *Judy: A Dog in a Million* (London: Quercus Editions Ltd., 2014), 177.

31. "Judy—P.o.W. Heroine—Gets Dog "V.C." To-Day," *Evening Standard*, May 2, 1946. PDSA Archives.

32. Varley, *The Judy Story*, 80.

33. Banno, who had served with the Allied forces during World War I, had some sympathy with his British prisoners. The same cannot be said of the commandants who followed him at Gloegoer.

34. Weintraub, *No Better Friend*, 208.

35. Sources vary as to the spelling of Captain Nishi's name. In *The Judy Story* Varley spells it Nissi rather than Nishi. And there is so little written about this man that it's hard to verify the correct spelling. But Nishi is a more common name, and Nissi is rare. So more than likely "Nishi" is the correct spelling. Robert Weintraub has a good explanation in *No Better Friend*, 352.

36. Ibid., 215.

37. Ibid., 225.

38. Varley, *The Judy Story*, 91.

39. Weintraub, *No Better Friend*, 227.

40. Varley, *The Judy Story*, 93.

41. Fryer, "Judy, the Dogged POW."

42. Varley, *The Judy Story*, 93.

43. Lewis, *Judy: A Dog in a Million*, 236.

44. Varley, *The Judy Story*, 94.

45. Weintraub, *No Better Friend*, 236.

46. Ibid., 230.

47. "Judy—Animal V.C. And Prisoner of War," *Wellington Evening Post*, September 24, 1949. PDSA Archives.

48. Weintraub, *No Better Friend*, 230.

49. Ibid., 233.

50. Local villagers often placed fruit on graves instead of flowers.

51. Fryer, "Judy, the Dogged POW."

52. Varley, *The Judy Story*, 101.

53. Weintraub, *No Better Friend*, 255.

54. Ibid.

55. Varley, *The Judy Story*, 113.

56. "Animal Hero—Exploits of a Dog—Prisoner of Japanese," *Otago Daily Times*, September 26, 1949. PDSA Archives.

57. Sources vary as to the actual date the camp was liberated, giving dates from August 15, 1945 (a day after V-J Day) to late August (after preliminary surrender documents were signed) to September 4, 1945 (two days after the Japanese formally surrendered). Judy's tombstone reports she was a POW from March 1942 to August 1945.

58. Weintraub, *No Better Friend*, 295.

59. Ibid., 293.

60. Ibid., 297.

61. Varley, *The Judy Story*, 120.

62. Weintraub, *No Better Friend*, 302.

63. Ibid., 303.

64. "Judy—P.o.W. Heroine."

65. Weintraub, *No Better Friend*, 309.

66. Fryer, "Judy, the Dogged POW."

67. Weintraub, *No Better Friend*, 310.

68. Sources vary on the number of days Judy was missing. At the time, newspaper reports said ten days: "Judy, V.C., Dies after Search," *Daily Express*, March 21, 1950. More recent accounts indicate four days; Lewis, *Judy: A Dog in a Million*, 318.

69. Weintraub, *No Better Friend*, 322.

70. Ibid., 323.

WAR BIRDS

1. Ward West, "But the Pigeons Still Get Through," New York Times, April 27, 1941.

NINE: WINGED WARRIORS

1. "Pigeons for Defense," *New York Times*, January 13, 1941.

2. "Army Registering Homing Pigeons for Conscription in an Emergency," *New York Times*, January 6, 1941, 17.

3. "Pigeons for Defense."

4. Flint Whitlock, "The National Pigeon Service: Our Fine Feathered Friends," Warfare History Network, April 4, 2017, http://warfarehistorynetwork.com/daily/wwii/the-national-pigeon-service-our-fine-feathered-friends/.

5. Mary Blume, "The Hallowed History of the Carrier Pigeon," *New York Times*, January 30, 2004, http://www.nytimes.com/2004/01/30/style/the-hallowed-history-of-the-carrier-pigeon.html.

6. Contrary to popular belief, "homing" and "carrier" pigeons are not the same. Homing pigeons are also called racing pigeons. Carrier pigeons carried messages until the nineteenth century, when the modern homing pigeon was developed. The carrier pigeon is now strictly a show bird and evidently has lost much of its strong homing instinct.

7. "The Homing Pigeon," in *Signal Corps Technical Manual TM 11-410*, 1945, 2.

8. Ward West, "But the Pigeons Still Get Through," *New York Times*, April 27, 1941.

9. "The Homing Pigeon," 2.

10. Wendell Levi, *The Pigeon* (Sumter, SC: Levi Publishing Co, 1974), 250.

11. Ibid., 596.

12. Ibid., 592.

13. Ibid., 593.

14. Marion B. Cothren, *Pigeon Heroes: Birds of War and Messengers of Peace* (New York: Coward-McCann Inc., 1944), 44.

15. "The Homing Pigeon," 14.

16. Ibid., 25.

17. Cothren, *Pigeon Heroes*, 43.

18. As the pigeon was a female, the gender-proper French spelling should have been Chere Amie. Ah, bien!

19. The Meuse-Argonne Offensive took place from September 26, 1918, to the signing of the Armistice, which ended the war on November 11, 1918.

20. "Pigeon Message from Capt. Whittlesey to the Commanding Officer of the 308th Infantry, 10/04/1918," National Archives, https://www.archives.gov/historical-docs/todays-doc/?dod-date=1004. Most sources—including even the National Archives in its description of this document—spell Maj. Whittlesay's name Whittlesey. But this original document itself is signed "Whittlesay." One has to assume this spelling is correct.

21. Major Charles Whittlesay was awarded the Medal of Honor for his actions during this battle. Yet, sadly, in 1921 his memories of war got the better of him. Whittlesay went missing from a ship at sea, an apparent suicide.

22. "Aerial Reconnaissance," Central Intelligence Agency, July 23, 2012, https://www.cia.gov/about-cia/cia-museum/experience-the-collection/text-version/collection-by-subject/aerial-reconnaissance.html.

23. "War Equines Vanish; Dogs, Pigeons Join Up," *New York Times*, January 28, 1945.

24. Levi, *The Pigeon*, 13–14.

25. Joe Razes, "Pigeons of War," *America in WWII Magazine*, August 2007, http://www.americainwwii.com/articles/pigeons-of-war/.

26. For great pictures of this vest, including original drawings, see Lindsay Keating, "Pigeons in Bras Go to War," Oh Say Can You See: Stories from the National Museum of American History, September 4, 2013, http://americanhistory.si.edu/blog/2013/09/pigeons-in-bras-go-to-war.html.

27. Razes, "Pigeons of War."

28. "Carrier Pigeon 'GI Joe' Wins Medal," World War II Today: Follow the War As It Happened, no date, http://ww2today.com/18th-october-1943-carrier-pigeon-gi-joe-wins-medal.

29. Ibid. Some sources report incorrectly that it was over one thousand instead of one hundred Allied lives that GI Joe saved. See Long, *Animal Heroes*, 37; Peter Hawthorne, *The Animal Victoria Cross: The Dickin Medal* (Barnsley, South Yorkshire: Pen & Sword, 2014), 64.

30. Otto Meyer, "GI Joe," www.pigeon.org/pdf/gijoe.pdf, no date.

31. St. Hill Bourne, *They Also Serve*, 212.

32. Ibid. The "Yeoman Warders" are also known as "Beefeaters."

33. "GI Joe (Pigeon) Gets His V.C.," *Daily Graphic*, November 7, 1946. PDSA Archives.

34. "Well Done, 'GI Joe'!," *London Calling*, November 14, 1946. PDSA Archives.

35. Sources vary as to whether Blackie was with the 132nd Infantry Regiment or the 164th. Both regiments were part of the Americal (23rd Infantry) Division. The 132nd Infantry Regiment was originally with the 33rd Infantry Division. When the Army reorganized and went from four down to three infantry units per division, the 132nd was relieved by the 33rd on January 14, 1942, and assigned to Task Force 6814, which then became part of Americal (23rd Infantry) Division in May 1942. The three infantry regiments of Americal were the 132nd, the 164th, and the 182nd.

36. In 1989, Burma's military rulers changed the country's name to Myanmar, but the legality of the change remains in dispute.
37. "Army Pigeons: Hall of Fame," *Racing Pigeon Digest*, December 1, 1998, 28. Reprinted from *Racing Pigeon Review*, January 1946.
38. Ibid.
39. Ibid.
40. Ibid.
41. Tony M. Kiser and Lindsey F. Barnes, *Loyal Forces: The American Animals in World War II* (Baton Rouge: Louisiana State University Press, 2013), 60.
42. Cothren, *Pigeon Heroes*, 16.
43. Levi, *The Pigeon*, 14.
44. Ibid., 27. Sadly, there is no information on what the message contained.
45. Ibid., 26.
46. Ibid., 26-27.
47. Zimmerman Brackett, "Museum Tells Signal Corps Story," *Augusta Chronicle*, December 21, 1999.
48. Ibid.
49. Cothren, *Pigeon Heroes*, 17.

TEN: BRITAIN'S BIRD BRIGADE

1. John M. Kistler, *Animals in the Military: From Hannibal's Elephants to the Dolphins of the US Navy* (Santa Barbara: ABC-CLIO, LLC, 2011), 244.
2. Garry McCafferty, *They Had No Choice: Racing Pigeons at War* (Stroud, Gloucestershire, England: Tempus Publishing, Ltd., 2002), 57.
3. "Pigeons Save Life in RAF, for Planes Forced Down at Sea or Those in Flight They Carry Messages," *New York Times*, July 11, 1943.
4. W. H. Osman, *Pigeons in Two World Wars* (London: The Racing Pigeon Publishing Company, 1976), 61.
5. Capital ships are the most important warships in a naval fleet. Battleships were considered capital ships at the start of World

War II, but aircraft carriers gradually took over the number one spot, and battleships took a secondary position in the fleet.

6. Ralph Barker, *Down in the Drink: Their Deadliest Enemy Was the Sea* (London: Pan Books, 1958), 185.

7. "The Use of Pigeons by the RAF in WW2: Extract from Military Reports on The United Nations: Number 15, Signal, February 15, 1944," Arcre: Independent Professional Research at the British National Archives (TNA), January 4, 2013, https://www.arcre.com/pigeons/pigeonsraf. Sources vary on what happened to this pigeon. One book states that after the bird was released because it was wet and darkness was approaching, "After performing a few perfunctory circles, the pigeon merely alighted back to the dinghy; and no amount of cajoling or beating about the head, could persuade it to resume its flight. Its fixed intention was obviously to make a fifth passenger." Martin W. Bowman, *Deep Sea Hunters: RAF Coastal Command and the War Against the U-Boats and the German Navy 1939–1945* (South Yorkshire, England: Pen & Sword Books, 2014), 108. Another source claims that the men were finally able to get the bird to take off. Barker, *Down in the Drink*, 188.

8. She may have hitched a nighttime ride on an oil tanker, as some sources reported.

9. Some sources state it was an eleven-man crew, but according to an oral history of the captain, Flight Officer Ronald Vaughn, it was a ten-man crew including himself.

10. Some sources say the plane was redirected to Aberdeen and Oban, instead of Invergordon and Bowmore, as Flight Officer Ronald Vaughn asserted.

11. Jim Carlo, *Three "Cats," a Pigeon, and 27 Brave Men of Coastal Command* (Kent, England: FVRepro, 2012), 13. This book is the personal account of Flight Officer Ronald Vaughn, as told to author Jim Carlo.

12. Rona, sometimes called North Rona, is a remote island in the Scottish Inner Hebrides, an island group just off Scotland's western coast.

13. St. Hill Bourne, *They Also Serve*, 203.

14. Some sources say that Taylor only had four birds at his disposal, not six. Long, *Animal Heroes*, 27.

15. "Hero Pigeon's WWII Medal on Show," BBC News, June 1, 2005, http://news.bbc.co.uk/2/hi/uk_news/england/hampshire/4600865.stm.

16. Osman, "Pigeons in World War II," in *Pigeons in Two World Wars*, 103.

17. Long, *Animal Heroes*, 45. Paddy was one of 46,532 British pigeons U.S. forces used during the war.

18. According to author David Long, no humans could join the Allied Forces Mascot Club; membership was strictly limited to animals. The club was formed to "recognize the increasingly important role being played by regimental and other service mascots." Members included dogs, goats, birds, monkeys, "and at least one fox." Ibid., xi.

19. "D-Day Fliers Decorated (1944)," YouTube, posted by British Pathé, April 13, 2014, https://www.youtube.com/watch?v=msqgZFvQk_E.

20. "Our War Pigeons," *Nottingham Evening Post*, November 22, 1944.

21. St. Hill Bourne, *They Also Serve*, 204.

22. "Well Flown!" *Herndon & Finley Times*, November 28, 1944.

23. Osman, "Pigeons in World War II," in *Pigeons in Two World Wars*, 73.

24. St. Hill Bourne, *They Also Serve*, 204.

25. Operation Varsity, on March 24, 1945, a later campaign involving Allied forces crossing the Rhine into Germany, was the largest airborne operation in history conducted on a single day and in one location. It involved more aircraft, gliders, and troops on the first day than Market. The number of troops flown in on subsequent days, however, made Market the larger overall operation.

26. William flew at roughly sixty miles per hour that day.

27. St. Hill Bourne, *They Also Serve*, 211.

28. Stuart Eastwood, Charles Gray, and Alan Green, *When Dragons Flew: An Illustrated History of the 1st Battalion The Border Regiment 1939–45*, 169–170. PDSA Archives.
29. Sources vary as to the number of German troops that were surrounded. Estimates range between 325,000 to as high as nearly 400,000.
30. W. H. Osman, ed., *Pigeons in World War II: The Official Records of the Performances of Racing Pigeons with the Armed Forces* (London: The Racing Pigeon Publishing Co., Ltd., 1950), 52.
31. St. Hill Bourne, *They Also Serve*, 205.
32. The famously speedy Per Ardua once covered one thousand ninety miles in roughly twelve days.
33. Some sources give Mary's ID number as NURP.40.WCE.249, instead of WLE. WLE comes from Major W. H. Osman's *Pigeons in Two World Wars*, from the section "Pigeons in World War II," which is considered the definitive record of war pigeons. While Mary's record is not listed, Osman does mention that she was a Dickin Medal winner and gives her ID number on p. 194.
34. These bomb attacks were also called the "Baedeker Raids." Hitler had been enraged by the RAF's bombing of the ancient German cathedral city of Lubeck on the night of March 28, 1942. So the German dictator launched a series of reprisal raids on some of England's most beautiful but strategically unimportant towns, chosen for their historical and cultural rather than military value. Hitler used the travel guide Baedeker's Great Britain to select the targets. Exeter was the first bombing target, followed by Bath, York, and Norwich.
35. "We've Not Another Just Like Mary, Romance of an Exeter Pigeon," *Exeter Express & Echo*, November 17, 1945. PDSA Archives.
36. The sequence of events after Tommy was discovered in the street varies, depending on the source. Some say Drijver found the bird. Others claim the boy found the bird and gave it directly to Drijver. Still others say the postman found Tommy and brought him to Drijver. The precise truth may never be known.

37. Sources at that time did not reveal any details of the message. More recent sources report that the coded message concerned either a munitions factory near Amsterdam or the location of a German U-boat base.
38. St. Hill Bourne, *They Also Serve*, 210.
39. "Lost Pigeon Brought Home Military Secrets, Wins Medal," *Manchester Daily Sketch*, January 1, 1946. PDSA Archives.
40. "Short History of the Australian Corps of Signals Pigeon Service from 1942," South Australian Homing Pigeon Association archives, no date, http://www.sahpa.asn.au/archives/flyers/dickinmedal.htm.
41. Ibid.
42. "Presentation of the Dickin Medal in Australia," *Animals Magazine*, October 1947, 6. PDSA Archives.
43. During Operation Overlord, the 21st Army Group controlled all ground forces, which included not only the British Second Army and Canadian First Army, but the United States First Army, and smaller units as well.
44. The story of the Duke's role on this mission is culled from the personal account of Sergeant William Thomas "Johnnie" Walker. Walker was attached to the 9th Parachute Battalion. PDSA Archives.

WAR HORSES
1. Richard Dempewolff, Animal Reveille, (Garden City, New York: Doubleday, Doran & Company, Inc.,1943), p. 229.

ELEVEN: HEROES WITH HOOVES
1. Christopher Miskimon, "Army Mules: The Beast of Burden in War," January 29, 2016, Warfare History Network, http://warfarehistorynetwork.com/daily/wwii/army-mules-the-beast-of-burden-in-war/. CBI stands for the China-Burma-India theater.
2. The Lend-Lease Act (H.R. 1776) signed on March 11, 1941, was the principal means for providing U.S. military aid to Great Britain and other foreign Allied nations during World War II.

It set up a system that allowed the United States to lend or lease war supplies to "the government of any country whose defense the President deems vital to the defense of the United States." The United States would provide Great Britain with the supplies it needed to fight Germany, but would not insist upon being paid immediately. Instead, the U.S. would "lend" the supplies to the British, deferring payment. In return for the aid, the U.S. was given ninety-nine-year leases on army and naval bases in Allied territory during the war, among other compensations. By allowing the transfer of supplies to Britain, China, the Soviet Union and other countries without compensation, the act permitted the United States to support its war interests without sending men into battle.

3. Erna Risch and Chester L. Kieffer, *The Quartermaster Corps: Organization, Supply and Services* vol. 2 (Washington, DC: Center of Military History, Department of the Army, 1955), 315–23. For more information on the role of the Army mule, see Toni M. Kiser and Lindsey F. Barnes, *Loyal Forces: The American Animals of World War II* (Baton Rouge, LA: Louisiana State University Press, 2013), 25–45.

4. Long, *Animal Heroes*, 219.

5. St. Hill Bourne, *They Also Serve*, 194.

6. A coronet marking is a white band about an inch wide just above a horse's hoof.

7. "Mobile Hospital for Sick Animals" [photo caption] *Times* (Evening Edition), December 24, 1947. PDSA Archives.

8. "Police Horse Heroes," *The Animals' Magazine*, PDSA, July 1947, 5. PDSA Archives.

AND A WAR... CAT?

1. Dorothea St. Hill Bourne, They Also Serve (London: Winchester Publications, Ltd., 1947), p. 41.

TWELVE: THE ONE AND ONLY—SIMON

1. Isabel George, "A Cat's Tale," *Lady*, May 1993. PDSA Archives.

2. Victoria Heuer, "Five Famous Cats of War," Pet MD, n.d., https://www.petmd.com/cat/slideshows/seasonal/five-cats-of-war.

3. Patrick Roberts, "Faith the London Church Cat," Purr 'n' Fur, n.d., http://www.purr-n-fur.org.uk/famous/faith.html.

4. Linda D. Kozaryn, "Pfc. Hammer Finds a Home," American Forces Press Service, April 24, 2004, http://archive.defense.gov/news/newsarticle.aspx?id=26813.

5. Some sources report that Simon boarded the ship on the shoulders of the captain, but not according to the first-hand account by George Hickinbottom as told to Patrick Roberts. Patrick Roberts, "Simon, of HMS *Amethyst*," Purr 'n' Fur, http://www.purr-n-fur.org.uk/famous/simon.html.

6. There is precious little written about Peggy. It's usually just her name mentioned in sources, nothing more.

7. Vera Cooper, *Simon the Cat* (London: Hutchinson & Co. LTD, 1950), 7.

8. C. E. Lucas Philips, *Escape of the "Amethyst"* (London: Pan Books. Ltd., 1958), 45.

9. Two days later, the death toll rose to twenty. The number of dead and injured, however, varies from source to source. The nineteen-to-twenty fatality figure appears in the official report about the Yangtze Incident delivered to Parliament, which also contains the names. J. S. Kerans, "HMS *Amethyst* Incident, Yangtse River, April to May 1949," Naval History, February 20, 2016, http://www.naval-history.net/WXLG-Amethyst1949.htm.

10. Roberts, "Simon of the HMS Amethyst."

11. Lucas, *Escape of the "Amethyst,"* 195.

12. "*Amethyst's* Cat Hero: Full Story," *South Wales Echo*, October 31, 1949. PDSA Archives.

13. "*Amethyst's* Cat Gets Dickin Medal for Catching Rats." Associated Press, August 5, 1949, http://www.maritimequest.com/warship_directory/great_britain/pages/sloops/hms_amethyst_u16_able_seacat_simon_page_2.htm.

14. Val Lewis, *Ships' Cats in War and Peace* (Middlesex, England: Nauticalia Ltd., 2001), 33.

15. Robert Green, "Able Seacat Simon, D.M., R.N. (1947–48)," http://www.maritimequest.com/warship_directory/great_britain/pages/sloops/hms_amethyst_u16_able_seacat_simon.htm.
16. *Time*, December 12, 1949, http://content.time.com/time/magazine/article/0,9171,854035,00.html.

EPILOGUE
1. According to Smoky's website, citing *Popular Dog*, 2001 and *Dog Fancy*, 2003.

APPENDIX
1. W. H. Osman, ed., *Pigeons in Two World Wars*.
2. Ibid., 28.
3. "'V.C.' for Ipswich Pigeon, Echo of War Exploit," *Ipswich Evening Star*, September 9, 1946. PDSA Archives.

Index